Services in World Economic Growth

Symposium 1988

Edited by Herbert Giersch

Institut für Weltwirtschaft an der Universität Kiel

J.C.B. MOHR (PAUL SIEBECK) TÜBINGEN

WESTVIEW PRESS * BOULDER, COLORADO

CIP-Titelaufnahme der Deutschen Bibliothek

Services in world economic growth: symposium 1988 / Inst. für
Weltwirtschaft an d. Univ. Kiel. Ed. by Herbert Giersch. -
Tübingen: Mohr, 1989
  ISBN 3-16-345482-8 brosch.
  ISBN 3-16-345483-6 Gewebe
NE: Giersch, Herbert [Hrsg.]; Institut für Weltwirtschaft <Kiel>

Distributed by
  Westview Press, Inc.
  5500 Central Avenue
  Boulder, Colorado 80301

Schriftleitung: Hubertus Müller-Groeling

Institut für Weltwirtschaft an der Universität Kiel
J. C. B. Mohr (Paul Siebeck) Tübingen 1989

ISBN 0-8133-7915-6 (Westview)

CONTENTS

Preface   Herbert Giersch   V

I. Services and the Changing Economic Structure

Modern Service Sector Growth: Causes and Effects	Herbert G. Grubel/ Michael A. Walker	1
Discussant	Richard Blackhurst	35
Defining and Measuring Output and Productivity in the Service Sector	Domenico Siniscalco	38
Discussant	Frank D. Weiss	59

II. International Aspects

International Transactions Involving Interactions: A Conceptual Framework Combining Goods and Services	Seev Hirsch	63
Services and Comparative Advantage Theory	H. Peter Gray	85
Discussant	Henning Klodt	104
Trade and Foreign-Owned Production in Services: Some Conceptual and Theoretical Issues	John H. Dunning	108
Discussant	Pan A. Yotopoulos	151

III. Sectoral Analysis

Telecommunications and the Scope of the Market in Services	Gerald R. Faulhaber	156
Discussant	Axel Busch	166
Telecommunications Policy – Assessing Recent Experience in the US, Japan and Europe and Its Implications for the Completion of the Internal Common Market	Günter Knieps	173
Discussants	Tyll Necker	190
	Herbert Ungerer	192

IV

Protection and the Structure of the
Banking Industry in an International
Context   Robert Z. Aliber   198

Discussant   Norbert Walter   219

Integrated World Markets in Services: Brian Hindley   222
Problems and Prospects

Discussant   Jürgen Müller   245

IV. Services and International
    Division of Labour

North-South Trade in Services: Some   Rolf J. Langhammer   248
Empirical Evidence

Discussant   J. Michael Finger   272

List of Contributors   274

Preface

This volume is the outcome of the 19th Kiel Week Conference held at the Institute of World Economics, 22-24 June 1988. It contains the revised versions of the papers and comments submitted after discussion.

As in previous years, the purpose of the conference was to explore a subject of relevance for economic policy. This time, we focused on services and their increasing importance for industrialized and developing countries and for world economic growth and trade.

The first paper, presented by Herbert Grubel, describes the origins of service-sector growth and the main driving forces behind it. Using Canadian data, Grubel demonstrates that the share of producer services in GDP has grown faster than that of other services. He also shows that producer services raise productivity in the production of goods. Finally, he points out that trade in producer services is linked more to capital flows or to trade in goods than directly to the movement of persons. Therefore, we should learn more about these indirect forms of trade in services.

The description of service-sector growth was expected to raise the conceptual problems of how to define and measure output and productivity in this sector. Domenico Siniscalco's paper addresses itself to this problem. It does this by explaining the standard approach and comparing it with an innovative alternative one.

Seev Hirsch, in the third paper, contributes to the debate on the role of services in international trade, his main point being that trade in services is not essentially different from trade in goods, since the latter also involves some form of interaction between users and suppliers. He comes to the conclusion that the potential for trade in services and service-intensive goods would be enhanced not only by reducing restrictions but also by new technologies, such as telecommunications, that curtail the need for face-to-face interaction.

The fourth paper deals with the question of how to incorporate trade in services into traditional comparative advantage theory. Peter Gray is sceptical because the characteristics of services are so manifold, just like those of goods. Therefore trade in services cannot be explained only by relative factor prices as emphasized by the neofactor proportions theory. Other variables such as technology differences or communications linkages are crucial to explain trade in services. He suggests a more empirical approach to look at individual sub-categories of services and their characteristics.

John Dunning, in the fifth paper, shows how the growth of the service sector is related to the proliferation of multinational enterprises. Firms, when preferring foreign production to trade in services, do not only consider factor endowments but also regulatory patterns as well as their own internal organizational structure.

In the two subsequent papers, the telecommunications sector is the focal point. While Gerald Faulhaber describes how important this sector has been for the development of financial and retail services in Europe, Günter Knieps analyses the results that have been achieved by deregulating it in the US, Japan and Great Britain. Both underline the importance of deregulating telecommunications for service-sector growth.

Robert Aliber looks at the banking industry in an international context. In his paper, he wonders why most of the banking offices are owned by domestic firms. In order to explain this, he considers locational advantages, barriers to entry and to take-overs, portfolio requirements and interest rate ceilings, etc.

Brian Hindley, in turn, concentrates on transportation services. On the one hand, they are a factor of market integration, on the other hand, they are heavily regulated, with barriers to entry rooted in bilateral agreements. He is not sanguine about whether a substantial improvement could result from multilateral negotiations. Indeed, even bilateral negotiations would be slow to bring progress.

In the last paper of the conference, Rolf Langhammer uses empirical data from four OECD countries to show that North-South trade in services is far from negligible and extends beyond mere "transport and travel" to other private services such as advertising, insurance, or construction. Furthermore, he considers that the specialization patterns in services of the four industrialized countries are similar to those for manufactured goods. He also points out that the importance of developing countries for service exports differs from country to country. Because government interventions and factor endowments are inextricably intertwined their separate impact on patterns of trade in services cannot be identified.

The Institute is indebted to the authors and discussants and to those who made this conference possible. The Deutsche Bundesbank provided financial support. We owe thanks to the Landeszentralbank Schleswig-Holstein, the City of Kiel, the Dresdner Bank and the Oberpostdirektion Kiel for their hospitality. Seev Hirsch gave valuable help in preparing the conference and Axel Busch ensured that it was organized efficiently. Credit is also due to Fiona Short and Dietmar Gebert for their painstaking efforts in giving this volume its final shape.

Kiel, March 1989   Herbert Giersch

I. SERVICES AND THE CHANGING ECONOMIC STRUCTURE

Herbert G. Grubel
Michael A. Walker

Modern Service Sector Growth: Causes and Effects

1. Introduction

The growth of service-sector employment and GDP in industrial countries has been significant in the 20th century and has reached levels which have given rise to all kinds of theorizing and speculation about its causes and effects. Figures 1 and 2 illustrate this development for Canada in terms of employment, showing that service-sector employment has grown from near 35 per cent to over 70 per cent of the total between the census years 1911 and 1981. Employment in the service sector has exceeded that in goods production since 1958. Very similar developments have taken place in other industrial countries and with respect to the growth in GDP, as is documented below.

In this study, we review briefly the existing body of knowledge relevant to an explanation of the causes and effects of this growth of the service sector. Part 3 presents a taxonomy of service industries and a pioneering approach to the estimation of consumer, government and producer services. The determinants and welfare effects of these services are discussed in Part 4.

2. Review of the Literature

Hill [1977] discusses definitions and conceptual issues surrounding the service sector. While these issues are interesting and important, in this study we approach them pragmatically. The service sector is what the UN system of national accounts and most national statistical offices record as such in terms of employment and GDP. The possible develop-

Figure 1 - Historic Employment Shares for Canada (census years)

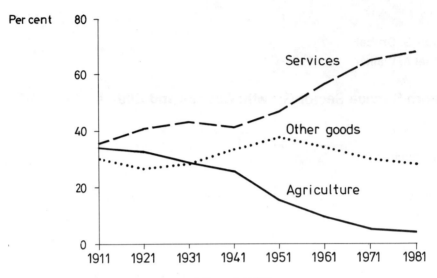

Source: Government Printing Office [1983].

Figure 2 - Employment in Canada by Industry Groups

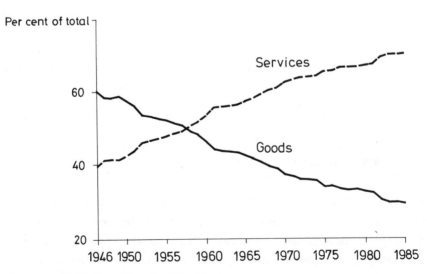

Source: Statistics Canada [b; d].

ment of new and better data in the future may require adjustments to our theories and results.

In a large and growing literature, the causes and welfare effects of the historic growth in the service sector are being analysed. At the risk of oversimplification, this literature may be divided into five classes.

Firstly, Adam Smith and other classical economists considered the production of services to be unproductive. This notion was based on their concept of exchange value and the perception that services are performed by servants for individuals. Such services, once produced, cannot be exchanged for money or other goods in the manner in which material goods can be. While modern value theory has discredited the validity of the view that the production of services involves an unproductive use of resources, the basic idea still pervades much public thinking in the West. In the Soviet Union's national income accounts personal services are not recorded as part of national output. In the 1950s, the United Kingdom imposed special taxes on personal services in order to discourage their production.

Secondly, the now classic studies by Stigler [1956], Baumol [1967] and Fuchs [1968] explained the growth of services as the result of a high income elasticity of demand for, and the low rate of productivity growth in the production of consumer services. The analytical focus of these studies has been on the implications of these characteristics on overall productivity growth and inflation. The conclusions of this analysis have entered the economics literature as the widely-known "Baumol Effect".

Thirdly, Fisher [1939] developed a model of primary (agricultural and other natural resource industries), secondary (manufacturing) and tertiary (service) sectors. Modern economic development in this model was seen to generate growth in output and productivity in the primary sector which, given the saturation of demand, led to the shrinking of this sector's share of employment and output. The labour released from this sector moved into the manufacturing sector. Eventually, manufacturing employment was expected to experience a relative decline for the same reasons that resulted in the shrinking of the primary sector. The surplus labour was then expected to find employment in the tertiary industries.

Literature of recent origin such as Shelp [1981], Bell [1979], Blackaby [1978] and Bluestone and Harrison [1982] builds on this model by Fischer. Broadly speaking, these authors argue that the service sector is encountering the same problems of saturation in demand that have befallen the primary and secondary sectors before. However, there is the new problem that labour not needed in this sector has nowhere to go. There is no corresponding fourth sector that expands and satisfies new types of demand.

This literature has attracted much attention among politicians and some economists since it offers an innovative explanation of the high unemployment rates and the balance-of-payments problems of the United States of the 1980s. It has given wide publicity to the concept of "de-industrialization", the existence of which is considered evidence of a fundamental pathology of free market systems and creating the need for industrial planning. In addition, this literature decries the growth of the service sector since it is alleged to reflect "doing each other's laundry" (with a zero gain in real output) and to result in a "bi-modal income distribution" (services requiring waiters at low wages and computer experts at high pay with a decline of the middle-income occupations and pay). These phenomena are also considered to create a need for industrial planning.

Fourthly, Riddle [1986], Ott [1987], Tatom [1986], Kutscher and Mark [1983] and Kravis [1983] have developed analytical models and empirical evidence largely in response to the arguments made by the most recent critics of service-sector growth. Their main findings are that recent trends are a continuation of past developments, especially the growth in demand for consumer services and that there is no reason for public intervention to prevent de-industrialization or any other allegedly undesirable developments.

For example, Ott [1987, p. 13] presents recent statistics and notes "The shift in output has reflected a relative shift in consumer demand toward services". Riddle [1986, pp. 218; 229] notes in the concluding section of her book entitled "Services and the Quality of Life" that "services are the housekeepers of the world".

The fifth set of studies like Gershuny and Miles [1983], Swan [1985] and Radwanski [1986] build on the preceding literature but add as an innovation a special emphasis on the role of producer and government services in the growth of the service sector.

The current study is in this tradition. Its main contribution lies in the quantification of the relative size of consumer, government and producer services. It will be shown that in Canada during the post-war years at least, the share of GDP originating with producer services has been twice that of consumer and government services. The share of the last two sectors has remained nearly constant in real terms since the 1950s and almost all real growth in Canada has come from producer services. Similar results have emerged from estimates made for other countries, though there are some interesting differences in the growth rates of the different sectors in the United States, Japan, Greece and Sweden, as will be seen below.

3. The Basic Taxonomy

The purpose of this section is to give a more precise definition of the analytical classes of consumer, government and producer service sectors and to present estimates of the size of each for a number of countries.

a. Consumer Services

Consumption expenditures are one of the cornerstones of the Keynesian models of the economy. Traditionally, they distinguish between spending on durable and non-durable goods and services. Here, we are concerned with spending on services which consist of the output of restaurants, hotels, financial and insurance firms, retail outlets, amusement and recreation facilities, personal service facilities for hair, clothing, shoes, automobiles and household goods and communication and public transportation systems. This list is not exhaustive and its precise statistical coverage is specified in the original sources of time series presented below.

b. Government Services

Government services are generated by the incurrence of exhaustive expenditures required in the administration of education, health, welfare, defence, justice and general government programmes. It is clear that under this definition government services exclude money spent in transfer payments, though they include the cost of carrying out these transfers.

We assume that all exhaustive government expenditures are made available free of charge to citizens and that they result in public consumption, except for real capital formation. This assumption results in an overestimate of total government service consumption if some government spending is used by producers, some education and health expenditures go towards net human capital formation and spending on defence is considered to be a form of investment in national security. It also leads to an over-estimate of government service consumption if there are charges to consumers and they are included in the category of service consumption spending discussed in the preceding section.

c. Producer Services

Producer services, which may also be called intermediate input services, are all those services not bought by private individuals or provided by governments. They consist of the output of industries known as Business Services, comprising computer, accounting, advertising, personnel, protection and similar industries. However, they also include a part of the output of several industries that are often better known as sources of supply for consumer services. These are the financial, insurance, real estate, transportation, engineering, legal, storage, communication, hotel, restaurant and many other service industries.

Several studies noted above have dwelled on the very rapid growth of Business Services in recent years. While this sector has experienced the most rapid growth of all service sub-sectors, in 1985 it still represented a relatively small proportion of total employment in Canada.[1] Below, we provide empirical information which reflects the increased use of business as well as the other producer services.[2]

d. Estimation Technique

The estimation of the relative size of the three service sectors has been dictated by the absence of any time series on producer services and the availability of the following three basic statistical time series in nominal and real terms. Firstly, the most basic is the series on GDP at factor cost for the sum of all service-producing industries. Secondly, there are time series on gross expenditures on services by consumers, and thirdly, exhaustive expenditures by government. Estimation of the value of producer services basically involves the subtraction of consumer service spending GDP and of exhaustive government spending from the total value of service GDP. The residual is equal to the value of producer services.

The estimation procedure required some minor adjustments to the basic time series data. Government spending was reduced by expenditures on government capital formation on the grounds that this involves mainly spending on construction of roads, schools and similar projects. However, no adjustment was made to eliminate material inputs from the remaining government services. These data thus count as service GDP

---

[1] The level of employment in Canada in Business Services in 1985 was 498 thousand and therefore less than that in Health and Welfare with 979 thousand, Education with 745 thousand and Accommodation and Food Services with 632 thousand (Statistics Canada 71-001, February 1986).

[2] Space limitations prevent us from discussing here the role of international non-factor trade in services. However, we should note that available statistics on Travel, Freight and Shipping, Business Services and Other tend to be weighted heavily in favour of producer services, since the only consumer services are virtually those absorbed by tourists. For more on the nature and magnitude of trade in services, see Grubel [1986; 1988], where it is argued that the bulk of services are traded internationally after they have been embodied as producer services in material substances or they have been produced or absorbed by persons or goods during temporary stays abroad.

the goods used up in the production of the government services, such as paper and computers.[1]

A second adjustment is based on the fact that the value of consumer service expenditures include the values of intermediate material inputs, such as the food served in restaurants.[2] The ratio of value added to gross output of these consumer service industries was about 0.6 for Canada during the 1970s. This figure was used to deflate the gross service consumption data for all of the countries in this study and for all years since the correct figures could not be obtained from available data sources. This procedure is likely to create a relatively small bias in the comparison of intertemporal developments within each country, since the consumer service industries are relatively labour intensive and have experienced little technological change. For the same reasons, comparisons of different countries should be subject to relatively small biases.

In sum, the estimating procedure derives producer services as a residual: Total Service Expenditure and Product minus Government Provided Services minus Consumer Service GDP equals Producer Service GDP.

---

[1] If the material inputs used by the government (and consumer service producing industries) are not deducted from the gross expenditures, it is possible in principle for the sum of these service expenditures to exceed the total GDP of the service industries measured through output. Therefore, the failure to deflate government exhaustive spending for material intermediate inputs results in an underestimate of the size of the demand for producer services. The same bias results from the failure to deduct the intermediate service inputs purchased by governments from exhaustive government spending. However, this treatment probably creates a relatively minor bias given the adjustment made for capital formation and the labour intensity of most government services. The exception, in this is spending on defence, which in the case of Canada is relatively minor (3 per cent of GDP). It should also be noted that if the proportion of material and intermediate service inputs used by governments in the provision of their services has remained constant, then there will be a relatively unbiased estimate of the rates of growth of the share of producer services in GDP.

[2] Use of the GDP of consumer service-producing industries eliminates from gross production figures not just material but also intermediate service inputs bought by the industry. These intermediate service inputs are thus attributed to the producer service sector, which is the intention of the exercise.

e. Empirical Results

At the end of 1987, Statistics Canada produced a revised set of statistics on real GDP at factor cost in 1981 prices for the years 1961-1986. These data were used to develop Figures 3 and 4 which show the shares of consumer, government, producer and total service expenditures as a percentage of GDP for those years in nominal terms, real terms and as an index to highlight changes in the size of shares. Required basic data for analogous estimates could be found in OECD National Accounts publications only for the years 1970-1984 and for a small set of countries. Estimates of the size of the different service sectors for some of these countries are contained in the appendix tables and only the changes in the index are presented in figures.

f. Results for Canada

Figure 3 shows the shares of nominal GDP represented by output of the total and different sub-sectors of the service industries. The growth of the total share closely parallels that of the growth in the employment share shown in Figure 2. It is also clear that consumer and government services in recent years have been about equal size and each have been slighly more than half the magnitude of producer services.

Estimates in terms of constant prices are shown in Figure 4. They reveal that in throughout the period as a per cent of GDP consumer and Government services have been of about equal size while producer services have been about 40 to 50 per cent greater as a share of GDP. The representation of the shares in terms of levels hides some interesting developments of the shares through time which are brought out effectively in Figure 4. Most notable in this representation is that producer services have grown, somewhat cyclically, 20 per cent as a share of GDP during the 25 years under observation. Consumer services, on the other hand, have represented a declining share of GDP between 1961 and 1973 but recovered their 1961 levels by 1986. Government services kept pace

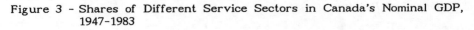

Figure 3 - Shares of Different Service Sectors in Canada's Nominal GDP,
1947-1983

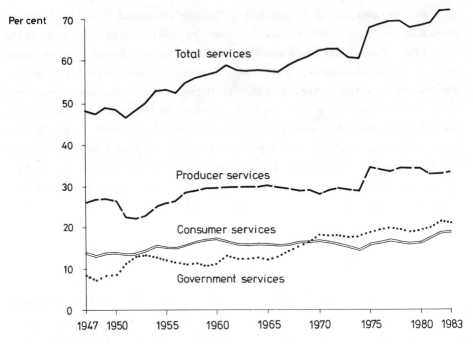

Source: Statistics Canada [a].

with the growth of the producer services until 1982. Thereafter, their
share fell to the level they had occupied in 1961. [1]

g. Some Thoughts on Prices

The preceding results depend heavily on the quality of the price
data used in the construction of the series. It is well known that price
and productivity data present particularly severe problems for statis-

---

[1] The finding on the relative decline of the government share points to
the importance of transfer payments in total spending. However, this
decline may also be a statistical artifact. See the next section for more
details.

ticians in the case of government services. These problems are mostly due to the absence of market prices and often units of output, as in the case of defence. To overcome these problems, statisticians assume that the real quantity of output is strictly proportional to real expenditures on inputs by governments.

Figure 4 - Shares of Services as a Percentage (1981 dollars)

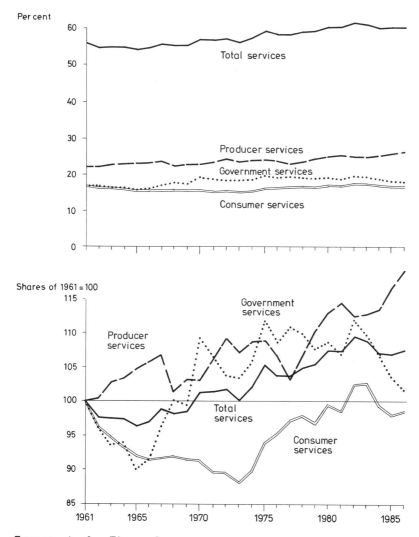

Source: As for Figure 3.

For example, a doubling of employees issuing pension cheques is assumed to result in a doubling of real service output. This procedure neglects the fact that the number of cheques issued may have grown more than 100 per cent through the simultaneous introduction of computers and the doubling of employees. Under such a condition the real quantity of government services produced has more than doubled while official statistics show only a growth of 100 per cent. By analogy, deterioration in the quality of services, such as the incidence of misdirected cheques, should be reflected as a factor lowering the real quantity of government services produced.

There is only inconclusive empirical evidence on the real quantity of output by governments adjusted for changes in productivity and other inputs. One may surmise that computers, word-processors and modern means of communication and travel have probably increased the productivity of civil servants and soldiers. On the other hand, Read [1983] has produced evidence on the decline of productivity in Canada Post, in spite of large increases in capital per worker.

There are also problems associated with the measurement of price and quality changes in privately-produced services. The bias in the data resulting from these problems appears to be less severe than that stemming from the measurement of government service output.

In the absence of reliable information, we have to accept the results reported above as the best systematically available. However, we can note, that if there is a systematic underestimate of productivity increases in the government sector, then the consumption of real government services has been greater than is indicated by current data. In other words, Canadians have been provided with pension cheques and defence at rates growing more rapidly than is implicit in Figure 4. Under these assumptions, the share of real government services in GDP has declined less or may even have increased. Most important, it is logically possible that, under these assumptions, the real share in producer services has remained constant or has fallen.

Below, we assume that bias in the measurement of real service production is sufficiently unsystematic and small to preserve the validity of the main findings: producer services represent about one half of all service output, consumer and government services one quarter each in nominal terms. The growth of real service output is dominated strongly by the growth of producer services.

h. Some Preliminary Evidence on OECD Countries

The OECD publication of the National Accounts of member countries contains the information needed to estimate the level and real growth rates of consumer, government and producer services for a number of countries. In the appendix tables, we present the shares of total services GDP made up of these components for the years 1970-1985 for these countries. From the analytical perspective of our study, the most important result emerging from these tables is that, in recent years, in both nominal and real terms the level of producer services has been somewhere between 28 and 33 per cent of all services. Canada is the outlayer with 41 per cent. The great similarity is remarkable in the sense that the sample covers such diverse countries as the United States, Japan, Norway, Sweden and Greece.

The proportion of consumer services has been around 15 per cent of the total for all countries except Sweden and Norway, where it has been roughly one half that size. The explanation for this is likely to be found in the much larger government service sector in these latter two countries.

For the purpose of theorizing, we have prepared Figure 5. It presents the time trend of the share of real producer services in total GDP for each of the countries in the sample (the data in the appendix give percentages with total service GDP as the base of 100). The data show an interesting similarity of the size of the share for the United States, Greece, Sweden and Japan, all of which have remained unchanged during the 15 years of observation. Canada stands out as the country with a rapid and consistent growth in the producer service sector. Norway, on the other hand, is notable for the consistent decline in this share.

A detailed analysis of this data cannot be presented here. However, it is tempting to suggest that in Norway, Sweden and Greece the very rapid growth and high level of government service spending may be due to the rapid growth in producer services put out by the government which in the other countries tend to be produced in the private sector.

Figure 5 - Producer Services as a Per Cent of GDP (constant prices)

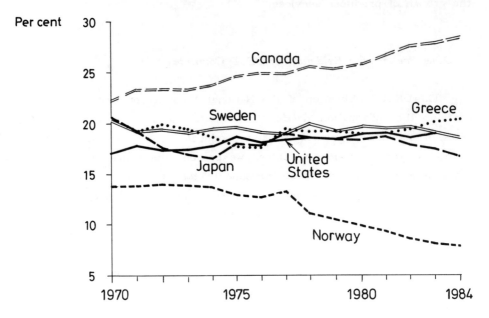

Source: OECD [various issues].

If this hypothesis is correct, then the main point of our basic model is reconfirmed by the international evidence. The bulk of the growth of service-sector GDP is due to the increased output of producer services. Obviously, these propositions need further investigation by a detailed analysis of the composition of government spending or correlation analysis between the growth rate of government and producer services. Also, constancy of the producer service-sector share in the United States and Japan, which has been unaccompanied by a growth in government services, needs to be explained.

In sum, the evidence on the levels and growth rates of different service sectors in different countries is presented here more for discussion than in definitive support of our model.

4. The Economics of Individual Sectors

a. Consumer Services[1]

The demand for individual goods and services in the budgets of consumers has been studied by Houthakker and Taylor [1966] and Prais and Houthakker [1971] in their path-breaking application of econometrics and the use of computers. Schweitzer [1969] and Tulpule and Powell [1978] have made similar studies for Canadian and Australian consumers respectively. Bernstein and Geehan [1988] used translogarithmic expenditure functions to estimate demand functions for Canada.

These and other studies have found that the income elasticity of demand for services ranges between 0.6 and 2, with an average of slightly above 1. The income elasticity of demand is high for some services, such as fancy restaurant meals and other traditional luxury services. On the other hand, for a wide variety of personal, household and recreation services, the income elasticity is quite low because modern technology has produced substitute goods such as appliances for household services and modern electronic devices for entertainment outside the home. Bernstein and Geehan [1988, p. 331] found an income elasticity of demand for insurance services of about 1.5.

The importance of the aggregate consumer services used in the preceding section suggests that it might be interesting to consider the demand for the sum of all consumer services, something which has been given little attention before. Only very recently Summers and Heston [1988] have studied total service consumption spending in 60 countries. They found that "service expenditures are somewhat income elastic with respect to consumption when allowance is made for relative prices" [ibid., p. 16]. Bernstein and Geehan [1988, p. 331] have found the demand for non insurance services in Canada to be about 1.25.

Below, we present data on Canada, though the application of the model to conditions in France and the United States has produced very

---

[1] The analysis in this section draws heavily on Grubel and Hammes [1987].

similar results.[1] Using aggregate data, a standard demand equation for total Canadian consumer spending on services for the 1961-1985 period was estimated[2] with the following results:

[1] $\ln(S) = -1.175 + 1.172\ln(TE) - 0.39\ln(PS)$
     (-8.6) (16.81) (-2.48)

where S is the real service expenditure per capita, TE is total real consumption expenditure per capita and PS is the relative price of services, ln means natural logs and the values in parenthesis are t-values. The number of observations is 25, R^2 is 0.989 and the uncorrected Durbin-Watson statistic is 0.42.

As can be seen, the estimated income elasticity in this equation is statistically significant, has the theoretically-expected sign and is consistent with that found in other studies. The price elasticity coefficient is significant and has the expected sign. However, the level of the Durbin-Watson statistic suggests the omission of a variable.

In the search for this omitted variable, we constructed a model of household behaviour in which changes in the female labour force participation rate is an exogenously-given, driving force. According to this model, the movement of women into the labour force reduces the production of certain types of services in the household and increases their purchase in the market. Accordingly, changes in the female labour force participation rates are hypothesized to result in shifts in the demand

---

[1] Grubel and Hammes [1987] and Hammes, Rosa and Grubel [forthcoming] contain results for the United States and France respectively. Trivedi [1988] used the basic model to estimate the demand for consumer services in India. In place of labour force participation rates for females he found the rate of urbanization to be a theoretically and empirically strong shift parameter for the demand function.

[2] The data were taken from Statistics Canada, CANSIM matrix 6708, series D 10131 and D 10147, both series as revised in 1986. Further information on prices, other independent variables, econometric techniques and a theoretical model of household behaviour is given in Grubel and Hammes [1987]. However, we should note that the demand equation is identified as a result of the assumption that the supply of consumer services is perfectly elastic. This assumption seems reasonable in the light of the fact that the consumer service industry is relatively small and most of the factors of production it requires, mostly notably labour, are good substitutes in use in other industries.

function for services and change the total expenditure and relative price coefficients in the estimating equation. The results of our calculations are:

[2] lnS = 1.009 + 0.348ln(TE) + 0.703ln(F) - 0.007ln(PS)
    (6.86) (6.09)   (15.42)   (-0.13)

The symbols are defined as before, F is the female labour force participation rate, the numer of observations is 25, R^2 is 0.999 and the uncorrected Durbin-Watson is 2.07. These results are consistent with our model and basic postulates of consumer behaviour. They imply that the income elasticity of demand for consumer services is well below one and that the growth in demand for them has been driven by the growth in the female labour force participation rate. At the mean, for every one per cent increase in the participation rate, the demand for consumer services has increased to 0.7 per cent.[1]

For our general analysis of the service sector, these estimates have three important implications. Firstly, they imply that the rise in the female labour force participation rate from 28.7 per cent in 1961 to 54.4 per cent in 1985 has been responsible for 63 per cent of the increased demand for consumer services. Secondly, this demand growth reflects a shift from unrecorded household production into the recorded formal sector by an amount equal to 16.4 per cent of the growth of GNP per capita during this period. Thirdly, if and when there is a change in the female labour force participation rate, the demand for consumer services and rate of measured economic growth may be expected to change correspondingly and by substantial amounts.

---

[1] The validity of our model finds support in the findings of Scarfe and Krantz [1988, p. 47] that, in econometric equations estimating the demand for restaurant meals in Canada, there is a significant difference in determinants of low (Chain) and high-priced (Independent) restaurants. The elasticity of demand with respect to total family expenditures is low for the former and high for the latter while the former shows statistically significant correlation with female labour force participation rates while the latter does not.

b. Government Services

During the immediate post-war period the dominant theory of the determinants and effects of government spending was that articulated most persuasively by Musgrave [1959], who, in turn, drew heavily on Pigou. This theory perceived government spending to be the outcome of a detached, rational calculus and administration by agents without any self-interest. It was postulated to involve the meeting of merit wants, the internationalization of externalities and the provision of public goods, all of which resulted in increased social welfare attainable with given resources.

The validity of Musgrave's public finance theory was challenged by the public choice model of Buchanan and Tullock [1962] and others. According to this view, government spending has been motivated predominantly by the efforts of politicians to secure votes from special interest groups that benefit from these expenditures. It is therefore likely to decrease rather than increase overall social welfare.

The spending data on Canada presented above lend some support to the public choice models. While government spending in total has been claiming ever increasing shares of GDP, most of the growth has been in transfer payments rather than exhaustive expenditures. As the data show, the latter in real terms actually represent a 20 per cent smaller percentage of GDP in 1986 than in 1961. According to the public choice approach, this is due to the fact that transfer payments can be aimed very well at special interest groups whereas real government services cannot.

The data on other countries, however, suggest that generalizations on this matter are difficult. US trends resemble those in Canada, especially if the growth of the 1980s in exhaustive expenditures were adjusted properly for increases in defence spending. Exhaustive spending in Japan fluctuated widely, but has been level for the period since 1971. Greece and Sweden, on the other hand, have experienced large growth in spending.

The future of government service production is difficult to predict. In North America, tax revolts have limited the ability and willingness of politicians to raise taxes while transfer payment programmes have a built-in growth. As a result, exhaustive expenditures are likely to shrink further in real terms. On the other hand, the deterioration of social overhead capital and real services may so reduce the quality of life and efficiency of the economy that pressures for increased spending will mount. Whether or not these pressures will succeed will depend significantly on the ability to bring under control the internal dynamics of transfer payment programmes and the tendency of politicians to buy votes by the initiation of new programmes for their constituencies. Undoubtedly, conditions in every country are different and we are not qualified to speculate on those.

c. Producer Services

According to neo-classical economic theory, growth in output per capita is an increasing function of society's ratio of capital to labour, where the former consists of real, human and knowledge capital. One of the ideas of the Austrian School of Economics expressed in the writings of von Boehm-Bawerk [1932] and found in Wicksell [1901] is that this capital-deepening involves increases in the "roundaboutness" and specialization of the entire production process.

Robinson Crusoe increased the roundaboutness of fish production when he constructed a fishing net. He did so because it enabled him, over the technical life of the net, to catch more fish than he could have through the use of the labour spent in making the net and the use of the same fishing effort without the net.

In a more complex society, fishing nets are produced by specialists who use machinery, human skills and scientific knowledge are produced by further specialists. All of these production processes increase roundaboutness and the "distance" between ultimate consumers of final output such as fish and the activities of these producers of intermediate inputs. The prices of these intermediate inputs must be high enough to earn producers at least normal returns. At the same time, these intermediate inputs must yield a positive net return to their users. Otherwise there is no market for them.

We think that it is useful to consider the providers of producer services to be one important set of specialists in this process which generates ever-increasing roundaboutness, specialization in production, capital-deepening and increases in labour and other factor productivity. It is difficult to generalize about the factor inputs and other technical characteristics of producer service industries.

Baumol [1984] has shown that some service industries have high capital-labour ratios, as for example the telecommunication industries and utilities. On the other hand, many firms providing producer services use workers with high levels of training, employ sophisticated techniques but have low levels of physical capital. These firms may be said to operate with high levels of human-knowledge capital per worker. Examples in this field are the computer and communications consulting firms that have developed since the electronic revolution of the 1970s. Birch [1979] shows that many of these firms are small and run by Schumpeterian entrepreneurs, but that there are also the large and more traditional firms in the financial, legal, accounting and engineering service industries. Finally, there are highly labour-intensive, low-tech producer services, such as janitors and retail clerks.

d. Schumpeterian Process

Seen in this perspective, the relative growth of the producer service sector can continue for as long as technological innovations maintain a marginal rate of return to capital greater than the rate of interest. In a market economy, this innovation is generated to a significant degree by Schumpeterian entrepreneurs. Of these, a large proportion fails, another large segment earns only normal rates of return, but they all are driven by the expectation of large, if temporary, returns, which accrue to only a few. As long as an environment favourable to these entrepreneurs is maintained, they venture into business with innovative technology, processes and services nd the dynamic process of accumulation and service-sector growth continues.

e. Productivity

One important implication of our model of the producer service sector is that its effect on the productivity of labour and other industries can be indirect but still very important. For example, consider the above model of fishing and capital-deepening through the use of nets. Assume that the net-making industry is without technological advances and that labour productivity in this industry is constant. Assume also that technological advances increase the effectiveness of nets in catching fish. Finally, consider that the fishing industry finds it profitable to increase the quantity of nets per worker. During the postulated period of innovation and capital-deepening, the price of fish may fall and demand increase sufficiently so that more workers are needed. Alternatively, the quantity of workers employed may fall. In either case, during the period under consideration the productivity of labour in the net-producing industry is unchanged but that in the fishing industry is growing since each worker catches growing numbers of fish in every new time period during which technology improves.

Computer, telecommunications, financial and similar service industries are much like the industries producing fish nets in the preceding example. They may be experiencing low or zero productivity gains,[1] but their inputs generate productivity increases in the industries purchasing their output. For example, productivity may have been constant in the firms which wrote the programmes required for the operation of the automated bank teller machines which were introduced in the banking sector in recent years. However, there is little doubt that the use of these teller machines raised the output of financial service industry workers in terms of cheque cashing transactions per time period.[2]

In modern economies, productivity gains generated by service industries may not even show up because of deficiencies in measurement procedures. For example, a town may initially be served by one shopping centre located at one end of town and operating at a certain level of productivity. Now consider that competition results in the establishment of a second shopping centre at the opposite end of town. In the new equilibrium, both centres operate profitably, each serving half the

---

[1] The validity of the following analysis is independent of the assumption about productivity developments in the service sector. We have chosen the present assumption because it is widely considered to be correct, although there is much argument over the validity of current measurement techniques [see Mark, 1982] used in arriving at this view.

[2] We owe this example to Chant [1988].

town's population. Under these conditions, it is easily possible that by traditional measures productivity in the retail sector serving the town has decreased, average retail margins have increased while at the same time there is genuine equilibrium in that all firms earn normal returns and the efficiency of household production has increased sufficiently to create an increase in overall welfare. [1]

f. Trade in Services

Our approach to the study of services in modern economies has some interesting implications for international trade in services, which have been discussed at greater length in Grubel [1988]. However, it is worth noting here two implications of the overwhelming importance of producer services in the economy.

Firstly, producer services are likely to play a significant role in the determination of comparative advantage. This is not a new idea since it is now widely accepted that the omission of human and knowledge capital underlies the Leontief paradox. These forms of capital enter the production process largely through the activities of producer service industries. More recent work in international economics by Krugman [1979] and Brander and Spencer [1983] have pointed to the potential role of comparative advantage played by industrial strategies in the development of new products and industries. In almost all of the examples used in this literature, but especially automobiles, computers and aircraft, these strategies require the use of high technology and other inputs which are typically provided by producer service firms.

Secondly, producer services are traded to a small degree by the temporary movement of delivery agents, as when professional consultants move abroad temporarily to provide a service. [2] There is also some pro-

---

[1] We owe this example to Acheson and Ferris [1988]. In some theoretical models the welfare gains from such locational differentiation are ambiguous. See, for example, Eaton and Wooders [1985].

[2] The permanent establishment of foreign operations by firms in the service sector involves international capital and therefore factor service flows. These are not the trade in services which has attracted the concern of policy makers and theorists in recent years. However, it

ducer service trade carried on by the temporary stay of capital equipment abroad, as in the case of leased drilling platforms and aircraft selling transportation to foreigners. The rest of the producer services are traded after they have been embodied in material substances.

According to Iococca [1984], Chrysler automobiles embody medical services worth more than the steel used in their construction. Of course, the steel in turn embodies many types of services and so on for the inputs used in steel production, in patterns which can be established through the use of input-output tables. Many producer services are embodied in paper, electronic storage devices and electronic signals. [1]

Our model of services implies that much theorizing about service as a special type of trade is unwarranted and that the standard theoretical treatment of services as essentially non-tradeable deserves to be retained. At the same time, the model invites theorizing about and measurement of embodied service trade.

5. Summary and Policy Implications

The main contribution of this study consists of the development of a taxonomy and measurement of consumer, government and producer services. The measurement technique, which can be applied in all countries with modern national income accounting systems, showed that in Canada about one half of all service GDP is used by producers, one quarter is consumed directly and one quarter is produced by government mainly for domestic consumption.

Our model of the demand for consumer services points to the importance of the monetization of household production as a driving force of

---

should be noted that service firms abroad tend to generate direct service trade to the extent that they generate income from patents, royalties, copyrights and other knowledge capital. Unfortunately, these sources of comparative advantage of foreign subsidiaries are not normally captured by existing balance-of-payments accounting procedures, as has been discussed by Rugman [1987].

[1] Some consumer services are traded in this manner after embodiment in such a form as life assurance contracts, but we believe this type of trade to be relatively unimportant.

demand. It also implies that the income elasticity of demand for services by consumers is much lower than suggested by the existing literature.

For economic policy, the most important finding is the relative importance and growth of producer services in the economy. The phenomenon falls readily into conventional theories of capital accumulation and specialization in production and suggests that the growth of the service sector will continue for as long as this accumulation continues.

Seen from this perspective, service sector growth is not a drag on economic development, as is implied by models which assume that consumer and government services dominate the sector and its growth. On the contrary, producer services are probably an important source of the productivity gains in the goods-producing sector. This may well be so in cases where productivity in the producer service industries proper is stagnant or even falling. In addition, producer services are part of the endowment which determines comparative advantage. Through embodiment in material substances generally and goods in particular, indirect trade in producer services is a source of gains from trade and specialization much like real capital and natural resources.

Our findings imply that it is inefficient to base development strategies on the subsidy of goods-producing industries at the expense of taxes on the service sector. In a growing and efficient world, much of the capital deepening is in the form of human and knowledge capital, which constitutes the main productive factor in the dynamic producer service industries. In a free market, marginal returns to investment in producer services and goods production tend to be equalized. Taxing one sector to benefit the other therefore may be presumed to reduce rather than raise income and welfare.

Appendix Tables

Table A1 - Proportions of Various Segments of Service Sectors in Nominal and Real Terms for Canada, 1970-1984

Year	Per cent in nominal terms				Per cent in real terms				Per cent in real terms set at 1970=100			
	G	C	P	T	G	C	P	T	G	C	P	T
1970	15.53	13.88	35.23	64.64	16.03	13.96	34.54	64.53	100.00	100.00	100.00	100.00
1971	15.33	14.06	35.87	65.26	15.33	14.06	35.87	65.26	95.58	100.76	103.85	101.13
1972	15.34	13.87	36.04	65.26	14.96	13.92	36.15	65.04	93.31	99.76	104.66	100.78
1973	15.01	13.23	34.84	63.07	14.75	13.47	36.28	64.50	92.01	96.51	105.02	99.95
1974	14.94	12.82	34.65	62.40	14.73	13.52	36.65	64.90	91.87	96.86	106.09	100.56
1975	16.16	13.35	33.97	63.48	15.14	13.97	37.22	66.33	94.44	100.08	107.74	102.78
1976	16.43	13.74	34.57	64.74	14.61	14.08	37.78	66.35	91.13	100.07	109.36	102.82
1977	17.08	14.04	34.02	65.14	14.82	14.14	37.52	66.42	92.44	100.88	108.62	102.93
1978	17.09	14.13	33.73	64.96	14.62	14.16	38.24	66.99	91.15	101.28	110.70	103.81
1979	16.57	13.87	32.58	63.01	14.37	14.54	38.14	66.67	89.62	101.45	110.41	103.31
1980	16.77	14.04	31.83	62.64	14.28	14.35	38.40	67.22	89.06	104.20	111.17	104.17
1981	17.11	13.95	32.83	63.89	14.16	14.91	39.46	67.97	88.31	102.83	114.22	105.32
1982	18.15	14.72	33.81	66.68	14.75	14.91	39.86	69.51	91.96	106.82	115.39	107.72
1983	18.45	14.80	33.69	66.95	14.54	14.72	40.29	69.55	90.71	105.43	116.64	107.77
1984	18.26	14.67	33.50	66.43	13.99	14.33	41.00	69.32	87.27	102.68	118.68	107.41

Note: G = Government provided services, C = Consumer service GDP, P = Producer service GDP, and T = Total GDP of the service-producing sectors. - Real terms variables are in 1971 prices.

Source: OECD [various issues].

Table A2 – Proportions of Various Segments of Service Sectors in Nominal and Real Terms for the US, 1970-1983

Year	Per cent in nominal terms				Per cent in real terms				Per cent in real terms set at 1970=100			
	G	C	P	T	G	C	P	T	G	C	P	T
1970	16.74	16.65	29.08	62.47	17.35	16.16	27.91	61.42	100.00	100.00	100.00	100.00
1971	15.93	16.85	30.54	63.31	16.38	16.26	28.96	61.59	94.42	100.59	103.76	100.28
1972	16.25	16.84	30.02	63.11	16.26	16.25	28.66	61.17	93.73	100.53	102.72	99.60
1973	15.57	16.58	29.85	62.00	15.39	16.12	28.83	60.35	88.73	99.74	103.31	98.25
1974	16.16	16.95	29.79	62.90	16.20	16.66	28.87	61.73	93.36	103.08	103.44	100.50
1975	16.80	17.34	29.46	63.60	16.80	17.34	29.46	63.60	96.83	107.30	105.55	103.55
1976	16.83	17.50	29.06	63.38	16.63	17.33	28.95	62.91	95.84	107.21	103.75	102.43
1977	16.48	17.62	29.03	63.13	16.18	17.20	29.57	62.95	93.29	106.42	105.95	102.50
1978	15.88	17.58	29.49	62.50	15.70	17.18	29.98	62.86	90.53	106.29	107.42	102.35
1979	15.77	17.75	29.45	62.97	15.76	17.38	29.61	62.75	90.85	107.49	106.12	102.17
1980	16.46	18.35	29.02	63.84	16.31	17.89	29.72	63.92	94.00	110.67	106.51	104.07
1981	16.59	18.43	28.50	63.52	16.34	17.75	29.97	64.05	94.18	109.78	107.39	104.29
1982	17.68	19.58	28.04	65.30	17.41	18.65	28.88	64.95	100.37	115.37	103.50	105.74
1983	17.78	19.86	28.68	66.31	17.17	18.70	29.36	65.23	98.97	115.70	105.19	106.20

Note: G = Government provided services, C = Consumer service GDP, P = Producer service GDP, and T = Total GDP of the service-producing sectors. – Real terms variables are in 1975 prices.

Source: As for Table A1.

Table A3 - Proportions of Various Segments of Service Sectors in Nominal and Real Terms for Japan, 1970-1984

Year	Per cent in nominal terms				Per cent in real terms				Per cent in real terms set at 1970=100			
	G	C	P	T	G	C	P	T	G	C	P	T
1970	3.11	13.12	31.04	47.27	5.01	15.26	36.55	56.82	100.00	100.00	100.00	100.00
1971	2.93	13.74	31.93	48.59	4.35	15.64	33.82	53.81	86.84	102.48	92.55	94.71
1972	2.69	14.11	32.12	48.92	3.49	15.62	33.75	52.86	69.75	102.38	92.34	93.05
1973	2.64	13.76	31.28	47.68	3.06	15.81	33.00	51.87	61.16	103.61	90.29	91.30
1974	3.90	13.65	32.19	49.75	4.30	16.33	31.85	52.48	85.91	106.99	87.15	92.37
1975	4.75	14.82	32.53	52.10	4.53	16.78	32.98	54.29	90.45	109.95	90.24	95.55
1976	4.70	14.91	32.60	52.20	4.59	16.28	33.23	54.11	91.72	106.70	90.93	95.23
1977	4.29	15.39	33.84	53.53	4.00	16.23	34.80	55.02	79.76	106.38	95.21	96.85
1978	3.54	16.10	34.06	53.70	3.31	16.54	34.56	54.41	66.05	108.36	94.57	95.76
1979	3.37	16.59	34.14	54.10	3.29	16.85	34.29	54.43	65.66	110.42	93.83	95.80
1980	3.70	16.49	34.21	54.40	3.66	16.50	34.19	54.36	73.13	108.16	93.56	95.68
1981	3.86	16.53	34.43	54.82	3.73	16.39	34.54	54.66	74.45	107.43	94.51	96.21
1982	4.12	17.16	34.11	55.39	3.86	16.75	33.57	54.18	77.12	109.74	91.85	95.36
1983	4.47	17.58	34.11	56.16	4.06	16.87	32.96	53.89	81.04	110.54	90.19	94.85
1984	4.79	17.53	33.63	55.95	4.25	16.59	32.02	52.86	84.78	108.73	87.61	93.03

Note: G = Government provided services, C = Consumer service GDP, P = Producer service GDP, and T = Total GDP of the service-producing sectors. - Real terms variables are in 1980 prices.

Source: As for Table A1.

Table A4 - Proportions of Various Segments of Service Sectors in Nominal and Real Terms for Greece 1970-1984

Year	Per cent in nominal terms				Per cent in real terms				Per cent in real terms set at 1970=100			
	G	C	P	T	G	C	P	T	G	C	P	T
1970	8.08	12.91	36.18	57.17	8.08	12.91	36.18	57.17	100.00	100.00	100.00	100.00
1971	8.40	12.92	35.08	56.39	8.39	13.08	34.66	56.13	103.87	101.38	95.80	98.19
1972	7.41	12.61	35.46	55.48	7.26	12.99	35.72	55.97	89.93	100.63	98.73	97.91
1973	6.99	11.54	34.09	52.63	7.72	12.82	35.20	55.75	95.61	99.36	97.30	97.52
1974	10.18	12.12	32.41	54.71	10.49	13.27	33.15	56.90	129.87	102.83	91.61	99.54
1975	11.02	12.17	33.69	56.88	10.60	13.06	33.36	57.03	131.32	101.23	92.21	99.76
1976	11.39	11.98	33.11	56.48	11.17	13.05	33.10	57.32	138.27	101.14	91.49	100.27
1977	12.18	12.11	33.65	57.95	11.57	13.23	33.58	58.38	143.25	102.51	92.82	102.13
1978	12.71	12.17	32.93	57.81	11.82	13.18	33.06	58.07	146.43	102.14	91.38	101.58
1979	13.10	11.77	33.17	58.04	12.21	13.32	33.11	58.64	151.18	103.21	91.53	102.58
1980	13.69	12.15	30.66	56.50	12.42	13.68	32.51	58.61	153.84	106.00	89.85	102.52
1981	14.17	12.64	29.27	56.09	12.74	13.91	32.75	59.40	157.79	107.77	90.51	103.90
1982	15.70	12.32	29.52	57.54	13.74	14.10	32.28	60.12	170.18	109.23	89.21	105.16
1983	15.83	12.05	30.85	58.73	14.26	14.23	32.88	61.37	176.57	110.30	90.87	107.35
1984	15.22	11.96	31.61	58.79	13.55	14.41	33.35	61.32	167.85	111.69	92.19	107.27

Note: G = Government provided services, C = Consumer service GDP, P = Producer service GDP, and T = Total GDP of the service-producing sectors. - Real terms variables are in 1970 prices.

Source: As for Table A1.

Table A5 - Proportions of Various Segments of Service Sectors in Nominal and Real Terms for Norway, 1970-1984

Year	Per cent in nominal terms				Per cent in real terms				Per cent in real terms set at 1970=100			
	G	C	P	T	G	C	P	T	G	C	P	T
1970	12.46	9.32	38.06	59.84	13.64	9.14	37.31	60.09	100.00	100.00	100.00	100.00
1971	13.21	9.26	37.56	60.03	13.57	9.09	37.33	59.99	99.49	99.49	100.04	99.83
1972	13.06	9.41	37.82	60.28	13.11	9.00	37.58	59.69	96.09	98.54	100.72	99.34
1973	13.50	9.30	38.28	61.09	13.56	8.91	37.45	59.93	99.41	97.56	100.38	99.73
1974	13.68	9.04	37.70	60.42	13.60	8.73	37.30	59.62	99.67	95.54	99.96	99.22
1975	14.51	9.16	34.88	58.56	13.78	8.80	36.21	58.78	100.99	96.25	97.04	97.82
1976	15.19	9.06	34.97	59.21	14.00	8.61	35.97	58.58	102.66	94.21	96.41	97.49
1977	15.30	9.25	35.46	60.02	14.17	8.69	36.57	59.43	103.85	95.11	98.01	98.90
1978	15.40	9.25	33.87	58.52	14.14	8.60	33.75	56.49	103.68	94.12	90.45	94.01
1979	15.19	8.89	32.66	56.74	14.43	8.53	32.76	55.72	105.76	93.33	87.81	92.72
1980	15.09	8.32	31.59	55.01	14.74	8.32	31.94	55.01	108.08	91.09	85.61	91.54
1981	15.57	8.73	30.73	54.66	16.00	8.44	31.08	55.51	117.26	92.34	83.30	92.38
1982	16.25	8.66	30.11	55.02	17.01	8.53	29.75	55.29	124.69	92.34	79.73	92.01
1983	16.40	8.89	29.39	54.68	16.96	8.56	28.86	54.37	124.30	93.72	77.33	90.49
1984	15.80	8.77	29.13	53.70	16.55	8.52	28.60	53.67	121.36	93.25	76.64	89.32

Note: G = Government provided services, C = Consumer service GDP, P = Producer service GDP, and T = Total GDP of the service-producing sectors. - Real terms variables are in 1980 prices.

Source: As for Table A1.

Table A6 – Proportions of Various Segments of Service Sectors in Nominal and Real Terms for Sweden, 1970-1984

Year	Per cent in nominal terms				Per cent in real terms				Per cent in real terms set at 1970=100			
	G	C	P	T	G	C	P	T	G	C	P	T
1970	16.40	9.82	33.62	59.83	20.72	9.47	32.39	62.59	100.00	100.00	100.00	100.00
1971	17.93	9.83	32.43	60.20	21.49	9.58	31.18	62.25	103.72	101.10	96.25	99.46
1972	18.54	10.06	33.11	61.71	21.86	9.66	31.09	62.62	105.52	102.01	95.97	100.05
1973	19.00	10.03	32.16	61.19	21.96	9.58	30.75	62.29	105.98	101.15	94.91	99.52
1974	19.62	9.75	28.50	57.87	22.13	9.63	30.99	62.75	106.81	101.70	95.66	100.26
1975	20.49	9.37	29.06	58.92	22.82	9.62	30.92	63.37	110.14	101.59	95.46	101.25
1976	21.66	9.43	28.87	59.96	23.54	9.69	30.20	63.42	113.59	102.31	93.22	101.34
1977	23.95	9.72	29.20	62.87	24.46	10.03	29.87	64.36	118.04	105.87	92.21	102.83
1978	24.23	10.01	30.40	64.64	24.57	9.96	30.84	65.37	118.59	105.10	95.22	104.45
1979	24.69	9.93	29.94	64.56	25.09	9.78	30.17	65.04	121.10	103.20	93.13	103.91
1980	25.28	9.75	30.30	65.33	25.28	9.75	30.30	65.33	121.99	102.96	93.53	104.38
1981	25.87	10.10	30.08	66.05	26.18	9.95	29.76	65.88	126.35	105.00	91.87	105.27
1982	25.98	10.48	30.18	66.64	26.36	10.05	29.68	66.09	127.20	106.08	91.63	105.59
1983	25.51	10.38	30.25	66.14	25.96	9.96	29.61	65.54	125.31	105.12	91.42	104.72
1984	25.07	10.22	30.55	65.84	25.81	9.77	29.04	64.62	124.59	103.09	89.65	103.25

Note: G = Government provided services, C = Consumer service GDP, P = Producer service GDP, and T = Total GDP of the service-producing sectors. - Real terms variables are in 1980 prices.

Source: As for Table A1.

Bibliography

ACHESON, Keith, Stephen FERRIS, Retail and Wholesale Trade Services in Canada. Fraser Institute Service Sector Project, Vancouver 1988.

BAUMOL, William, "Macroeconomics of Unbalanced Growth". The American Economic Review, Vol. 57, 1967, pp. 415-426.

--, Productivity Policy and the Service Sector. Fishman-Davidson Center for the Study of the Service Sector, Discussion Papers, 1, April 1984.

BERNSTEIN, Jeffrey, Randall GEEHAN, The Insurance Industry in Canada. Vancouver 1988.

BELL, David, The Coming of Post-Industrial Society: A Venture in Social Forecasting. New York 1979.

BLACKABY, Frank (Ed.), De-Industrialization. London 1978.

BLUESTONE, Barry, Bennett HARRISON, The Deindustrialization of America. New York 1982.

von BOEHM-BAWERK, Eugen, Capital and Interest: A Critical History of Economical Theory. (1st edition 1884.) Reprinted New York 1932.

BRANDER, James A., Barbara J. SPENCER, "International R&D Rivalry and Industrial Strategy". Review of Economic Studies, Vol. 50, 1983, pp. 707-722.

BUCHANAN, James M., Gordon TULLOCK, The Calculus of Consent: Logical Foundations of Constitutional Democracy. Ann Arbor 1962.

CASSON, Mark, The Firm and the Market. Cambridge, Mass., 1987.

COASE, Ronald, "The Nature of the Firm". Economica, Vol. 4, 1937, pp. 386-405.

CHANT, John F., The Market for Financial Services: The Deposit Taking Institutions. Fraser Institute Service Sector Project, Vancouver 1988.

EATON, Curtis, Myrna WOODERS, "Sophisticated Entry in an Address Model of Product Differentiation". Rand Journal of Economics, Vol. 16, 1985, pp. 282-297.

FISHER, Allan G.B., "Production, Primary, Secondary and Tertiary". Economic Record, Vol. 15, 1939, pp. 24-38.

FUCHS, Victor, The Service Economy. National Bureau of Economic Research, New York 1968.

GERSHUNY, Jonathan I., Ian MILES, The New Service Economy: The Transformation of Employment in Industrial Societies. New York 1983.

32

GINZBERG, Eli, George J. VOTJA, "The Service Sector of the US Economy". Scientific American, Vol. 244, 1981, pp. 48-55.

GOVERNMENT PRINTING OFFICE, Historical Statistics of Canada, Series D8-55. Ottawa 1983.

GREY, Rodney de C., Services and Intellectual Property Rights. Institute for Research on Public Policy, Discussion Paper Series on Trade in Services, Victoria, BC, March 1988.

GRUBEL, Herbert G., "All Traded Services are Embodied in Materials or People". The World Economy, Vol. 10, 1986, pp. 319-330.

--, "Direct and Embodied Trade in Services: Or, Where is the Service Trade Problem?". In: Chung LEE, Seiji NAYA (Eds.), Trade and Investment in Services in the Asia-Pacific Region: An Emerging Issue. Boulder 1988.

--, David L. HAMMES, Household Service Consumption and its Monetization: Or, How Much of Each Other's Laundry Are We Doing? Fraser Institute, Discussion Papers, 4, Vancouver 1987.

--, Michael A. WALKER, The Canadian Service Industries. Fraser Institute Service Sector Project, Vancouver 1989, forthcoming.

HAMMES, David, Jean-Jacques ROSA, Herbert G. GRUBEL, "Consumer Demand for Services". Kyklos, forthcoming.

HILL, T.P., "On Goods and Services". Review of Income and Wealth, Vol. 23, 1977, pp. 315-338.

HOUTHAKKER, Henrik S., Lawrence D. TAYLOR, Consumer Demand in the United States, 1929-1970, Analysis and Projections. Cambridge, Mass., 1966.

IOCOCCA, Lee, Iococca: An Autobiography. Toronto 1984.

JONES, Ronald, Frances RUANE, Appraising Options for International Trade in Services. Institute for Research on Public Policy, Discussion Paper Series on Trade in Services, Victoria, BC, March 1988.

KUTSCHER, Ronald E., Jerome H. MARK, "The Service Producing Sector: Some Common Misperceptions". Monthly Labor Review, Vol. 106, April 1983, pp. 21-24.

KRAVIS, Irving B., Services in the Domestic Economy and World Transactions. National Bureau of Economic Research, New York 1983.

KRUGMAN, Paul, "Increasing Returns, Monopolistic Competition and International Trade". Journal of International Economics, 1979, pp. 469-479.

McFETRIDGE, Donald G., Douglas A. SMITH, The Economics of Vertical Disintegration. Fraser Institute Service Sector Project, Vancouver 1988.

MARK, Jerome H., "Measuring Productivity in Services". Monthly Labor Review, Vol. 105, June 1982, pp. 3-8.

MOMIGLIANO, Franco, Domenico SINISCALCO, "The Growth of Service Employment: A Reappraisal". Banca Nacionale del Lavoro Quarterly Review, Vol. 142, 1982, pp. 269-306.

MUSGRAVE, Richard, The Theory of Public Finance. New York 1959.

ORGANISATION FOR ECONOMIC CO-OPERATION AND DEVELOPMENT (OECD), National Accounts - Detailed Tables. Paris, various issues.

OTT, Mack, "The Growing Share of Services in the US Economy - Degeneration or Evolution?". Federal Reserve Bank of St. Louis Review, Vol. 69, 1987, pp. 5-22.

PRAIS, S.J., Henrik HOUTHAKKER, The Analysis of Family Budgets. Cambridge 1971.

RADWANSKI, George, Ontario Study of the Service Sector. Ministry of Treasury and Economics. Toronto 1986.

READ, Lawrence M., "Canada Post: A Case Study in the Correlation of Collective Will and Productivity". In: Donald J. DALY (Ed.), Research on Productivity of Relevance to Canada. Ottawa 1983, pp. 129-136.

RIDDLE, Dorothy I., Service-Led Growth: The Role of the Service Sector in World Development. New York 1986.

RUGMAN, Alan M., "Multinationals and Trade in Services: A Transactions Cost Approach". Weltwirtschaftliches Archiv, Vol. 123, 1987, pp. 651-667.

SCARFE, Brian L., Murray KRANTZ, The Market for Hospitality. Fraser Institute Service Sector Project. Vancouver 1988.

STIGLER, George J., Trends in Employment in the Service Industries. Princeton 1956.

SHELP, Ronald K., Beyond Industrialization: The Ascendancy of the Global Service Economy. New York 1981.

SUMMERS, Robert, Alan HESTON, The International Demand for Services. University of Pennsylvania, Discussion Papers, 32, January 1988.

SWAN, Neil M., "The Service Sector: Engine of Growth?". Canadian Public Policy, Vol. XI, 1985, pp. 344-350, supplement.

SCHWEITZER, Thomas T., Personal Consumer Expenditures in Canada, 1926-75. Economic Council of Canada, Ottawa 1969.

STANBACK, T.M., Jr., Services: The New Economy. Montclair, NJ, 1981.

STATISTICS CANADA [a], GDP at Factor Cost by Industry. Series 13-531, 61-213, Occasional Papers, 15-001.

-- [b], GDP by Industry. Cat. No. 61-213, 1981, 1986 for years after 1971.

-- [c], The Labour Force, Cat. No. 71-001, February 1986.

-- [d], National Income and Expenditure Accounts, Vol. I, The Annual Estimates 1926-74. Cat. No. 531, Occasional Papers, 1976 for years up to 1971.

TATOM, John A., "Why has Manufacturing Employment Declined?". Federal Reserve Bank of St. Louis Review, December 1986, pp. 15-25.

TULPULE, Anthony, Alan A. POWELL, Estimates of Household Demand Elasticities for the ORANI Model. University of Melbourne, Impact Project Research Centre, Preliminary Working Papers, OP-22, 1978.

TRIVEDI, Vish, The Service Sector in India. Dissertation, Simon Fraser University, Burnaby, BC, 1988.

WILLIAMSON, Oliver, "Transactions Cost Economics: The Governance of Contractual Relations". Journal of Law and Economics, Vol. 22, 1979, pp. 233-261.

WICKSELL, Knut, Lectures on Political Economy. London 1901.

Comment on Herbert G. Grubel and Michael A. Walker, "Modern Service Sector Growth: Causes and Effects"

Richard Blackhurst*

I found this to be a very interesting paper. As with most work on services industries, the data present serious problems (both conceptual and practical, but for the most part the authors are candid about these limitations and there is no need for me to dwell on them.

The parts of the paper I liked best were those which dealt with "producer services". In particular, the authors' emphasis on the import-ance of producer services to efficient production in an increasingly technologically sophisticated world meshes very well with much of the current literature on the evolution of the world economy.[1] Clearly there is in every economy a very large number of firms producing goods and services whose ability to successfully confront world market competition is heavily influenced by the availability - or lack thereof - of competi-tively priced producer service inputs.

This emphasis on the importance of producer services to efficient production makes it all the more difficult to understand the authors' curt dismissal of the importance of international trade in services. In par-ticular, their advice "that the standard theoretical treatment of services as essentially non-tradable deserves to be retained" (p. 23) sounds rather odd when we consider the level of attention that has been devoted to services trade in the current round of multilateral trade negotiations. It is no secret that there was a wide range of views on the issue of including services trade in the Uruguay Round, but to the best of my knowledge, no government argued that services are essentially non-

---

* The opinions and conclusions in this comment are my own and do not necessarily reflect the views of the GATT Secretariat.

[1] For example, a recent paper by Henryk Kierzkowski and Ron Jones ("The Role of Services in Production and International Trade: A Theoretical Framework", June 1988, mimeo) notes that "Service links have the function of connecting production blocks in separate lo-cations, perhaps among several countries". This seems very close to the authors' use of the term "roundaboutness".

tradeable. In any case, there is now no doubt that trade in services is one of the key topics in the Round.

To a large degree, this difference in perception is probably explained by the authors' use of a very narrow definition of trade in services - in effect, that trade in services is limited to face-to-face delivery achieved by the strictly temporary cross-border movement of either the supplier or demander of the service.[1] Even those services which move across frontiers embodied in paper or electronic signals seem to be excluded from their definition.

The extent to which their general approach to the issue differs from that of most other analysts, and of the officials engaged in the Group of Negotiations on Services (GNS), is also strikingly evident from the first part of the footnote on page 22: "The permanent establishment of foreign operations by firms in the service sector involves international capital and therefore factor service flows. These are not the trade in services which has attracted the concern of policy makers and theorists in recent years". The claim in the latter sentence would certainly be news to those people in Geneva and in national capitals who are involved in the GNS, where the conditions governing market access, including issues relating to rights of establishment and/or commercial presence, as well as the mobility of productive factors, both capital and labour, are still very much live issues. It would also surprise a number of academics who have worked on this topic.[2] Clearly the world at large has adopted a much wider definition than the authors of which activities fall under the heading of "trade in services".

To sum up: if we combine (i) the authors' important insights about the size and central role of the producer services sector in a modern economy, with (ii) a broader definition of which activities and types of transactions are included under the heading "trade in services", I

---

[1] See footnote 2 on page 22 and the third full paragraph in 4.f., "Trade in Services", in Grubel and Walker's paper. Even within the confines of their very narrow definition of trade in services, the authors could be accused of making an unwarranted leap from the conclusion that most trade in services is not face-to-face to the conclusion that face-to-face trade in services is so insignificant that we can safely ignore it.

[2] See, for example, Brian Hindley, "Introducing Services into the GATT". February 1987, mimeo.

believe we have a very persuasive case for creating a liberal, multi-lateral, rules-based system for trade in services. As with the present GATT system covering trade in goods, the aim of such a services trade regime would not be to maximize trade in services, but rather to promote two complementary goals:

- a reduction in uncertainty about future market access for services; and

- a reduction over time in barriers to trade in services in order to bring domestic prices of services in each country closer to world market prices.

Given the importance they attach to the services sector in modern economies, it seems very unlikely that the authors would wish to quarrel with either of these goals.

Domenico Siniscalco

Defining and Measuring Output and Productivity in the Service Sector

1. Introduction

The falling share of manufacturing and the growing share of service sector in total employment is a clear feature in the process of structural change of the most advanced countries. From a statistical point of view, the reason for the change in the relative shares of industry and service sector employment lies in two factors: the relative growth of productivity and the relative growth of total (final and intermediate) demand. For many years, the economic debate about the determinants and the implications of the growth of service sector employment has revolved around the relative quantitative importance of these two factors. But the measures of productivity in the service sector are themselves the object of a lively controversy. Several authors, as we shall see, assert that the very measurement of productivity in many service branches is a meaningless exercise, given the peculiar characteristics of this sector. Other authors dismiss the above considerations as nonsense.

Generally speaking, productivity is a ratio of some measure of output to some index of input use. Labour productivity indices relate output to labour inputs (employees in standard units, hours worked and so on); global productivity (or total factor productivity) indices relate output to the whole set of inputs such as labour, capital, energy, materials and other inputs. As is quite obvious, the meaning and the quality of the productivity measures depend on the definition and the quality of their ingredients, and on the particular formula used to aggregate the various components into one output and one input index.

The specialized literature discusses a whole set of theoretical and empirical problems related to the measurement of productivity [cf. Kendrick, 1977; Kendrick, Vaccara, 1980; Griliches, 1987]. In the case of services, however, the controversy is basically confined to the meaning and the accuracy of the data, with special reference to the definition and the measurement of real output. Given the widespread dissatisfaction with the actual measurement of real output in many service branches, this matter is somehow preliminary to other problems in the measurement of productivity. For this reason, in this paper I shall first concentrate on the issues related to the measurement of output in the service sector, and discuss only later some other problems specifically related to productivity.

The paper is organized in three main sections. Section 2 reviews the standard approach to the measurement of output in the service sector, showing that services in the current systems of national accounts are treated as "immaterial goods". Section 3 discusses the main problems related to the measurement of real output of services in the systems of national accounts and contrasts the standard treatment with an innovative approach, based on a definition of services proposed by Hill [1977] and further elaborated in the literature. In this new context, service output is not conceived as an immaterial good, but as a change in the condition of an economic unit which occurs as a result of the activity of another economic unit. This definition is alternative to the standard treatment of services and leads to different measures of output and productivity. Against this background, Section 4 examines the main implications of the two approaches, proposes some criteria to choose among them, and discusses the scope for future research with special reference to the concept and measurement of productivity in the service sector.

2. The Standard Approach to the Measurement of Service Sector Output

The difference between goods and services was emphasized by the classical economists who considered many service activities as "unproductive labour". This conception is still reflected in the Material Production System (MPS) of accounts of the Centrally-Planned Economies, which treats non-material services as a form of consumption of national income and does not measure their output as such.

In Schumpeter [1954, p. 628], the debate on productive and unproductive labour is labelled as a "dusty museum piece" and, indeed, with the advent of the marginal utility theory there is no need to distinguish between productive and unproductive labour, since all activities producing objects of exchange are intrinsically productive. Accordingly, neo-classical theory does not logically distinguish goods from services, but treats them as different elements of the same class of commodities.[1] In general equilibrium theory, in fact, a good is defined by its physical characteristics, its location in space and the date of its delivery. In this theoretical context, services are regarded as goods. The different types of human labour are equally treated as goods [cf. Arrow, Debreu, 1954; Debreu, 1982]. For this reason, some authors maintain that the distinction between goods and services is not relevant to economic theory, and that it basically concerns applied work.

As argued in the last section, I disagree with the latter proposition. It is true, however, that in current orthodox theory goods and services (and even labour) are not considered as logically different entities, and that the theory does not provide any criterion to distinguish among them.

The orthodox approach is reflected in the system of national accounts (SNA) of the market-type economies, where services are treated as immaterial goods and are defined in a pragmatic way, by enumeration. Most approaches consider as services those products defined in the four major divisions (6, 7, 8 and 9) of the International Standard Industrial Classification (ISIC), i.e.: wholesale and retail trade, hotels and restaurants (ISIC 6); transport, storage and communications (ISIC 7); finance, insurance, real estate and business services (ISIC 8); community, social and personal services (ISIC 9).

Other approaches, such as the European System of Accounts, first distinguish "market" from "non-market" services and then list the branches which "conventionally" belong to these two sectors [cf. Eurostat, 1981, n. 308-314]. The homogeneity among the national systems of accounts of the market-type economies has greatly reduced some primitive ambiguities in the classification of services as a whole, even if some differences among countries can arise at a disaggregate level [for a discussion, cf. Ochel, Wegner, 1987].

---

[1] For a discussion of the treatment of service activities in the history of economic thought, cf. Delaunier, Gadray [1987] and Kenessey [1987]. A recent survey of the treatment of services in the MPS, with a discussion of several shortcomings, can be found in Gajecki and Kasiewicz [1987].

For both goods and services, in each given year the SNAs record a number of standard operations such as production, final consumption, intermediate consumption, import, export etc. As far as gross output is concerned, the measurement is first carried out in nominal terms, using the same criteria followed for goods, i.e. measuring the value of production as proxied by sales, whatever the price charged may be called (selling price, fee, rate, toll, duty, and so forth). The only notable exceptions to this rule, are non-market services and the "intermediation branches".

Since non-market services, by definition, are not the object of transactions, the value of their output is conventionally proxied by the value of their costs, namely by the sum of intermediate and labour costs, and depreciation.

In the branches of intermediation (trade and the intermediation activity of the banking and insurance institutions) gross output is measured by the margin, since the gross output of these sectors is defined as the increase in the value of the goods or funds which are the object of intermediation. In the retail and wholesale trade, the margin is calculated as the difference between the value of the goods sold by traders and the value of the goods bought for resale. In insurance institutions and pension funds, it is measured by the amount by which the gross premium earned exceeds the sum of claims due, supplementary payments, and so on. In the banking institutions, as far as their service concerns financial intermediation, the margin is measured subtracting the amount of interest paid to creditors from the amount of interest received from borrowers[1].

---

[1] The treatment of banks' output is the object of a big debate: cf., e.g., Gorman [1969], Ruggles, Ruggles [1982], Goldberg [1985], Nomisma [1985], Haig [1986]. Mamalakis [1987] identifies six different types of services provided by banks and proposes an interesting approach to analyse the interdependence among the commodity-type services and the intermediation activity. The output of the commodity-type bank services is currently calculated by means of quantity indicators. The output of financial intermediation, instead, is measured as the difference between the amount of interest received minus the amount of the interest paid on the borrowed funds, and is usually treated as "imputed banking services". Since the methodology for imputing banking services concerns the distribution of these services among the different branches and final demand, but not their measurement, we do not discuss it here, but refer to the specialized literature.

If we except non-market services and the intermediation activities, however, the concept of gross output in the service sector always corresponds to total sales; value added is then calculated as the difference between gross output and intermediate costs.

Starting from the data in nominal terms for a base year, the central statistical offices (CSO) decompose the flows in prices and quantities. The data on the volume of services provide the basis for all the calculations of real output and productivity changes; but this is the area where the main theoretical and empirical problems arise.

Technically speaking, the CSOs follow two main methods to calculate real output in services: either they deflate nominal output by a price index, or they extrapolate the output of the base year by an appropriate quantity indicator. The more complete surveys of the actual methods followed by the different CSOs can be found in Fuchs [1969], Hill [1971], Smith [1972], Kendrick [1982] and OECD [1987].

In a now classic study, Hill [1971] provides evidence of the fact that, in measuring gross output in the service branches, the CSOs of OECD countries use the deflation method in 41 per cent of the cases, and the extrapolation method in 59 per cent of the cases. In measuring value added, the deflation was used in 35 per cent of the cases and the extrapolation in the remaining 65 per cent. These practices have not changed substantially in more recent years.

As far as the individual countries are concerned, a survey carried out by Noyelle and Stanback [1988] shows that the extrapolation by quantity indicators (often input measures) is predominant in the US and in the UK, while deflation is preferred in the continental European countries and in Japan. In the LDCs, the estimates seem to rest on more heroic methods [for Latin America, cf. Mamalakis, 1985].

Both the extrapolation and the deflation method suffer from several shortcomings, in theory and in practice. In deflating nominal output, the price indices are often related to a sub-set of services in the relevant branch, or even, when specific price indices are not available, to the output units of similar branches. In extrapolating the base-year output, the volume indicators are physical quantity estimates, but often rely on input measures (such as employment, work hours or real wages), sometimes corrected for an estimate of productivity growth.

The choice among deflation and quantity extrapolation has been the object of a lively debate among statisticians and among users. Some authors, such as Marimont [1969], seem to prefer deflation since the quantity indicators are often based on input measures, and therefore, as productivity rises, they tend to underestimate output. Other authors seem to prefer quantity extrapolations, arguing that price indices are even less reliable than input measures [cf., e.g., Kendrick, 1969], and they lead to fictious measures of output [de Bandt, 1985; 1987]. A few contributions in this area tried to assess the sensitivity of the results to changes in methodology. Smith [1972] showed that, following the two different methodologies (and under different hypotheses), the annual growth rate of service output in the UK, for the years 1951-1966, ranges from 1.9 to 2.8 per cent. Trogan [1985] found a smaller sensitivity with regard to French data. The issue, however, is mainly conceptual, and concerns the definition of an output unit for intangible commodities.

While material goods, at an appropriate level of disaggregation, can always be identified as something physical, with defined characteristics, and often measurable with reference to standard units, the output of services cannot be observed *per se*. The identification of a product unit for services, therefore, requires an abstraction which, in any case, implies some degree of arbitrariness.

According to Nusbaumer [1987, p. 59], in order to define a service output unit, one has to follow different logical steps: "first it is necessary to identify indicators of performance which are adapted to the nature of service acts being performed, such as time, intensity, distance travelled, availability, speed, etc. Second, it is necessary to identify operational concepts related to these performance indicators and which make it possible more or less arbitrarily to mark off bundles of service acts representing unit of services. For example an hour of screenplay, a mile of transportation, a day of gardening, a roundgard of duty, a piano lesson, a bus journey".

In this procedure, however, one can incur several difficulties, which, in turn, can lead to "conventional" (i.e. highly approximate) methods in measuring output.

First of all, in many service branches alternative measures of the same output unit, with different meanings, exist. Even in relatively easy

cases, such as transport, one has to choose among measures of the service produced, i.e. traffic units supplied, and measures of the service
consumed, i.e. traffic units actually bought [cf., e.g., Marimont, 1969;
Nomisma, 1985; Nusbaumer, 1987; Delaunay, Gadray, 1987].

Secondly, for some branches there is no conceptual agreement on
what to measure: health services or educational services are typical
branches where there is still substantial uncertainty about the object of
measurement (on these points see, for example, Reder [1969], Klarman
and Feldstein [1969], Hill [1971; 1977], Eurostat [1981]).

Thirdly, in many service branches a "true" output unit can hardly
be identified and defined: examples can be found in legal or business
consulting, administrative services, R&D services, advertising, maintenance and engineering services [cf. Hill, 1971; Eurostat, 1981; de Bandt,
1987]. The case of wholesale and retail trade and financial intermediation
is even more problematic. Since gross output is measured as the intermediation margin, the definition of a unit of physical output is logically
difficult: indeed, what is the volume of a margin? This explains the frequent proposals to adopt other kind of output measures for these services, based on the number of transactions or on the volume of goods
intermediated.

The methodological notes to the official statistical publications are
often elusive on the actual procedures which are followed to calculate the
output data in the different cases. The specialized literature, however,
contains a large body of evidence on these indices: the already referred
to surveys by Marimont, Hill, Smith and Kendrick provide a discussion
of the indicators which can be used in the various branches. A recent
analysis by Nomisma [1985] considers the main procedures used in Italy,
the US and Japan, in view to construct productivity indices. Finally, a
very large literature which cannot be surveyed here for reasons of
space, discusses the main alternative methods for individual sectors,
with special attention to the most problematic cases, such as credit,
health services, education, and the like.

From all these sources, a main conclusion can be drawn: in the
definition of output units in the various service branches there is always
a clear inclination to prefer the indicators which make services resemble
"things", through direct definitions or indirect estimates. For this reason, it is legitimate to say that services, in the standard practice of the

CSOs, are generally treated as "immaterial goods". As an important implication of this output is usually defined and measured from the producer (i.e. from the technical) point of view. This often happens when output is defined directly with reference to quasi-physical properties, and it happens a fortiori whenever output is proxied with input measures.

3. The Innovative Approach to the Definition and Measurement of Output in the Service Sector

The standard approach to the measurement of output in the service sector is the object of dissatisfaction on both empirical and on conceptual grounds. On empirical grounds, the main critics argue that the standard methods tend to underestimate the actual growth of output and overestimate the price increase. This bias depends on a number of problems.

The first problem is a direct consequence of the specific indicators which are used in the quantity extrapolations. Using simple quantity indicators, often based on input measures, it is very difficult to account for the actual productivity changes taking place in the service branches. The recent literature [eg. Kutscher, Mark, 1983; Gershuny, Miles, 1983; Ochel, Wegner, 1987] and ad hoc surveys [IRER, 1984; Cipolletta, Freschi, 1983; Rosa, Barbieri, 1988] show that many service activities are capital intensive, that their accumulation rate is very fast, and that the growth of output per man (appropriately defined) is often higher than that found in many manufacturing sectors.

A second problem has to do with quality changes, which conceptually have to be treated as quantity changes, and not as price changes. This is a classical issue, which affects the measurement of goods as well: in the service branches, however, changes in quality are particularly frequent (also as a consequence of changes in the product mix within each branch) and tend to be treated as changes in prices whenever the volume of output is extrapolated with simple indicators, or it is measured by deflating value data using a "conventional" price index (on this point, see Fuchs [1968], Marimont [1969], Hill [1971], Petit [1986], Ray [1986]).

A third problem, conceptually similar to the previous one, is the bias which may arise from the production of new services. Innovative services in finance, business services, entertainment, and so on have been a typical feature of the service development in the last few years, but they tend to be ignored when the CSOs use simple indicators to extrapolate real output.

A fourth problem is the redistribution of activities between producer and consumers taking place in the reorganization of some services.[1]

All in all, given a certain increase in nominal output, the current methods may tend to underestimate the output growth and overestimate the price increase. For a given employment change, the underestimation of output is reflected in an underestimation of productivity growth. The slow dynamics of productivity, in turn, can be used to explain the fast growth of services prices in a sort of circular reasoning: starting from correct data on service employment and output in nominal terms, real output, prices and productivity changes can be made mutually consistent, no matter how biased they are. This remark can be crucial in the debate on the relative growth of service employment, where the (alleged) fast growth of prices and slow growth of output are "explained" with the slow dynamics of productivity estimated from the same set of data.

If these are the main empirical criticisms to the standard approach,[2] the theoretical dissatisfaction traditionally concerns the defini-

---

[1] An old example provided by Kravis [1969] points out that the measurement of trade has to cope with the fact that the shift from traditional retail shops to supermarkets involves a shift of activities from the producer to the consumer itself. Similar examples can be made for the shift from restaurant to fast-food and self-service, from traditional to self-service petrol stations and the like. A generalization of these examples can be found in a paper by Hill [1979] on the relationship between "do-it-yourself" and GDP.

[2] An additional empirical problem, which can create a downward bias in the measurement of service output not only in real but also in nominal terms is finally determined by the very high birth rates in service firms. As a consequence of this trend, an increasing portion of service output tends to be ignored in the national accounts. This kind of bias, which can be really substantial, can be observed when the national accounts are revised following a Census. The most recent revision of the Italian National Accounts [ISTAT, 1987] provides a rather shocking example in this sense. In the base year (1982) GDP was increased by 15.4 per cent with respect to the old estimate for the same year. The revision was mainly concentrated in market services, whose output has been increased by 31.8 per cent. Within the service sector output was

tion of services. In the modern literature, it is possible to identify three different definitions of services corresponding to different phases of the debate.

In a first phase, from the classic analyses of Fisher [1935; 1939] and Clark [1940] to the work of Kuznets [1957; 1966], services have been defined as a residual entity - the "tertiary" sector - following the approach adopted in the 'thirties by the Australian and the New Zealand CSOs. This early definition, which is based on a negative criterion (viz. whatever is not classified as agriculture or industry), implied some uncertainty in setting the borderlines between secondary and tertiary sector[1] and was not particularly helpful in organizing the economists' thoughts about services. On the latter point, cf. among the others Stigler [1956]; Momigliano, Siniscalco [1982; 1986]; Gershuny, Miles [1983]; Petit [1986]; Delaunay, Gadray [1987].

In a subsequent phase, services have been analysed by use of a positive approach, which defined them on the basis of some attributes common to services as opposed to material goods. The most important study in this phase is Fuchs [1968]. In Fuchs, services are defined as those commodities which are intangible, instantaneous (in that "they perish in the very instant of production") and are produced next to the consumer and with its own participation; they cannot be stored, nor transported, nor accumulated [Stanback, 1980]. The analysis, then, highlights many characteristics and implications of the service sector per se and its relation with industry and with society as a whole.

Fuchs' way of defining services has been widely held in the literature since the 1970s. By now, it is clear that none of the above properties is sufficient to define services as opposed to goods; but taken to-

---

revised as follows: "wholesale and retail trade, lodging and catering services": +47.5 per cent; "transport and communication services": + 9.6 per cent; "services of credit and insurance institutions": +4.8 per cent; "housing": +21.6 per cent; "miscellaneous and business services": +52.2 per cent.

[1]

The maximum extension of the tertiary sector can be found in the third edition of the famous book by Clark [1957], where the tertiary sector includes the public utilities (electricity, gas, water) and even building and construction; the minimum extension is to be found in Kuznets [1966], where industry includes transport and communication.

gether they can provide a grid which captures many dimensions of the service activities.

In 1977, finally, a path-breaking paper by Hill provided a general definition of services, which classifies them according to a single sufficient criterion. According to Hill [1977, pp. 317-318], "a good may be defined as a physical object which is appropriable and therefore transferable between economic units. A service - on the contrary - may be defined as a change in the condition of a person, or of a good belonging to some economic unit, which is brought about as the result of the activity of some other economic unit, with the agreement of the former person or economic unit".

This concept of service is discussed at lenght in Hill's paper, which also introduces some important distinctions. Services affecting goods (such as transportation of goods, postal deliveries, repair, maintenance, cleaning) occur when goods which already belong to some economic unit are transformed in some way as the result of the activity of the producer unit (the two economic units are normally different, but production on own account can always happen: this can provide a definition of "implicit services", i.e. services provided within an industrial firm). Services affecting persons, in turn, can be divided into services changing the physical and the mental condition of the person. Passenger transportation, hairdressing and various forms of health treatment are examples of the former. Education, communication, entertainment, legal advice are examples of services affecting the mental condition of the person (from the examples it should be obvious that "services affecting persons" is a much broader category than personal services). In addition to this, other contributions in the literature have enlarged Hill's classification to comprise services affecting firms, defined as the sub-set of business services which affect the knowledge and the organization of the firm (e.g. external R&D, administrative services, business and financial advice).

Hill's general definition of services has several implications. As far as the classification is concerned, services are no longer defined as immaterial goods; goods and services, on the contrary, are treated as logically different entities. A service is a change in the condition of an economic unit which is the result of the activity of another economic unit: being a change, it is essentially different from a good which is an object. As Hill [1977, p. 318] makes clear, "when a service is provided for by one economic unit for another, nothing is actually exchanged between them in the way the ownership of goods is transferred from one unit to another. It is therefore quite inappropriate to think of services as "immaterial goods" which can be traded on the market". To support this view several instances can be provided: for example, in the transportation of a good, the change of location cannot be considered as an immaterial good, just as medical treatment cannot be considered as an immaterial drug or the cleaning of clothes as an immaterial detergent.

As far as the measurement of output is concerned, the implications of Hill's definition are equally important. As a service is defined as a change, the mere performance of some activity is not enough if the consumer unit is not affected in some way. "In the great majority of cases, the change in the consumer unit can be observed by comparing it before and after the provision of the service. The amounts of services produced must be measured by recording the extent of these changes in the consumers and not by observing the activity of the producer" [Hill, 1977, p. 318]. This notion, which can be found also in other authors [e.g. de Bandt, 1985; 1987], has more to do with value added than with gross output, and this, again, can have several implications for our way of understanding services.

4. The Two Approaches Compared: Criteria to Choose Among Them, Implications and Scope for Further Research

Hill's new definition of services has been quite successful in the literature. Some authors have developed it [e.g. Riddle, 1986], a large majority of the recent contributions refer to it, and it is presented as the definition of services in the "New Palgrave Dictionary of Economics".

Since this definition differs from the definition of services as immaterial goods, the obvious question to ask is how useful and fruitful it is vis-à-vis the standard approach. Below, I shall address this issue by considering three different dimensions of the question: how useful it is as a classification scheme, i.e. as a "filing system"; how useful it is to arrive at a better measurement of output in the service sector; and how fruitful it is as a conceptual device to organize our thoughts on the service sector.

The most obvious advantage of Hill's definition lies in its power as a filing system. With a single sufficient criterion it is possible (for the first time) to define a whole set of heterogeneous service activities, drawing precise borderlines with respect to goods. This borderline does not stem from technology nor from commodity attributes; rather, it depends on the object of the transaction: an object versus a change in the conditions of a good or a person.

This criterion seems to be a powerful device in providing an "essential" definition of services. In addition to this, Hill's concept of services allows us to endogenize many of the attributes of services, as defined in the literature of the 1960s and 1970s. Take, for instance, the example of intangibility: a service, being a change, cannot be logically tangible. The same reasoning applies to non-storability: a change cannot be logically stored.

Finally, it may be interesting to note that, contrary to the concept of services as immaterial goods, this innovative definition is consistent with the treatment of services in the legal systems of continental Europe. Following the civil-law distinction, goods can be the object of "rights", e.g. property, use and so on, while services, being acts, can only be the object of obligations, e.g. of carrying them out.

As far as the measurement of output is concerned, we do not have enough elements to assess the usefulness of this approach. Hill's definition compells us to abandon the current indicators which measure service output from the producer's point of view (as a process and not as a product in Hill's own terminology). At the moment, however, we do not yet have a set of alternative measures to discuss. As is well known, measuring the intangible requires a compromise between optimal concepts and operational measures. While Hill provides a few pragmatic examples of operational indicators related to his concept of service output (e.g. in transport, in health services, in education), other authors seem to take a more radical position and propose "to reject the notion of an autonomous and identifiable volume of production for services and to measure output and productivity through the user activity" [de Bandt, 1987].

The most serious problems, however, are on the theoretical side, and concern the usefulness of Hill's definition as a framework within which to organize our thoughts on services. As we discussed in detail, the two approaches surveyed in this paper rest on alternative definitions of service. By alternative I mean that a compromise between the two is conceptually impossible.

The standard approach, which defines services as immaterial goods, is well rooted in the neo-classical theory of value and, in a sense, is an important complement to it. Indeed, as Lancaster [1966] makes clear, the precise definition of an output unit is important since it allows a correspondence between a set of values and a set of well-defined things, i.e. prices to be explained. Otherwise, we would be left with a theory of value which refers to abstract entities (wants) and a set of prices referring to actual goods and services. [1] In this sense, the effort of defining service output per se, in a precise and quasi-material way, is important in the theory; but the logical difficulties we discussed in Sections 2 and 3 show that the attempt of defining an output unit and a price for services as immaterial goods may be an illusion, so that the theory of the demand for goods can hardly be applied to service transactions.

Hill's definition might offer a solution to this impasse. Service output is not a commodity, but is an act which affects the user's goods or personal conditions. For this reason, service output cannot exist per se but strongly resembles value added or even labour, in that the usual action by a firm's employee is to achieve some change in the condition of an input (or in the state of the firm's knowledge). The difference with labour, indeed, seems to rest on the institutional setting in which the service is provided: employment relationship versus market relationship, or, in other words, hierarchy versus market. The difference between the two approaches is even clearer when we consider how the different definitions of output are reflected in the notion of productivity. The productivity measures which can be constructed on the notion of service output as an immaterial good are conceptually similar to the notion of productivity in manufacturing industry. This concept purports to measure the efficiency in producing standard reproducible commodities (in this sense it is typically a "Fordist" notion). The notion of productivity stemming from Hill's definition has instead to do with the contribution of

---

[1] These observations are the rationale of the so-called "characteristics' theory of demand", as elaborated by Johnson [1958] and Lancaster [1966], and recently discussed by Millgate [1987].

services to the efficiency of the user;[1] for this reason service productivity can hardly be considered per se [cf. de Bandt, 1985; 1987].

In the literature, there are few examples of the latter approach.
Kuznets [1981], commenting on a paper by Fuchs, questions the very
meaning óf measuring output and productivity in sectors which are closely integrated. Gupta and Steedman [1971] measure labour productivity in
the UK by vertically integrated sectors and this implies, among other
things, a measurement of the contribution of services to the productivity
of goods. Momigliano and Siniscalco [1982] measure labour productivity in
Italy by vertically integrated sectors, showing that the higher productivity in manufacturing occurs in those branches which are more closely
integrated with services. But the notion of indirect productivity implied
by Hill is probably more than this: in the case of education, for example, it implies the consideration of the productivity advantage for the
whole society stemming from greater human capital.

To sum up, I do not believe we have enough objective elements to
decide among the two definitions yet. Hill's definition seems to be more
powerful as a classification scheme, but its implications for the SNA and
as a framework within which to organize our thoughts still have to be
fully explored.

If we re-consider the conceptual treatment of service activities in
the history of economic thought, from the pioneering works of Gregory
King at the end of the 17th century (as quoted by Marx in the "Theories of Surplus Value") to Adam Smith, to Karl Marx himself, and to the
reaction by the neo-classical economists (which prepared the ground for
the current treatment of services), we can see that the different definitions and measurements the service activities have been always closely
related to the authors' theory of production, and even more to their
Weltanschauung. In this context even the classifications by Fisher [1935;
1939] and Clark [1940] were strictly functional to their view of the
world.[2]

---

[1] In neo-classical terms one could think of a production function which
explicitly embodies intermediate services among its arguments.

[2] Very interesting surveys of this literature with special reference to
the treatment of services in economic theory and social accounting are
to be found in Studentski [1958] and in a recent book by Delaunay
and Gadray [1987]. The former is a classic. The latter is very inter-

The current systems of national accounts of the market-type economies apply to the conceptual categories of services which have been developed to describe economic systems primarily based on the production of manufacturing goods. The sectoral accounts, in particular, seem to be tailored for the Fordist mode of production, in that they assume the homogeneity of products, technologies, and so on.

This treatment is progressively perceived as inadequate when describing societies where the production of services represents more than 50 per cent of GDP and where even industrial production is much less standardised than it was twenty years ago. The Planned Economies' MPS accounts raise even greater dissatisfaction, and imply even greater dilemmas in the treatment of services [for a recent discussion, cf. Gajecki, Kasiewicz, 1987].

In the last twenty years, increasingly interesting studies have been produced on structural change in the industrial countries, showing the role of services within the productive systems and the economies. These studies have allowed us to correct some earlier perceptions and to appraise many dimensions of the service activity. I believe that, as soon as these studies are unified in a modern view of the economic system, this will give rise to a new treatment of services in the national accounts. By this I mean that the decisions on the most adequate way of treating services in the national accounts have to come from theory.

Bibliography

ARROW, Kenneth J., Gerard DEBREU, "Existence of Equilibrium for a Competitive Economy". Econometrica, Vol. 22, 1954, pp. 256-290.

CLARK, Colin, The Conditions of Economic Progress. London 1940.

--, The Conditions of Economic Progress. London 1957.

DE BANDT, Jacques, "La Productivité dans les Activités de Service: Sens et Non-Sens". In: MINISTERE DE LA RECHERCHE ET DE LA TECHNOLOGIE, Programme Mobilisateur "Technologie, Emploi, Travail", Cahier 1, La Productivité dans les Services. Paris 1985, pp. 9-32.

---

esting, since it pays detailed attention to the French reaction to Adam Smith's treatment of services as unproductive activities.

DE BANDT, Jacques, Production in Constant Prices and Productivity in the Service Activities. Paper presented at the Biennial Conference on Current Issues in Productivity at Rutgers University, December 1987, mimeo.

DEBREU, Gerard, "Existence of Competitive Equilibrium". In: Kenneth J. ARROW, Michael J. INTRILIGATOR, Handbook of Mathematical Economics, Vol. 2. Amsterdam 1982, pp. 697-743.

DELAUNAY, Jean C., Jean GADRAY, Les Enjeux de la Société de Service. Paris 1987.

EUROSTAT, Sistema Europeo di Conti Economici Integrati (ESA). Statistical Office of the European Communities, Luxemburg 1981.

FISHER, Alan G.B., The Clash of Progress and Security. London 1935.

--, "Primary, Secondary, and Tertiary Production". Economic Record, Vol. 21, 1939, pp. 280-296.

FREY, Luigi, Terziario Avanzato e Lavoro. ISTAT, Rome 1985, mimeo.

FUCHS, Victor R., The Service Economy. National Bureau of Economic Research, General Series, 87, New York 1968.

-- (Ed.), Production and Productivity in the Service Industries. National Bureau of Economic Research, Studies in Income and Wealth, 34, New York 1969.

GAJECKI, Ryszard, Stanisław KASIEWICZ, "Provision of Services in Poland: a Theoretical and Statistical Study". The Review of Income and Wealth, Vol. 33, 1987, pp. 273-304.

GERSHUNY, Jonathan J., After Industrial Society? The Emerging Self-Service Economy. London 1978.

--, Ian D. MILES, The New Service Economy. London 1983.

GOLDBERG, Simon A., "The Treatment of Interest in the National Accounts: a Review. Paper presented at the 19th General Conference of the International Association for Research in Income and Wealth, held 25-31 August 1985 at Noordwijkerhout, NL, mimeo.

GORMAN, John A., "Alternative Measures of the Real Output and Productivity of Commercial Banks". In: Victor R. FUCHS (Ed.), Production and Productivity in the Services Industry. National Bureau of Economic Research, Studies in Income and Wealth, 34, New York 1969, pp. 115-189.

GRILICHES, Zvi, "Productivity: Measurement Problems". In: John EATWELL, Murray MILGATE, Peter NEUMAN (Eds.), The New Palgrave Dictionary of Economics, Vol. 3. London 1987, pp. 1010-1030.

GUPTA, S., Ian STEEDMAN, "An Input-Output Study of Labour Productivity in the British Economy". Oxford Institute of Economics and Statistics, Bulletins, 1, 1971, pp. 21-34.

HAIG, Bryan, "The Treatment of Interest and Financial Intermediaries in the National Accounts of Australia". The Review of Income and Wealth, Vol. 32, 1986, pp. 409-424.

HILL, T.P., La Mesure de la Production en Termes Réels. OECD, Serie des Etudes Economiques, Paris, February 1971.

--, "On Goods and Services". The Review of Income and Wealth, Vol. 23, 1977, pp. 315-338.

--, "Do-it-Yourself and GDP". The Review of Income and Wealth, Vol. 25, 1979, pp. 31-39.

ISTITUTO CENTRALE DI STATISTICA (ISTAT), La Revisione dei Conti Economici Nazionali. Rome 1987, mimeo.

ISTITUTO REGIONALE DI RICERCA DELLA LOMBARDIA (IRER), I Servizi per lo Sviluppo delle Imprese. Milan 1984.

JOHNSON, Harry G., "Demand Theory Further Revisited: Or Goods are Goods". Economica, Vol. 25, 1958, pp. 322-340.

KENDRICK John W., "Discussion". In: Victor R. FUCHS (Ed.) Production and Productivity in the Service Industries. National Bureau of Economic Research, Studies in Income and Wealth, 34, New York 1969, pp. 44-49.

--, Understanding Productivity. London 1977.

--, Measurement of Output and Productivity in the Service Sector. Paper presented at the Wharton Conference on the Future of the Service Economy, Philadelphia, November 1982.

--, Beatrice N. VACCARA, New Developments in Productivity Measure Analysis. National Bureau of Economic Research, Chicago 1980.

KENESSEY, Zoltan, "The Primary, Secondary, Tertiary and Quaternary Sectors of the Economy". The Review of Income and Wealth, Vol. 33, 1987, pp. 359-386.

KLARMAN, Herbert E., Martin FELDSTEIN, "Discussion". In: Victor R. FUCHS (Ed.), Production and Productivity in the Service Industries. National Bureau of Economic Research, Studies in Income and Wealth, 34, New York 1969, pp. 132-146.

KRAVIS, Irving B., "Discussion". In: Victor R. FUCHS (Ed.), Production and Productivity in the Service Industries. National Bureau of Economic Research, Studies in Income and Wealth, 34, New York 1969, pp. 84-93.

KUTSCHER, Ronald E. , Jerome A. MARK, "The Service-Producing Sector: Some Common Perceptions Reviewed": Monthly Labor Review, April 1983, pp. 21-24.

KUZNETS, Simon, "Quantitative Aspects of the Economic Growth of Nations, II. Industrial Distribution of National Product and Labor Force". Economic Development and Cultural Change, Vol. II, 1957.

--, Modern Economic Growth. New Haven 1966.

--, "Comment". In: Herbert Giersch (Ed.), Towards an Explanation of Economic Growth. Symposium 1980. Tübingen 1981, pp. 249-252.

LANCASTER, K. , "Change and Innovation in the Technology of Consumption". The American Economic Review, Papers and Procedings, Vol. 56, 1966, pp. 14-23.

MAMALAKIS, Markos J. , The Service Sector in Latin America. Paper presented at the 19th General Conference of the International Association for Research in Income and Wealth, held 25-31 August 1985, at Noordwijkerhout, NL, mimeo.

--, "The Treatment of Interest and Financial Intermediaries in The National Accounts: The Old 'Bundle' versus the New 'Unbundle' Approach". The Review of Income and Wealth, Vol. 33, 1987, pp. 169-192.

MARIMONT, Martin L. , "Measuring Real Output for Industries Providing Services: OBE Concepts and Methods". In: Victor R. FUCHS (Ed.), Production and Productivity in the Service Industries. National Bureau of Economic Research, Studies in Income and Wealth, 34, New York 1969, pp. 15-40.

MILGATE, Murray, "Goods and Commodities". In: John EATWELL, Murray MILGATE, Peter NEWMAN (Eds.), The New Palgrave Dictionary of Economics, Vol. 2. London 1987, pp. 546-549.

MOMIGLIANO, Franco, Domenico SINISCALCO, "The Growth of Service Employment: a Reappraisal". Banco Nazionale del Lavoro (BNL) Quarterly Review, No. 142, 1982, pp. 269-302.

--, --, "Mutamenti nella Struttura del Sistema Produttivo e Integrazione fra Industria e Terziario". In: Luigi PASINETTI (Ed.), Mutamenti Strutturali del Sistema Produttivo. Bologna 1986, pp. 13-59.

MONTANI, Guido, "Productive and Unproductive Labour". In: John EATWELL, Murray MILGATE, Peter NEUMAN (Eds.), The New Palgrave Dictionary of Economics, Vol. 3. London 1987, pp. 1008-1010.

NOMISMA, Alcune Proposte per la Misura della Produttivita nell' Industria e nei Servizi in Italia. Report to the National Council for the Economy and Labour (CNEL), Bologna, December 1985.

NOYELLE, Thierry, Thomas M. STANBACK, Productivity Changes and Employment Growth in the Services. Research Paper, Conservation of Human Resources Project, Columbia University, New York 1988, mimeo.

NUSBAUMER, Jacques, The Services Economy: A Lever to Growth. Dordrecht 1987.

OCHEL, Wolfgang, Manfred WEGNER, Service Economies in Europe. Opportunities for Growth. London 1987.

ORGANIZATION FOR ECONOMIC COOPERATION AND DEVELOPMENT (OECD), Measurement of Value Added at Constant Prices in Service Activities. Paris 1987.

PETERSON, William A., "Total Factor Productivity in the UK: A Disaggregated Analysis". In: K.D. PATTERSON, K. SCHOTT (Eds.), The Measurement of Capital. London 1979, pp. 213-225.

PETIT, Pascal, Slow Growth and the Service Economy. London 1986.

RAY, George F., "Productivity in Services". National Institute Economic Review, February 1986, pp. 44-47.

REDER, Melvin W., "Some Problems in the Measurement of Productivity in the Medical Care Industry". In: Victor R. FUCHS (Ed.) Production and Productivity in the Service Industries. National Bureau of Economic Research, Studies in Income and Wealth, 34, New York 1969, pp. 95-131.

RIDDLE, Dorothy I., Service-Led Growth, The Role of Service Sector in World Development. New York 1986.

ROSA, Giuseppe, Giovanni BARBIERI, Terziario Avanzato e Sviluppo Innovativo. Confederation of the Italian Industry, Rome 1988, mimeo.

ROWTHORN Robert E., John R. WELLS, De-Industrialization and Foreign Trade. Cambridge 1987.

RUGGLES, Richard, Nancy RUGGLES, "Integrated Economic Accounts of the United States: 1947-1980. Survey of Current Business, Vol. 62, 1982.

SCHUMPETER, Joseph A., History of Economic Analysis. New York 1954.

SMITH, A.D., The Measurement and Interpretation of Service Output Changes. London 1972.

STANBACK, Thomas M., Unterstanding the Service Economy. Baltimore 1980.

STIGLER, George, Trends in Employment in the Service Industries. National Bureau of Economy Research, Princeton 1956.

STUDENTSKI, Paul, The Income of Nations, Part 1: History. New York 1958.

SUMMERS, Robert, "Services in the International Economy". In: Robert P. INMAN (Ed.), Managing the Service Economy. Prospects and Problems. Cambridge 1985, pp. 27-48.

TROGAN, Philippe, "La Mesure de la Productivité des Services Marchand". In: MINISTERE DE LA RECHERCHE ET DE LA TECH-NOLOGIE, Programme Mobilisateur "Technologie, Emploi, Travail", Cahier 1, La Productivité dans les Services. Paris 1985, pp. 51-58.

Comment on Domenico Siniscalco, "Defining and Measuring Output and Productivity in the Service Sector"

Frank D. Weiss

Were the present conference to have been held in June 1788, the title of this paper might have read "Defining and Measuring Output and Productivity in the Manufacturing Sector", and one might have compared and contrasted various properties of agricultural produce with manufactured goods, and seen what measurement problems arose. Let me say at the outset that the difficulties of measuring output in services are generally overdrawn (there is one important exception to this statement, and I shall turn to it below), particularly at the conceptual level but also at the practical level.

A useful prelude to these comments is given by Siniscalco on page 52, where he suggests that from the intellectual historical record "we can see that the different definitions and measurements of service activities have been always closely related to the authors' theory of production". (The ensuing reference to their Weltanschauung is superfluous because that's also what a theory of production is.) The author lists, as evidence, Gregory King, Smith, Marx, the neo-classicals, and for good measure A. G. B. Fisher and Colin Clark. Lengthening this list by one name will show directly how problems of measuring net output in services and goods are similar: Gary Becker. To him, final output, which is known as "utils", is produced in the household with market goods, market services and the consumers', no, the producers' time. My purpose here is not to propagate this production theory or world view, but to use it to suggest that (market) goods and services benefit from symmetrical treatment. Were Becker to suggest his own system of national income accounts, he would have to measure the contribution of the stock of consumer durables to the flow of utils. Note that this flow is a service.

Yet, I doubt that this system of national accounts would give rise to much of a valuation problem. After all, the price of a washing machine is observable. It's price would surely have to be distributed over time. One could argue about how to do this, but the argument would not turn out to be very fruitful.

Siniscalco in his paper carefully compares and contrasts what he calls "traditional" measurement concepts, i.e. concepts actually used, with Hill's conception of services as acts which change the state of the consumer. Discussions like this remind one of the search for the "essence" of an object or an idea. Everyone has his favorite idea of the "essence" of services, or the demarcation line. I believe Kravis' is the extreme perishability of services. Others focus on the personal interaction between consumer and producer. It is easy to discredit such notions individually with counterexamples from the world of goods. Once upon a time, strawberries were extremely perishable. Now an intermediate service - freezing - preserves them and even makes them eminently tradable. If Hill focuses on changing the state of the consumer of services, I can counter from the world of goods - use of the washing machine cleans my clothes and makes me a better person.

Moving away from the plane of counterexamples, one can generalize a bit to say that such distinctions may or may not be valid, depending on the state of technology. I think Bhagwatis' suggested categories "splintering and disembodiment" of services illustrate this point very well. Bhagwati constantly refers to the state of technology. But my criticism of this "Essentialist" approach to measuring output in services is more fundamental: I believe the approach is misguided; it will lead nowhere. There is no reason to suppose we will ever discover the final essence of anything and I know of no field of science where progress was predicated on discovering the essence of anything.

Siniscalco could have exploited his insight (mentioned above) about the theory of production much further: the current national accounts are certainly *not* predicated or built on a "Fordist" notion of production. Uniformity and standardization of goods certainly aid in measurement, but that is all. The present national accounts are rather faithful reflections of the neo-classical world view: value, for goods and services, is determined in markets. If things flow through markets they have value - they are given a price - a valuation - by those markets. Of course this strictly neo-classical world view leads to patent absurdities from time to time - the valuation of a housewife's time in the national accounts being the most infamous.

A chain of reasoning like this one is consistent with Baumols' sur-prise, at another conference on services, about what the problem was at all: services have prices, so the benefit of the consumer can be mea-sured. Full stop. That is all there is to it.

Note that standardization of commodities or services - the "Fordist" view again - makes the valuation of these things more precise. Markets for standardized commodities work better. Otherwise there are informa-tional and strategic problems which make market valuations less precise and in the limit nonexistent. The oriental bazaar with individualized transaction is probably some intermediate form between a modern price-making market and a nonmarket.

But this leads one toward the practical problems of measurement on existing, more or less well functioning price-making markets. At this stage there is no longer a problem of principle. One merely has to calcu-late a price index. Services, like goods, have multiple characteristics. The market inputes a value to the whole bundle. All one needs to do is experiment with a Lancastrian hedonic regression until one finds a good fit. (There is no guarantee, and no requirement, that the outside ob-server will get the fit exactly. It does not matter for practical applica-tion.) Get the bundles of characteristics each year and price it with the equation. The practical problem is solved. Thus, one can suggest to national income account producers to refrain from using input based extrapolators of service output. They should use price indexes more frequently. This method would work, more or less well, even for what Kravis calls "comparison resistant services", like medical care. We do not need to know the "essence" of the output of medical care. We need only know that it is valued, and by a method of trial and error, see if we can explain what it is valued for. This may be tedious or complicated or costly, but it is not a matter of principle.

Of course, this market-determined view of value shows the lacunae in the market approach to valuation and national income accounting. Some services are not provided by markets, though they are undoubtedly valued by consumers. And this sphere of activity - government provided services - is growing, or at least it seems to be. But as a practical mat-ter, one can impute values to goods and services through relying on market analogues. This has been done for much of household production - housewives services and household production of goods. If there are no market analogues, one might get an imputation through preference revelation schemes. All this may sound far fetched, or expensive, but it is not a problem of services.

II. INTERNATIONAL ASPECTS

Seev Hirsch

International Transactions Involving Interactions: A Conceptual Framework Combining Goods and Services

1. Introduction

The 1987 *World Development Report* states that the share of
services in the United States' gross domestic product rose from 59 per
cent in 1965 to 67 per cent in 1985, while their share in employment in
the same period rose from 60 per cent to 66 per cent.[1] The share of
services in the output and employment of other "industrial market economies", though somewhat lower, is also high and rising, thus justifying
the label of "the service economy", which has been used to describe the
structural changes which high-income countries have undergone in recent
decades.[2]

---

[1] The 1987 edition of the *World Development Report* gives the following
percentages concerning the share of services in the GDP and employment of various country groups:

Country groups	1965		1985	
	GDP	employment	GDP	employment
Low-income countries	32	14	35	15
Middle-income countries	50	27	52	34
Industrial market economies	55	48	61	58

Source: World Bank [1987, pp. 205; 264-265].

For an insightful interpretation and evaluation of the statistics concerning the share of services in world output and employment, cf.
Summers [1985].

[2] See, for example, Giarini [1987], Gershuni and Miles [1981], and Shelp
[1981].

Both economists and policy makers disagree on whether the emergence of the service economy should be welcomed or regretted. Disagreements about the inevitability of the process, about its desirability, and about its social and economic implications abound. While some writers [Shelp, 1981; Nussbaumer, 1987] welcome the service economy and regard it as a harbinger of social and material progress, others [Lawrence, Dyer, 1983; Reich, 1983; Cohen, Zysman, 1987] regard it with dismay and advocate steps to halt the decline of the industrial sector.

The controversy over the role of services in the economy extends to international trade as well. The United States and the European Community have been demanding that trade in services should be put on the agenda of the Uruguay Round and that trade in services, like trade in goods, should be liberalized. Certain developing countries led by Brazil and India have objected, claiming that the liberalization of trade in services would harm their national interests since they have a comparative disadvantage in services which are vital for the development of the technologically advanced sectors of the economy.

Some writers disagree with this assessment claiming that developing countries have a comparative advantage in some services and that a liberalization of trade in services is just as beneficial to all parties as a liberalization of trade in goods [Sapir, Lutz, 1980; Sapir, 1985; Bhagwati, 1984; 1987; Giarini, 1987].

Other writers claim that services should not be treated as a special category in trade negotiations. Liberalization in the treatment of factor movement and in the rules of establishment by foreign firms will liberalize international transactions in services as a by-product [Grubel, 1987].

Writers on services during the last decade have tended to accept the distinction between goods and services offered by Hill [1977, p. 317] who defined a good as "a physical object which is appropriable and, therefore, transferable between economic units".[1] He defined services as "a change in the condition of a person, or a good belonging to some economic unit, which is brought about as a result of the activity of some other economic unit" [ibid., p. 318]. While, like material goods, services

---

[1] See, for example, Bhagwati [1984], and the entry on "Services" in the *New Palgrave Dictionary* (1987).

are transferable between economic units, the transfer must be accomplished by means of interaction between the producer of a service and its user or consumer. Moreover, since services are a process rather than a thing, they are not storable.

Services, according to Hill's definition, are conceptually different from goods. They are not merely intangible goods which can be exchanged in the market place; "a surgical operation is not some kind of immaterial drug; the cleaning of clothes is not some kind of immaterial detergent" [ibid., p. 318]. And he goes on to state: "Thus the fact that services cannot be held in stock is not a physical impossibility, but a logical impossibility" [ibid., p. 319].

Tangible goods and services do not cover the entire universe of "products". There remains yet another category, that of intangible goods. Information, and more generally, knowledge are examples of this last category. Unlike Hill-type services, information may be stored, and its production or consumption does not necessarily require producer/user interaction. Information may be stored in the human mind, in written records, or electronic storage media. Like material goods, information represents a stock of future services consumed or absorbed at the discretion of the user.

While the transmission of information constitutes a service in the Hill sense of the word, information itself, regardless of how it is stored, is more akin to a good, albeit an intangible good, which, in addition, has the properties of a public good. Failure to distinguish between intangible goods and services may lead to confusion concerning the economic role and properties of either group. The public goods characteristic of intangible goods may give rise to additional confusion.

This paper seeks to make a contribution to the on-going debate about the role of services in the national economy and in international transactions by introducing an analytical framework combining goods and services, and by demonstrating how the framework can be applied to the analysis of positive and normative aspects of the debate on services.

Section 2 outlines a formal model which introduces and utilizes the concept of simultaneity factor (or S-factor), which focuses on the interaction between suppliers and users of the output of production processes. The relationship between the S-factor and different modes of supplier/user interaction is discussed in Section 3. The following section considers the impact of the S-factor on the international tradability of services and of goods with varying service-intensities. Empirical evidence on international tradability is presented in Section 5. Section 6 examines alternative modes of domestic and international transactions in services and in service-intensive goods. Some conclusions are discussed in Section 7.

2. The S-Factor Model

The conceptual differences and similarities between tangible goods, intangible goods and services may be usefully analysed within the framework of a formal model. The model, which has been elaborated upon by this writer elsewhere, identifies the following components of a typical transaction between producer and user [cf. Hirsch, 1988]:

[1] $U = P_i + P_s + R_i + R_s,$

where:
- U represents the total value of the transaction from the user's point of view;
- P denotes costs incurred by the producer, R the costs incurred by the user;[1]
- i stands for costs incurred in isolation, s for simultaneous costs i.e., costs incurred during interactions between supplier and user.

Every service transaction between separate economic units can be broken down into two basic components: a component which requires interaction between the supplier and the user, $P_s + R_s$, and a component which represents costs incurred by the two parties in isolation, $P_i + R_i$.

Next consider the S-factor, formally defined as follows:

[2] $S = (P_s + R_s) / U.$

S can vary between zero and unity. It equals zero when the transaction involves no interaction between supplier and user, i.e., when the

---

[1] The latter include costs of search, and costs of absorbing the product or service in question into the user's organization.

transaction in question concerns what might be termed a "pure good". S equals unity when interaction between supplier and user spans the entire process of production and consumption. When production and consumption entirely overlap, this kind of transaction may be termed a "pure service".

Pure services abound in the real market place. Services such as hairdressing, a private music lesson or a public concert are examples of such services. Many services, however, do not require interaction between producer and user throughout the entire production process. A medical consultation, which involves interaction between the doctor and his patient, may be followed by a laboratory analysis which is performed without the patient being present. A legal consultation may likewise be followed by a lengthy analysis performed by legal experts in isolation. These transactions are services: production involves interaction between supplier and user, the end product is intangible and it is not storable. They are, however, not "pure services", i.e., the interaction between supplier and user does not span the entire production process. Applying the terminology developed above to medical, legal and similar services, it may be said that their S-factor, while being positive, is less than unity.

"Pure goods" also exist in the real world. The value of goods belonging to this category is approximated by the ex-factory cost of tangible goods, and by the costs involved in producing information or other kinds of knowledge. However, pure goods, whether tangible or intangible, are of no value to the users in their pure form. To be useful, tangible goods must reach the buyers. They must, in other words, be transported. Often additional activities are required before they are usable. These may include warehousing, distribution functions such as wholesaling and retailing, instruction, installation, maintenance, and finance, to mention just a few. Clearly every one of these activities is properly labelled a service.

Intangible goods, like information and other forms of knowledge, must also, as was noted earlier, be transmitted to the user, before they can be absorbed by him. Intangible goods therefore must also be accompanied by services before they can be used.

Thus, while the concept of a pure good may be analytically valid, real economic transactions concerning both tangible and intangible goods, invariably encompass combinations of goods and services, i.e., goods with different service intensities.

It may be concluded that, as a rule, actual market transactions, regardless of whether they involve tangible goods, intangible goods or services, contain a positive S-factor. In other words, transactions of all kinds require some form of interaction.

3. The S-Factor and Modes of Interaction

The S-factor was shown in the last section to represent those elements of the total cost of a transaction which is incurred during interactions between the producer and the user. Since such interaction is not normally required during the manufacture of tangible goods, the interactions themselves take place only during the rendering of services. The modes of interactions, their duration, and their costs have a profound effect on the economic characteristics of services and of the goods with which they are associated.

It is possible to distinguish between the following interaction modes: face-to-face interaction, interaction via the telecommunications media, and interaction via written communication. The mode actually used in the process of rendering a specific service depends on the nature of the required or preferred interaction between supplier and user of the service. This, in turn, is determined by the characteristics of the service.

Provision of certain services requires physical interaction between the user and equipment provided by the supplier. Use of cash dispensers, public telephones, and laundrettes belong to this category.

Physical interaction may also characterize services rendered to inanimate objects. Painting, repair jobs, installation, and maintenance of buildings and of equipment belong to this category. In some cases the services have to be "produced" or rendered on the premises of the user. In other cases there may be a choice as to the location where the "production" of the service actually takes place.

Face-to-face or direct and simultaneous interaction between the producer or service supplier and its user, between the supplier and goods belonging to the user, or between the user and goods or equipment provided by the supplier probably account for a high proportion of service transactions. Other modes of interaction are, however, also possible, as was noted above.

One alternative is to provide a given service by different technical means which often also affect the institutional relations between the supplier and user. Substitutes which cater to the same needs as the original service, but take a different form, may be offered. A restaurant meal may be substituted for by a home-cooked meal or by a take-away meal; a public concert can be substituted for by a musical record, or a concert transmitted by radio or television; a washing machine may replace the services rendered by a laundrette; a private car may replace public transport, and so on.

These forms of service substitution, which often involve the replacement of services rendered by independent suppliers by services provided largely by equipment owned by the user, has been labelled by Bhagwati [1984] as "splintering and disembodiment". In assessing these developments, Bhagwati [ibid., p. 134] distinguishes between services-from-goods splintering which "yields service activities which are technically progressive and possibly capital intensive, whereas the goods-from-services splintering process, reflecting the disembodiment effect, generally leaves behind a residue of service activities which are technically unprogressive and generally labour intensive".

Face-to-face interaction is required when the service in question is supposed to affect the physical condition of the user. A haircut, a medical examination, a paint job, and an air trip belong to this category. In other cases, face-to-face interaction may be considered necessary or preferred, even though the physical condition of the user is unaffected by the service. Banking and retailing belong to this group. In both cases, simultaneous interaction between the supplier of the service and the user is considered advantageous. The interaction, however, does not affect the physical condition of the user. Its purpose is to facilitate an exchange of information which, in turn, affects the decision regarding the specifications of the service transaction being contemplated.

The need for simultaneous supplier/user interaction does not necessarily have to be satisfied by face-to-face interaction, however. Simultaneous interaction may also be facilitated by the use of modern means of telecommunication such as the telephone. Technological developments in telecommunications such as the telex, facsimile, electronic data transmission and videotext have further increased the speed of communication, improved its quality, and reduced its cost.

Traditional mail may of course also provide a means of interaction between supplier and user of services. Services which are unaffected by the speed of communication, i.e., services which do not require simultaneous interaction may continue to be provided by this time-honoured method of communication. Availability of electronic mail, which considerably shortens the time between the sending of a message and its receipt, may further reduce the need for direct face-to-face communication between service suppliers and their customers.

The relationship between the mode of interaction and the S-factor is straightforward. The S-factor consists of two partially independent components: the mode of interaction with its associated costs and the duration of the interaction. [1]

The mode of interaction clearly has a profound effect on its cost. Face-to-face interaction is, as a rule, the most costly mode, since it requires either the supplier of the user to spend time on travel, in addition to the time spent on the interaction proper. The cost of interaction is likely to be reduced substantially when face-to-face interaction is not required.

The technological developments in telecommunications mentioned above have facilitated instantaneous and reliable communication between supplier and user at remarkably low unit costs. As was shown above, such developments provide, in some cases, acceptable substitutes for face-to-face interaction, thus making it possible to expand the range of services and their scope.

It may in fact be argued that the impact of the telecommunications revolution on the development of services may be as profound as the impact which the transportation revolution had on industrial development. Bearing in mind that industrial products have a positive service compo-

---

[1] Other characteristics of the supplier/user interactions must also be considered. The duration of the interaction and its frequency clearly affect the S-factor as well as the total cost of the service. The interaction may be long or short in relation to the total time required to "produce" the service. There may be a single interaction or multiple ones and they may occur at the beginning, the middle or the end of the process. Clearly, every one of these factors affects both the S-factor and the total cost of the service in question.

nent and hence a positive S-factor, it may be concluded that the impact of the telecommunications revolution is not limited to the services sector. The industrial sector may also be affected.

4. The S-Factor and International Tradability

A major thesis of this paper is that interaction between producers and users of services determine their tradability, i.e., whether or not they are internationally traded, and the form in which international transactions take place. The paper also argues that interaction between producers and users of services influences the tradability of tangible goods since the latter invariably have a positive service content. [1]

In this section, it is shown that the service content of goods (or, more precisely, their S-factor) has a decisive influence on their tradability, i.e., on whether they are internationally traded and on the mode of international transactions. The analysis which follows builds on and extends the S-factor framework outlined in Section 2. To simplify the analysis, the tradability of services is considered first.

If the producer of a service is located in one country and the user in another, those elements of the service cost which are associated with the S-factor are bound to be more costly than when the producer and user are located next to each other. Some cost elements, such as transportation and communication costs, tend to rise with distance. Other costs, such as financing, rise because of the need to operate within two currency systems and under more than a single jurisdiction. When costs incurred due to cultural distance, in the form of language and legal barriers, are added to the costs mentioned above, it follows that interna-

---

[1] In fact, several of the ideas developed in this paper were inspired by a study of Israel's electronics industry which analysed the international operations of electronics equipment manufacturers who sought to sell their products in distant export markets. Analysis of the components of specific transactions showed that the cost of goods sold, which roughly represents the ex-factory cost of the transaction in question, typically accounted for less than 50 per cent of the total value. Thus, less that half the value consisted of the cost of the tangible product. The remaining half consisted of services produced *after* the completion of the production process. For details, see Hirsch [1987].

tional transactions in services generally involve a cost premium over domestic service transactions.

This cost premium varies with the level of the S-factor, the mode of communication required between the producer of services and their users, and with the number and duration of the interactions required for the performance of a specific service. It is highest when the service involves physical contact or face-to-face interaction between producers and users. The premium is lowest when the required interaction is indirect, involving, for example, written communication. Even in this case, however, a positive premium is associated with the exportation of the services in question.

Using the notation employed in equations [1] and [2] in Section 2 with some modifications, these points are formally stated below: Consider the costs of providing a given service in two countries, 1 and 2. The superscripts 1 and 2 denote the country in which the service is being produced or consumed:

[3] $\qquad U^1 = P_i^{\ 1} + P_s^{\ 1} + R_i^{\ 1} + R_s^{\ 1}$

[4] $\qquad U^2 = P_i^{\ 2} + P_s^{\ 2} + R_i^{\ 2} + R_s^{\ 2}.$

Next consider the case where a service in country 1 is less costly than in 2, and where a producer in 1 seeks to export the service. Total costs of providing the service to country 2 are as follows:

[5] $\qquad U^{12} = P_i^{\ 1} + R_i^{\ 2} + P_s^{\ 12} + R_s^{\ 21}.$

While the first two cost elements, i.e., those incurred by the country-1 producer and the country-2 user in isolation, remain unchanged, the internationality of the transaction affects the cost elements associated with the S-factor. $P_s^{\ 12} + R_s^{\ 21}$ may be replaced by $(P_s^{\ 1} + R_s^{\ 2})$ $(1 + T^{12})$, which reflects the outcome of a process whereby the producer and user agree on an interaction mode which minimizes total costs of the service. T^{12} represents the rate of excess of foreign over domestic interaction costs.

[6] $\qquad P_s^{\ 12} + R_s^{\ 21} = (P_s^{\ 1} + R_s^{\ 2})\ (1 + T^{12}).$

For the service to be exportable to 2 it is necessary that $U^{12} < U^2$. Substituting [6] into [5] to rewrite U^{12}, deducting U^2 from U^{12} and denoting $P_i^1 - P_i^2 = dP_i$ and $P_s^1 - P_s^2 = dP_s$, the condition of tradability may be written as follows:

[7] $dP_i + dP_s + (P_s^1 + R_s^2) \, T^{12} < 0.$

Tradability of a service depends on the difference between the sum of the cost savings of the low cost producer, and the cost premium associated with international producer/user interactions. The service is tradable only if the cost savings of the low-cost producer exceed the export cost premium. Stated in relative terms – for a service to be tradable, it is necessary that:

[8] $$\frac{|dP_i + dP_s|}{U^{12}} < \frac{P_s^1 + R_s^2}{U^{12}} \, T^{12}.$$

Recalling the definition of the S-factor, note that the ratio $(P_2^1 + R_s^2)/U^{12}$ may be defined as S^{12}. The tradability condition thus becomes:

[9] $$\frac{|dP_i + dP_s|}{U^{12}} > S^{12} T^{12}.$$

The right-hand side of equation [9], which represents the international S-factor, consists of two independent elements: the first, S^{12}, is conceptually similar to the domestic S-factor formally defined in equation [2]. The second element is T^{12}, represents as was noted above the excess of foreign over domestic interaction cost per service "unit". S^{12} and T^{12}, which have positive values, combine to inhibit the tradability of services.

5. Tradability of Services - Some Empirical Evidence

The thrust of the analytical framework developed in this paper is that the S-factor is trade inhibiting. Since the trade-inhibiting effect of the S-factor is manifested through pure services and the service contents of goods, it is to be expected that ceteris paribus services are less tradable than material goods. The figures in Table 1 provide a preliminary test of this hypothesis.

The table shows the share of services in GDP and in the total exports of five industrial economies: the United States, Japan, the Federal Republic of Germany, the United Kingdom and France. It is immediately evident that the share of services in GDP is far higher than their share in exports. This observation lends credence to the assertion that, in general, the S-factor outweighs the traditional comparative advantage factor, and that services are, on the whole, less tradable than material goods.

The figures in Table 1 cannot in themselves be regarded as conclusive proof of the services' poor tradability hypothesis. National account statistics include outlays on defence, education, health and other public services provided by national and local governments. These services are by definition non-tradable, and should therefore be excluded from the figures.

In the calculations cited above, non-tradable public services were included in the left-hand column, while being excluded from the right-hand column. The figures are therefore not strictly comparable.

Moreover, it is frequently alleged that tradability of services is hampered far more than tradability of goods by government restrictions.

Table 1 - Share of Services in GDP and in Total Exports of Selected Countries, 1980

Country	GDP	Total exports
United States	63	11
Japan	55	12
Federal Republic of Germany	49	14
United Kingdom	63	22
France	60	19

Source: World Bank [1982]; Stern, Hoekman [1987].

Thus, the figures may be consistent with two partly contradictory hypotheses, namely the poor tradability hypothesis, and the excessive regulation hypothesis. One of these effects has to be neutralized before it can be determined which of the two hypotheses better explains the poor trade performance of services. The liberalization of intra-EEC service flows scheduled for 1992 should provide a suitable opportunity for testing the explanatory powers of the two hypotheses.

The services' poor tradability hypothesis is also supported by the figures in Table 2 which contains data on the percentage distribution of services exports of the five countries listed in Table 1. The figures strongly indicate that a high proportion of those services which enter international trade, consist of services which are not traded for their own sake. These services facilitate movement - movement of goods, movement of people, and movement of information.

Movement of goods and of people is depicted in Columns 2 and 3. Services concerned with the movement of information, e.g., telecommunication services, are listed in Column 5, depicting "other private" services.

The figures in this column also include services such as trade financing and trade insurance which, like transportation, facilitate international movement of goods and services. These services (labelled by Deardorff [1985] as "traded" services, by Sampson and Snape [1985] as "separated" services and by Bhagwati [1984] as "long-distance" services) are not demanded for their own sake. They are a by-product of international trade in goods and in other services.

Table 2 - Distribution of Services Exports in Selected Countries, 1980 (per cent)

Country	Shipment and passengers services	Other transport and tourism	Travel private services	Other	Total
United States	10	35	27	29	100
Japan	38	31	3	27	100
Federal Republic of Germany	16	19	19	46	100
United Kingdom	16	30	19	36	100
France	4	32	25	39	100

Source: IMF [1985].

Travel and tourism (Column 4) constitute another group of services which account for a significant proportion of service exports earned by four of the five countries listed in Table 2. In this case too, international movement is the motivating factor. Bearing in mind that trade finance and insurance plus telecommunications are all contained in the last column, it may be concluded that services which do not involve the international movement of goods, of services, and of people account for a rather low proportion of international trade in services.

These figures are consistent with the hypothesis that international trade in those services which are not a by-product of trade in goods, and which are not intended to facilitate the movement of people or information across national boundaries, is severely limited by the dominance of the export premium associated with the S-factor over the traditional trade-enhancing comparative advantage factors.

6. Domestic and International Transactions of Industries with Different Service Intensities

Application of the S-factor framework to the analysis of transactions in goods follows from the assertion that in the market place pure goods do not exist. To be useful to the consumer, all goods have to be associated with services.

Incorporation of goods within the formal model developed in Section 4 is straightforward, and requires only minor modifications. The revised condition of tradability now becomes:

$$[10] \qquad \frac{\left| dP_i^* + dP_s^* \right|}{U^{*12}} > S^{*12} \cdot T^{12}$$

where:

- U^{*12} is the total cost of a transaction between countries 1 and 2 involving a service or a good with a positive service content;

- S^{*12} is the simultaneity factor of a transaction involving a service or a good with a positive service content;

- dP_i^* and dP_s^* represent the intercountry differences between producers' costs incurred in isolation and during their interaction with users;
- P_i^{*2} and P_i^{*1}, the components of dP_i^*, now represent the cost components of a good with a given service content, or those components of a
service which do not involve interactions between supplier and user.
These costs provide the basis for the advantage (if any) of the coun-
try-1-based exporter, which must exceed the cost premium associated
with the S-factor.

The S-factor, which is invariably present in services, tends, as
was shown above, to inhibit international trade and to render many services non-tradable. Even though ceteris paribus the S-factor of goods
with a positive service content is smaller than that of pure services, it
inevitably also inhibits the tradability of the former and influences the
institutional modes of international transactions in these goods.

The modes of transaction in different goods are influenced both by
their service intensity per se and by types of services with which different goods are associated.

For the purpose of illustration, consider an elementary classification
scheme which distinguishes between universal and specific services. Universal services, which include transport, warehousing, finance and insurance, can be purchased from specialist organizations which provide
them on a general basis, unrelated as a rule to the goods with which the
service happens to be associated, hence the term universal service.
Specific services are inseparable from the goods with which they are
associated. Computers, for example, cannot be used without software
incorporated in operating programmes, which in turn must be learned by
the operators. Other durables, such as production machinery, medical
equipment, cars and household appliances, also have a fairly significant
specific service content. The specificity of many services, however,
tends to diminish over time as the knowledge about the technical specification of the equipment is diffused and ceases to be controlled by the
manufacturer.

The relative importance of specific services, and indeed their level
of specificity is in some sense associated with the phase of the product
cycle. New products whose specifications frequently vary tend to have a
relatively high specific service component. As products mature, the
specific service content tends to diminish. Certain technical services

become embodied in the hardware as the need for changes in the specifications declines due to accumulated experience. Other services cease being specific as the knowledge required for their provision becomes more diffused, and is acquired by users or by independent service organizations.

These product-cycle related, changing characteristics can be accelerated or retarded by deliberate policies of the manufacturer. He has some degree of freedom in substituting software for hardware. He also has some control over the diffusion of the proprietary information concerning specific services and its sharing with customers and with other organizations.

Specific services can, but need not necessarily be provided by the manufacturer. He can opt for comprehensive forward market integration and provide the entire range of required services himself. Alternatively, he may authorise partly or wholly independent organizations to provide the services to the user. Or he may choose partial forward integration, providing some specific services, leaving the provision of other services to independent organizations.

The S-factor framework can be employed in the search for the optimal level of forward integration. The outcome will be influenced by the interaction of the components of the S-factor with other variables, such as market power and cost of entry, commonly included in industrial organization models.

Serving foreign markets does not raise problems which differ in kind from those involved in supplying domestic markets.
Response to these problems, however, is more complicated due to the trade-retarding effects of the S-factor.

The S-factor framework suggests that the choice of the institutional mode in international markets is strongly influenced by the two opposing forces - the export cost premium associated with the S-factor, and market power, reflected by the level of forward market integration. Comparison between the costs associated in domestic and export markets indicate that the latter are consistently larger than the former. Demand for goods with different service intensities is, on the other hand, unlikely to depend on the location of the supplier; potential users would presumably be prepared to pay a given price for a specified bundle of goods services, regardless of whether the supplier resides locally or abroad.

Location of the supplier would influence a user's purchasing decision only to the extent that they associate risk levels and quality of service with it. marginal costs and revenues associated with successive levels of forward integration are consequently likely to intersect at a lower forward integration level in the export than in the domestic market.

These conclusions are consistent with the casual empirical observation that many firms which are fully integrated in their home market tend, in the international markets, to assign the provision of some or all services to independent organizations and also that licensing is more common in international than in domestic markets.

International trade is not the only form in which services are being transacted internationally. Foreign production by multinational firms has become an important, if not dominant mode of international transactions in services. Other institutional modes such as franchising, licensing and operations through joint ventures and other forms of partnerships have also been quite common.

One is led to hypothesize that the choice of the institutional mode of international transactions in services and not their tradability alone is influenced by the interaction between the trade-enhancing properties of the H-O-S factor and the trade retarding characteristics of the S-factor.

Equation [11] illustrates the argument. Consider an example where the condition of tradability is not fulfilled, i.e., where:

$$[11] \quad \frac{dP_i^* + dP_s^*}{U} \quad < \quad S^{*12} \cdot T^{12}.$$

In this case country-1 suppliers cannot export their services to country 2 even though their domestic production costs are lower than the costs incurred by their country-2 competitors. A country-1 firm seeking to supply country-2 customers under such conditions may consider doing so by utilizing an operating subsidiary located in the target market. Note, however, that this outcome will be economically feasible only if the country-1 firm enjoys a firm-specific advantage which can be transferred to its subsidiary in country 2, and provided further that the cost of transfer is not excessive.[1]

---

[1] Cf. Hirsch [1976] for a discussion of how firms choose between exporting to a specific market from their home country and supplying the

The firm-specific advantage may consist of proprietary know-how relating to operations, marketing or organization which can be translated into cost savings of product differentiation.[1] The firm possessing the proprietary know-how must in turn be able to withold it effectively from country-2 competitors. If the country-1 firm does not possess such an advantage which must be both proprietary and internationally transferable, its cost advantage under autarky is of no use to it in the market of country 2, since, like other firms in that market, it will have to depend on local inputs to produce the services it seeks to sell. These inputs are, by assumption, less efficient and hence more costly than in country 1.

The inability of the country-1 service supplier to export his service to country 2 may be explained by the conditions specified in equation [11], i.e., by the failure of the production cost advantage to exceed the export cost premium associated with the S-factor. It could also be explained by the inherent non-tradability of certain services. Examples belonging to the latter include tourist services such as hotels and restaurants, and other "location bound" services which are non-tradable by definition. Regardless of the motivation for country-1 firms' establishment or acquisition of subsidiaries in country 2, their ability to compete in this market depends on the possession of a firm-specific competitive advantage which can be denied to their competitors.

Technological developments in telecommunications, and the gradual merging of telecommunications and data processing technologies ought, however, to reduce the export cost premium and to enhance the tradability of those services which do not require face-to-face interaction. A growing list of business services such as accounting and even research, development and engineering may, thanks to the above-mentioned developments, be provided from distant locations. With the aid of videotext, even shopping may be computerized in future; the substitution of the

---

target market from a subsidiary located in the target market. The model may with a few modifications be applied to both goods and services.

[1] Dunning [1977] uses the term "ownership advantage" to describe the advantage which the foreign investor must possess in relation to domestic competitors in the target country. Ownership advantage is contrasted with location advantage which is the basis of the traditional comparative advantage enjoyed by a country.

traditional stock exchanges by computerized dealer networks makes traditional markets superfluous. The advent of computer-controlled cash dispensers and of terminals providing up-to-date financial information is dramatically diminishing the dependence of the public on physical banking facilities. Every one of these developments has positive implications for tradability, since they provide efficient and relatively inexpensive substitutes for face-to-face interaction, the main source of the trade-inhibiting export cost premium.

It may be said in conclusion that the choice of the institutional mode of international transactions in services and not their tradability alone are influenced by the interaction between the trade-enhancing properties of traditional comparative advantage and the trade-inhibiting properties of the S-factor. This hypothesis, however, need not be confined to services; it can be extended to goods as well.

7. Summary and Concluding Remarks

The point of departure of this paper is what goods and services are clearly distinguishable from each other. Goods, whether tangible or intangible, can be produced in isolation, they are storable and, with few exceptions, can be appropriated by whoever happens to own them. Services are intangible processes; the supplier produces changes in the user's person or his property. For services to be provided it is necessary for the producer and user to interact.

Further analysis leads to the conclusion that the above-mentioned distinctions, which are derived from Hill's definition, are more apparent than real. Hill's definition does indeed apply to real-world services. It is also applicable to real-world goods, however. This is so since tangible and intangible goods are useless unless they are accompanied by services. Thus, all transactions between the users and suppliers of both goods and services involve some form of interaction between them. [1]

---

[1] The only meaningful difference between goods and services in this context is that while services can be supplied only directly by their producers, goods may be supplied indirectly, by intermediaries who did not produce them.

When the cost of the interaction accounts for a high proportion of the transaction it is said to be characterized by a high S-factor. Ceteris paribus, services tend to have a higher S-factor than goods since the production process of goods does not require producer/user interaction while the production of services does. However, before a good becomes useful it must, as was noted above, be accompanied by a whole range of post-production services. These services may be characterized by a high S-factor which can have a trade-inhibiting effect of the entire transaction.

Transactions involving tangible goods, intangible goods and services proper may thus be indistinguishable from one another, from the point of view of the S-factor with which they are associated.

The international tradability of services and of goods with varying service components is inhibited by an export cost premium, which is determined by the mode of interaction and its duration. The premium is highest when face-to-face interaction between the producer and user is required, since this interaction mode involves international travel. Lower export premiums are associated with other modes of interaction.

To overcome the trade-inhibiting effect of the export cost premium associated with services, suppliers sometimes choose the route of international direct investment. They establish operating subsidiaries in close proximity to their customers, thus saving the export cost premiums. However, international investment, like international trade, involves extra costs which the domestic supplier does not have to bear. To compensate for these costs, the international investor must enjoy a firm-specific cost advantage over his domestic competitors.

Technological developments in telecommunications and the gradual merging of telecommunications and computer technologies reduce the need for face-to-face interaction between producers and users of services, and expand the scope of international trade in services. As a result of such developments, financial, legal, accounting and other business as well as personal services may be offered across national boundaries.

Bibliography

BHAGWATI, Jagdish, "Splintering and Disembodiment of Services and Developing Nations". The World Economy, Vol. 7, 1984, pp. 133-143.

--, "International Trade in Services and Its Relevance for Economic Development". In: Orio GIARINI (Ed.), The Emerging Service Economy. Oxford 1987, pp. 3-34.

COHEN, Stephen, John ZYSMAN, Manufacturing Matters: The Myth of the Post-Industrial Economy. New York 1987.

DEARDORFF, Alan, "Comparative Advantage and International Trade and Investment in Services". In: Robert STERN (Ed.), Trade and Investment in Services: Canada/US Perspectives. Toronto 1985, pp. 39-71.

DUNNING, John H., "Trade, Location of Economic Activity and the MNE: A Search for an Eclectic Approach". In: Bertil OHLIN, Per Magnus WIJKMAN, Per-Ove HESSELBORN (Eds.), The International Allocation of Economic Activity. London 1977, pp. 395-418.

EATWELL, John, Murray MILGATE, Peter NEWMAN, The New Palgrave Dictionary of Economics, Vol. 4. London 1977, p. 315.

GERSHUNI, Jonathan, Ian MILES, The New Services Economy: The Transformation of Employment in Industrial Societies. London 1981.

GIARINI, Orio (Ed.), The Emerging Service Economy. Oxford 1987.

GRUBEL, Herbert, "All Internationally Traded Services Are Embodied in Materials or People". The World Economy, Vol. 10, 1987.

HILL, T.P., "On Goods and Services". Review of Income and Wealth, Vol. 23, 1977, pp. 315-338.

HIRSCH, Seev, "An International Trade and Investment Theory of the Firm". Oxford Economic Papers, Vol. 28, 1976, pp. 258-270.

--, Services and Service-Intensity in International Trade. Tel Aviv, 1988, mimeo.

--, The Internationalization of Israel's Electronics Industry. Jerusalem Institute of Management (JIM), Tel Aviv 1987, mimeo.

INTERNATIONAL MONETARY FUND (IMF), Balance of Payments Statistics. Washington 1985.

LAWRENCE, Paul, David DYER, Renewing American Industry. New York 1983.

NUSSBAUMER, Jacques, Services in the Global Market. Boston 1987.

REICH, Robert, The Next American Frontier. New York 1983.

SAMSON, Gary, Richard SNAPE, "Identifying the Issues in Trade in Services". The World Economy, Vol. 8, 1985, pp. 171-182.

SAPIR, André, "North-South Issues in Trade in Services". The World Economy, Vol. 8, 1985, pp. 27-42.

--, Ernst LUTZ, Trade in Non-Factor Services: Past Trends and Current Issues. Washington 1980.

SHELP, Ronald, Beyond Industrialization: Ascendancy of the Global Service Economy. New York 1981.

STERN, Robert M., Bernard M. HOEKMAN, "Issues and Data Needs for GATT Negotiations on Services". The World Economy, Vol. 10, 1987.

SUMMERS, Robert, "Services in the International Economy". In: Robert P. INMAN (Ed.), Managing the Service Economy: Prospects and Problems. Cambridge 1985, pp. 27-48.

THE WORLD BANK, World Development Report. New York 1982 and 1987.

H. Peter Gray*

85 - 103

4 / / 2

Services and Comparative Advantage Theory

6 3 ℓ0

1. Introduction

Is there such a thing as distinct and separately-identifiable international trade in services? Can "comparative advantage theory" explain the pattern of international trade in non-factor services?[1] These questions, which are fundamental to any analysis of international trade in services, are the subject matter of Section 2. Section 3 confronts the possibility that, if services are to be differentiated from tangible goods in terms of the causes of international trade, it is by virtue of differences in the need for special foreign "delivery systems" or in a "foreign presence" as well as in differing availability of technology in the exporting and importing countries rather than in differences in the endowments of natural resources or of the generic factors of production. The importance of multinational subsidiaries in the foreign market as a special form of delivery system or foreign presence is investigated in Section 4. Finally, Section 5 examines the possibility that no single model of international trade will satisfactorily explain which goods and services a country exports or imports: international trade in both goods and services covers far too wide a range of both tangible goods, from bauxite to brussel sprouts to Boeing 747s, and services, from medical services to wanderlust tourism to computer software. The inevitable heterogeneity in traded goods and services requires that economists recognize the need for less all-embracing and more adaptable models of international trade.

---

* I am indebted to Axel Busch, Willliam S. Milberg and Karl P. Sauvant for comments on an earlier draft. The usual disclaimers apply.

[1] Grubel [1987, pp. 322 f.] points out that repatriated profits are likely to include payment for non-factor services provided by the parent corporation.

2. Definitions: Traded Services and Comparative Advantage

In an important paper, Grubel [1987] asserts that, because services are consumed as they are produced (i.e. they are non-storable), international trade in non-factor services must be embodied either in internationally-mobile goods or in internationally-mobile people. This argument leads to the questionable conclusion that "there is no valid distinction between trade in goods and trade in non-factor services" - particularly insofar as goods-embodied services are concerned [Grubel, 1987, p. 328]. [1] Grubel's position derives from an input-output approach to the question of the degree to which domestically-produced intermediate services are ultimately involved in international trade in downstream but not necessarily final products. Use of this approach inextricably mixes goods production and services production and the question of a separately-identifiable body of international trade in services becomes moot. Each traded good has some service content and that content is necessarily less than 100 percent. However, Grubel himself adumbrates the possibility considered in Sections 2 and 3 below when he states [ibid.] "efforts should continue to be focussed on negotiation in the well-established tradition of aiming for free trade in goods *and assuring rights of establishment of firms and service-producing individuals*" (emphasis added).

In other words, the ability of suppliers of services to provide their own marketing-and-distribution (m&d) services in foreign markets is important in the realization of total potential gains from trade in goods-embodied services. What Grubel has correctly shown is that relative cost efficiency in the production of intermediate services can affect a nation's relative efficiency in the production of final goods (and services). This is a valuable point to have made.

Even so, there is an identifiable group of services traded internationally which deserves separate analysis: the group includes people-embodied services; services which are produced for foreigners by means of extant communication systems (much of this kind of trade comprises the provision of information, i.e. data transmission and processing); and

---

[1] Grubel runs into difficulty in extending his argument to include electronic signals and "capital-embodied services" such as transportation services.

services which are embodied in goods for the *sole* purpose of making possible delivery of the service to a user separated in time and space. Thus, a computer program is committed to paper or disc merely for purposes of delivery, be it domestically or internationally, but the essence of the transaction is the provision of the service of programming. A blueprint or an architect's drawing is embodied in paper solely for the purpose of delivery and use through time. These practices (or goods) do not make the programmer, the engineer and the architect providers of goods in their domestic economies nor should they in the international economy. Indeed, many services which are embodied in paper products solely for the purpose of the transmission to the user can now be transferred internationally by computer-communication systems (including Fax machines) so that the proportion of international trade in goods-embodied services may be expected to decrease through time. Similarly, a transaction in financial assets is conducted by means of communication equipment and the service is embodied in a good only when (and if) the stock certificate, for example, is mailed to the buyer. In terms of the input-output approach, the suggestion here is that if the final stage of production is predominantly a service *and is seen as such domestically*, then the transaction should be included in international trade as a service irrespective of whether the product is temporarily embodied in a good for delivery purposes.

It is useful to amend Grubel's distinction and to divide internationally-traded services into the two categories of people-embodied or "communication-embodied and other services".[1] The second category is probably the main focus of the current interest in services and includes such internationally-traded services as data and financial services and other knowledge-intensive services some of which are embodied in goods (solely for the purpose of delivery).

Due largely to the work of Deardorff [1980; 1982], the expression "comparative advantage" has become linked to the factor-proportions model of international trade. Deardorff defines comparative advantage in these papers as requiring that countries export the goods which use

---

[1] This distinction receives further development below when transportation services are linked with people-embodied services; cf. also Gray [1983].

relatively intensively the factors of production which are relatively cheap in autarky. While it is easy to see how this definition came about, it is unfortunate because it leads to semantic confusion and a lack of expositional clarity. The principle of comparative advantage states that firms will export those goods in which they and their country are relatively (cost-)efficient and makes no contribution to the problem of the determinants of that relative efficiency. David Ricardo, of course, in his original example of positive-sum gains from trade, posited non-identical production functions. In so doing, he directly contravened one of the basic tenets of the factor-proportions model: that conditions of production are "everywhere the same" [Ohlin, 1933, p. 14]. The factor-proportions model is only one, albeit the most widely-accepted explanation of the causes of differences in relative efficiency in the production of individual goods. The model does *not* provide an adequate empirical explanation of international trade in tangible goods [Bowen et al., 1987]. The use of the expression "comparative advantage" in an analysis of the determinants of international trade in services (or goods) is potentially misleading insofar as it may be identified with a model which incorporates an assumption of a zero or negligible role for international differences in technology: the principle itself could, incorrectly, be seen as being refuted by an empirical rejection of the factor-proportions theorem with all of its highly-limiting assumptions.

Any analysis of the patterns of trade of different groups of products must countenance the possibility that one item contributing to the difference in the observed patterns of internationally-traded tangible goods and services, is a difference in the degree of technological contribution (including economies of scale) at the national and firm levels. To avoid the confusion resulting from the embodiment of comparative advantage in the factor-proportions theorem, the paper will use the terms "relative efficiency" or "competitive advantage" to denote export potential.[1] Thus a model of international trade should identify "relative ef-

---

[1] It is worth distinguishing between "relative efficiency" as defined in terms of opportunity costs, and "competitive advantage" as being defined in terms of money costs in some international numeraire. The former is more in keeping with assumptions underlying the pure theory of international trade and, in particular, assumes balanced trade on current account.

ficiency"and its causes rather than to allow the principle of comparative advantage to be identified with any particular model.

3. Are Services Different?

Consider four different categories of trade in services:

(i)   Services which are location-joining such as communications and transportation services;

(ii)   Services which require the user to move to the location of the supplier. This category is people-embodied and tourism is the obvious but not the only example;

(iii)   Services which require the supplier to move to the location of the user: this category is also people-embodied and construction is the obvious example;

(iv)   Professional services which can be made available to clients in other countries by having the service transmitted over communications equipment or by being temporarily embodied in a good.

It is the fourth category that is the main focus of current attention and which will dominate the attention of negotiators in the Uruguay Round. These services, insurance, banking, engineering, consultancy services and, above all, data-services, are those which the Office of Technology Assessment [OTA, 1986, Ch. 5] found to have the greatest estimated underreporting of the value of international trade. [1] They also have high degrees of reliance on technological innovation and on the existence of "related delivery systems". Services which are people-embodied are likely to grow at slower rates (with the possible exception of medical services and education) although pleasure travel (tourism) has always been found to be income-elastic.

Given that the factor-proportions model is by no means a complete explanation of relative efficiency in international trade in tangible goods (it also encounters serious difficulties with intra-industry international

---

[1] The separation of these categories is not "watertight" and technological change can alter the category in which a kind of service can most suitably be included. Sauvant has pointed out that the third category is a focus of current interest in some developing and middle-income countries.

trade as well as in trade in goods with a high technology content), the question of any difference in the causes of relative efficiency between trade in tangible goods and in services must be considered in a broader framework. Differing degrees of reliance of goods and services on technology and on a greater need by services for related (affiliated) delivery systems in the export market must be included. Here "technology" must be seen as including not only the ability of the exporting economy to utilize technology in the public domain but must also recognize the existence of proprietary (product and process) technology under the control of producing firms. "Related delivery systems" could comprise well-established mutually-serving working relationships as well as wholly-owned or joint-venture m&d subsidiaries but an affiliate is more probable (see Section 4 below). [1]

Consider a continuum of forces contributing to relative international efficiency of different goods and services ranging from complete reliance on differences in national factor endowments at one end (with technology everywhere the same) and, at the other end, complete reliance on differences in technological endowments with endowments of traditional factors of production identical in all countries. [2] It would be possible to construct a profile of a country's trade pattern in tangible goods by attributing either the value of exports above the line and/or imports below the line for each good according to the degree to which the relative efficiency is determined by factor endowments and/or technological advantage. (Alternatively, the profile could be constructed by simply entering categories of goods irrespective of value traded.) In this way, extractive minerals would be found at the left end of the continuum as would standard grey cloth and trade in agricultural products: goods in which

---

[1] It is also possible to argue that some services have relatively higher transportation costs than do tangible goods and are for this reason, less commonly traded between suppliers and consumers at some geographic distance. The importance of (round-trip) transportation costs in tourism is self-evident although much tourism can be an extension of travel costs incurred for business purposes. The sheer perishability of services (possibliy requiring embodiment in a good for delivery purposes) is also likely to make delivery costs higher.

[2] The extreme possibilities are highly improbable. At the right-hand extreme, it would be necessary for a country to have different technological capabilities without any relatively generous endowment of human capital.

the exporting country has a dominant lead in technology (e. g. RAM chips by Japan and long-range wide-bodied aircraft by the United States currently) would be at the right end of the scale.[1] Intra-industry trade will appear as a bulge in the right half of the continuum and will characterize the industrialized countries particularly in Europe. Developing countries may be expected to have a less complex profile as they show exports above the left half of the continuum and imports below the right-half. (There is no need for each category of good to be located at the same point on the continuum for each country.) A similar profile of international trade in services can be constructed. In the services profile, wanderlust tourism and resort tourism will be located well towards the left of the continuum and medical and information-intensive services and insurance in the right half. Trade in services will only require a distinct body of analysis if its profile is significantly different from that of international trade in tangible goods. Since both tangible goods and services comprise widely heterogeneous activities and each category has elements which can be identified over almost the full length of the spectrum, the burden of the proof must lie with those who would argue that trade in services has a different set of causal factors than does trade in tangible goods.

The second dimension of interest is the degree to which a "related delivery system" (as distinct from a network of indigenously-owned outlets such as hotels for tourism) is more important for the supply of services than it is for tangible goods. Here the analysis may focus virtually exclusively on socalled communications-embodied and other services including mainly the knowledge-intensive activities. The factor-proportions theorem neglects the role of innate barriers to trade due to cultural differences, to a lack of established linkages, or to difficulties in establishing an m&d organization in the importing country.[2] Exporting re-

---

[1] These are technological non-competitive imports identified in Gray [1976]. (Resource-based non-competitive imports are at the left end of the continuum.)

[2] The theory of intra-industry trade does acknowledge the need for similar tastes and this feature has received empirical support from Loertscher and Wolter [1980]. Recently the difficulties faced by foreign manufacturers in establishing effectual m&d outlets in Japan has concerned policymakers but not theorists.

quires that a good (services) be generated for foreign clients by home-country inputs and there is general recognition that exportation of services requires a well-established foreign presence: Sauvant [1986, p. 32] distinguishes between the provision of services through "pure trade", "pure foreign direct investment" in which the whole operation is performed in the country of sale, and "transactions requiring market presence". The latter can take many forms including partial local production and total production in one country and m&d only in the country of sale. Sauvant cites a Canadian study to the effect that "This third case (or variations on it) tends to be the most common in practice". A major purpose of the foreign affiliate is to provide local support in the foreign market. There are three main reasons why a service firm might need to have a related presence in the client's country of residence: (i) Local after-sales support systems and after-sales servicing of the product are necessary for many products but particularly for management consultation and software; (ii) cultural adaptation of the service produced abroad may be necessary and can require an on-going presence in the foreign market allowing the exporter to establish a long-term working relationship with the client; and (iii) economies of scale and scope encourage centralization of some complex operations in the headquarters of the exporting firm and the output of these resources can and often must be combined with local inputs in the importer's country to provide a competitive service-product. The value of international trade is, of course, the value of services provided by the parent company to the foreign outlet/subsidiary and must be clearly distinguished from the revenues of the foreign affiliate [Gray, 1988]. The contribution of a local-"owned" affiliate is enhanced if the type of service provided requires a knowledge of the client's operations so that services supplied are client-idiosyncratic. Under these conditions, orders placed will be influenced by any past association between the parent *or* the supplier's local affiliate and the client: a continuing presence in the foreign market becomes essential. It is important to distinguish between apparent affilitate relationships such as exist in the accounting and advertising industries where the service is so culture-specific that related partnerships are largely referral services and guarantees of quality of product and generate very little international trade [OTA, 1986, pp. 47-52]. In contrast, firms providing financial services benefit greatly from having subsidiaries located in foreign markets. In addition to allowing banks to follow multinational clients to foreign countries, local subsidiaries of financial firms are prerequisite to permission to solicit general business in the foreign market. Usually, this requirement derives from regulatory considerations concerning the safety of the subsidiary's creditors.

To the extent that a foreign presence is necessary for exports of services (i.e. service exports are transactions which effectively require a foreign presence), foreign governments can protect their domestic suppliers of services by restricting freedom to connect up with local delivery networks (right of presence) and/or by refusing foreign firms permission to establish affiliate firms in the country (right of establishment). It is also possible to protect home-country suppliers by refusing to grant "national treatment" to foreign affiliates [Walter, Gray, 1983]. Thus the inclusion of services in the new round of mulitlateral trade negotiations and the possibility of a legally-binding framework for trade in services poses some serious questions about the expansion of the scope of the GATT beyond its traditional and well-defined concern with international trade in goods and its non-involvement with matters of foreign direct investment.

4. The Case for "Owned" Foreign Affiliates

In principle, an exporter of services could rely on a well-established foreign firm with which it has had a good long-standing relationship. In practice, the exporter is likely to find it is more efficient to have the foreign affiliate be a wholly-owned subsidiary or, if need be, a joint venture. This is likely to be particularly true in information-intensive industries although in others franchising or even licensing may prove the most appropriate m&d strategy.

When the source of competitive advantage of a service firm is proprietary process technology acquired by a firm over a period of years, the firm will be unwilling to risk revealing those skills to a potential rival and will also seek to appropriate any quasi-rents which the proprietary knowledge may generate [Magee, 1977]. In activities in which the local agent has to be privy to the processes of production in the parent corporation, there is a strong preference for a wholly-owned subsidiary: local staff are likely to work better with headquarter's staff and to have a greater interest in preserving the firm's proprietary technology.

The benefits that accrue to having a wholly-owned subsidiary derive in part from "economies of common governance" (i.e. economies of intra-firm trade and interaction). These advantages [Casson, 1986; Williamson, 1979] may be attributed to economies of vertical and horizontal integration; the greater efficiency of intra-firm operations compared with arm's-length relationships; and the ability to exercise control over the quality of the service provided and, in this way, to safeguard the firm's reputation.

The economies of vertical and horizontal integration posit that activities conducted within a single firm will be less costly than arm's-length transactions between unrelated parties. Vertical integration allows a reduction in costs and possible improvements in the quality of the service by improving inter-unit scheduling efficiency through common control over sequential activities. An example of the potential savings to be achieved lies in the ability of a vertically-integrated firm to eliminate one inspection for quality by imposing the inspection either at the upstream or the downstream factory but not at both [Casson, 1986]. Horizontal integration may be less significant for services-producing firms than for their goods-producing counterparts although the transferability of reputation will apply equally. In addition to obvious benefits from appropriability, some firms will be able to enjoy production sharing by using excess capacity in one unit to relieve pressure in another. There are also gains to be achieved by avoiding the costs of contract negotiation among separate firms: it is probable that the costs of negotiation of the last marginal detail are significantly higher than the average costs and, if both parties subscribe to the same bottom line, much effort can be saved. Franchising operations in service industries stand to reap similar benefits as do their goods-producing counterparts particularly in terms of the assurance of quality of output and in economies of training.

The gains from closer operational ties among units are likely to be particularly important when there exists a strong cultural or environmental difference between the countries of the exporter and the importer. In context, "cultural" and "environmental" must be quite broadly interpreted to enfold tax law and regulatory differences as well as the differences in national social cultures. Economies of this kind depend upon the history of interaction between subsidiary and parent and on the development of a homology of attitude and outlook between people in the two units. Such homology is likely to contribute to the efficiency of communication within the larger organization as common goals and common jargon combine to transmit information more rapidly and more precisely. Egelhoff [1986, p. 97] reports the existence of much more efficient communication among people who have worked in the same firm environment for many years. Similar effects will derive from the development of mutual reliance among groups of people working regularly with each other even at some considerable geographical difference - including relationships among people in different subsidiaries as well as between subsidiaries and parent.

Where a corporate name serves as a guarantee of the quality of the service provided, the foreign presence serves as more than a simple link between two units: it ensures that the client abroad will be able to rely on the same quality of service as it has obtained from the parent. With the worldwide spread of (goods) multinational corporations, this is an important source of increased marketing efficiency.

The existence of a "foreign presence" is desirable for any kind of international trade in other than standardized products for which indigenous marketing outlets are perfectly adequate to assure efficient distribution of imports. Most services are non-standardized, particularly the knowledge-intensive services, and exportation of these kinds of service requires a presence abroad that includes access to a delivery system if that is under state control. To the extent that a greater proportion of services are non-standardized or client-specific, this feature of international trade is likely to be more important for services than for goods. The distinction is likely to become still more important when set out in terms of the desirability of subsidiary status for the foreign representative/outlet. While services do not require a different model of international trade from goods in terms of the technology/factor-proportions distinction, the question of the kind of foreign representation may indeed require a separate dimension in any positive model of international trade and any analysis of liberalization of trade in (information-intensive) services.

5. Multiple Sources of Competitive Efficiency in Services

Two features of international trade in services stand out: the problem of linking suppliers and consumers (users) who are resident in different countries and who cleave to different cultures, and the heterogeneity of service activities. The former problem is partly solved by recognizing the possibility that the consumer or the producer can be internationally-mobile on a temporary basis so that residence and geographic location do not always coincide. Such services can be usefully categorized as "factor-embodied" (obviously derivative from Grubel's dichotomy) where the factor involved can be either a factor of consumption (tourist, invalid or student) [Gray, 1970, p. 3] or a factor of production (construction equipment, a cargo vessel or a passenger aircraft). Internationally-traded services which are not factor-embodied ("other services"), are delivered to their user through extant delivery systems and through temporary embodiment in a tangible good for delivery purposes so that proximity of producer and user is not necessary. The heterogeneity of services, while important in the determination of any satisfactory model of service trade, is no greater than that of trade in goods so that generic classification of trade in goods and services does not require separate models.

The wide variety of individual transactions included in both kinds of trade raises the very fundamental question of whether it is possible or useful to think in terms of a single explanatory model of international trade which will effectively encompass all of the many kinds of trade in goods or services - international trade being defined quite simply as the use or consumption by residents of one country of the fruits of an activity performed by residents of another country. The heterogeneity involved relates not only to the characteristics of the tangible goods and services actually traded but also to the differences in the trading partners: e. g. North-South trade will have different important causal variables than will North-North trade. To attempt to capture the diversity of international trade within a single model is heroic but such attempts necessarily compress quite distinct activities into a single entity and impair the richness of analysis of at least one of the categories of trade included. Currently the theory of international trade has a dominant model which is a variant on the Heckscher-Ohlin-Samuelson or Heckscher-

Ohlin-Vanek theorems and which rests squarely upon identification of generic factors of production and the relationship between (demand-compensated) supply proportions and autarkic factor prices. The analysis then hinges on the factor intensities of production of individual traded goods. Some variables are excluded from these models in order to be able to identify the role of factor proportions more clearly: notable among these exclusions is the possibility of differences in technological resources in different nations.[1] Recently, the realities of multinational corporations, international trade in services, intra-industry trade and trade in high-technology goods, among others, have forced international economists to confront activities which do not adapt well to the basic model. Consider, as an example, Deardorff's [1985] attempt to fit services into his theory of comparative advantage. To force analysis of a category of trade into a model which is not suitable for the task is Procrustean in outlook and the added category of trade is deprived of the appropriate degree of detail in the analysis. Deardorff considers three[2] features of international trade in services and to be able to adapt services to his model is required to impose stringent limitations on the characteristics of services. As an example, consider the extreme assumption Deardorff is forced to make to attempt to "fold" the need for or existence of an affiliated subsidiary into his model: he conceives of management in the exporting country as an "absent factor" located in the exporting country but, magically, have its product in the importing country (even though he follows Hill's [1977] requirement that the service can only be produced when the producer and user are effectively in the same location). The requirement that the characteristics of international trade in services be fitted into the basic model, does not allow the analysis to countenance anything other than quite particular service activities and attributes. The matter closely resembles the inability of the mainstream model successfully to accommodate the existence of trade in high-technology goods.

---

[1] Deardorff [1985] does include one example of Hicks-neutral technology difference.

[2] Two of the examples are overlapping and relate to the need for a related foreign presence. The third, trade in trade-related services, is fitted into the basic model only by imposing quite severe assumptions on the form of trade-related services.

Table 1 presents a different approach to the problem of heterogeneity: it lists different kinds of international trade activities and variables
which might contribute *importantly* to those individual categories of
trade. Neither list is exhaustive and indeed the explanatory variables
are only marked as affecting the individual categories of trade if their
role is substantial so that the absence of an "X" does *not* imply a zero
role for the explanatory variable. Clearly, positioning the "X"s requires
individual judgement and other economists would probably generate a
different pattern: that said, it is evident that not every category of
trade has the same list of explanatory variables and that no explanatory
variable appears in every category of trade. (The number of activities
could be increased by identifying categories of trading partners as well
as goods traded.)

The focus of this paper is "services" in general and "other services" in particular. The variables needed to explain the pattern of
trade in factor-embodied services are fairly self-evident: by far the most
important of these services by value are tourism (or international travel)
and transportation: these two, between them, validate most of the "X"s
in the column. "Other services" tend to be more technology-intensive
and, except for the role of related distribution units and barriers to investment, have most of the same explanatory variables listed as international trade in high-technology goods. What is perhaps the most surprising thing about Table 1 is the relative unimportance of the simple factors
proportions of land, labor and capital. This causal variable shows up as
having importance only for low-technology, standardized goods, agricultural goods, and factor-embodied services (mainly tourism) and needs
broadening to be able to incorporate some of these kinds of trade.

The important point that derives from this table is that any general
model of international trade must either encompass an extraordinarily
large number of causal variables (thirteen are listed, barriers to trade
are not considered, and each of the thirteen is capable of refinement).[1]
All variables are excluded from some kinds of international trade (none
is featured in more than one half of the different categories of trade).

---

[1] Particularly technology which must ultimately encompass the ability of
an economy to use technology in the public domain, i.e. to have the
necessary infrastructure, and to allow for proprietary product and
process technology.

Table 1 - The Multidimensionality of International Trade

Explanatory variable	Trade in					
	agricul- tural	natural resource	lo-tech	hi-tech	other	factor- embodied
	goods		manufactures		services	
Climate	X					X
Natural resource endowments(a)		X				X
Simple factor proportions(a)	X		X			X
Human capital(a)				X	X	X
Technology differences				X	X	
Scale economies				X	X	
Differentiated goods				X	X	
Lancastrian tastes(b)				X		X
Transportation costs	X	X				X
Communication linkages					X	X
Internal dynamics				X	X	
Related distri- bution unit					X	
Barriers to in- vestment					X	

(a) Variables comprise the neofactor-proportions model. - (b) Consumer tastes are diffused over many differentiated products [Lancaster, 1980].

What this suggests is that a single theory of international trade - be it neofactor proportions, neotechnology or some mixture of the two - cannot hope to account satisfactorily for all of the kinds of international trade which is undertaken in this world. What is needed, then, is a more flexible body of analysis which will allow studies of specialist sub-categories to be undertaken without encountering all of the difficulties of definition and all the data problems which afflict the broad empirical tests of the kinds undertaken by Bowen et al. [1987] und Balassa and Bauwens [1985] and similar studies.

    Instead of a general model of international trade into which international trade in services must be compressed, there is a need for a series of models for separately-identifiable categories of international trade.

The more refined the model, i. e. the more similar the components of any trade category analyzed, the greater is the degree of detail which is achievable. Table 1 provides a firt step towards such a series of models. Trade in factor-embodied services requires seven (important) variables and "other services" eight variables if the phenomena are to be accounted for satisfactorily. Anything less detailed will lose some necessary or very desirable feature in the explanation of the determination of these categories of service trade. The fact that the model does not identify relative autarkic costs does not imply contravention of the principle of comparative advantage: services are obtained from foreign suppliers if those suppliers can provide a better service at a better price [Ohlin, 1933, pp. 12-13]. There are gains from trade and gains from trade are what the principle of comparative advantage is all about.

What matters in trade theory is the selection of the appropriate explanatory variables and the form or structure of the model. Clearly for "other services", economies of scale, the existence of in-place supply mechanisms, and the availability of product-specific technology and human capital are decisive. It would be extreme to say that autarkic factor prices "have nothing to do with the case" but it would not be very far from the mark.

Appendix

The approach to the modelling of international trade laid out in the main text requires that the whole subject of international trade be broken down into several sub-component areas and that these be modelled separately. There is a fundamental problem with this approach which must be made explicit: the (net barter) terms of trade and relative factor prices cannot be solved endogenously unless a model of *all* international trade is created and is solved simultaneously. This problem of the inability to solve for the terms of trade endogenously is not as unusual as might be supposed and afflicts the orthodox model by virtue of the latter's exclusion of non-competitive imports of natural-resource goods and of other kinds of international trade. This weakness of the mainstream model can be straightforwardly illustrated: Caves and Jones [1973, p. 11] assert that such exclusions are not important. Doing a severe injustice to Hawaiian coffee-growers, they argue: "If you live in the United States and have a taste for coffee, you have your coffee imported from Brazil or some other coffee-growing country because it is not produced in your own country. If such imports were cut off, your level of well-being or your "real income" would surely be reduced. If all trade were of this kind ... there would be little need for the economist either to expound on the virtues of trade or to explain the pattern of trade ... But many items in international commerce cannot be described or explained in this way ... What are the reasons for the large volume of international trade in these items?"

Caves and Jones then proceed to construct a model of international trade which is based exclusively on imports potentially competing with home production, and which generates endogenously the equilibrium terms of trade. The restrictiveness of the assumptions of such a model is covert.

To produce a model in which the endogenously-determined net barter terms of trade are not affected by the omitted trade, the following assumptions must hold: levels of income are unaffected; trade in the omitted goods is balanced; and non-competitive (omitted) goods use generic factors in the same proportions as do competitive goods so that the relative prices of generic factors are unaffected.

The solution is to allow the terms of trade to be imposed on each component sub-model exogenously. This has the advantage of making the assumption explicit as well as of ridding the model of the need for the assumption of balanced trade overall and in each sub-component. As a practical matter the terms of trade can be introduced in terms of existing absolute levels of factor prices in and the rates of exchange between the currencies of the countries included in the model.

Bibliography

BALASSA, Bela, Luc BAUWENS, "Comparative Advantage in Manufactured Goods in a Multi-Country, Multi-Industry, and Multi-Factor Model". In: Theo PEETERS, Peter PRAET, Paul REDING (Eds.), International Trade and Exchange Rates in the Late Eighties. Amsterdam 1985, pp. 31-52.

BOWEN, Harry P., Edward E. LEAMER, Leo SVEIKAUSKAS, "Multicountry, Multifactor Tests of Factor Abundance Theory". The American Economic Review, Vol. 77, 1987, pp. 791-809.

CASSON, Mark (Ed.), Multinationals and World Trade: Vertical Integration and the Division of Labor in World Industries. London 1986.

CAVES, Richard E., Ronald W. JONES, World Trade and Payments. Boston 1973.

DEARDORFF, Alan V., "The General Validity of the Law of Comparative Advantage". Journal of Political Economy, Vol. 88, 1980, pp. 941-957.

--, "The General Validity of the Heckscher-Ohlin Theorem". The American Economic Review, Vol. 72, 1982, pp. 683-694.

--, "Comparative Advantage and International Trade and Investment in Services". In: Robert M. STERN (Ed.), Trade and Investment in Services: Canada/U.S. Perspectives. Toronto 1985, pp. 39-71.

EGELHOFF, William G., Business Strategies and Competition in the Semiconductor Industry: A Comparative Study across U.S., Japanese and European Firms. Troy, N.Y., 1986.

GRAY, H. Peter, International Travel: International Trade. Lexington, Mass., 1970.

--, A Generalized Theory of International Trade. London 1976.

--, "A Negotiating Strategy for Trade in Services". Journal of World Trade Law, Vol. 17, 1983, pp. 377-388.

--, "International Trade in Services: Four Distinguishing Features". In: Khosrow FATEMI (Ed.), International Trade and Finance: A North American Perspective. Westport, Conn., 1988, pp. 15-23.

GRUBEL, Herbert G., "All Traded Services are Embodied in Materials or People". The World Economy, Vol. 10, 1987, pp. 319-330.

HILL, T.P., "On Goods and Services". The Review of Income and Wealth, Vol. 23, 1977, pp. 315-338.

LANCASTER, Kelvin J., "Intra-Industry Trade under Perfect Monopolistic Competition". Journal of International Economics, Vol. 10, 1980, pp. 151-176.

LOERTSCHER, Rudolf, Frank WOLTER, "Determinants of Intra-Industry Trade within Countries and Across Countries". Weltwirtschaftliches Archiv, Vol. 116, 1980, pp. 289-293.

MAGEE, Stephen P., "Information and Multinational Corporations: An Appropriability Theory of Foreign Direct Investment". In: Jagdish BHAGWATI (Ed.), The New International Economic Order. Cambridge, Mass., 1977, pp. 317-340.

OFFICE OF TECHNOLOGY ASSESSMENT (OTA), U.S. CONGRESS, Trade in Services: Exports and Foreign Revenues - Special Report. OTA-ITE-316, Washington, September 1986.

OHLIN, Bertil, Interregional and International Trade. Cambridge, Mass., 1933.

SAUVANT, Karl P., Trade and Foreign Direct Investment in Data Services. Boulder, Col., 1986.

WALTER, Ingo, H. Peter GRAY, "Protectionism and International Banking: Sectoral Efficiency, Competitive Structure and National Policy". Journal of Banking and Finance, Vol. 7, 1983, pp. 597-609.

WILLIAMSON, Oliver, "Transaction Cost Economics: The Governance of Contractual Relations". The Journal of Law and Economics, Vol. 22, 1979, pp. 233-261.

104-07

Comment on H. Peter Gray, "Services and Comparative Advantage Theory"

Henning Klodt

Trade in services is commonly perceived to be something special. But it is still an open question what the main differences to trade in goods are. Peter Gray's paper contributes significantly to a better understanding of these differences.

The factual evidence suggests that the international tradeability of services is quite low. Services account for about 60 per cent of total output in developed countries and 50 per cent in developing countries, whereas the share of non-factor services in world trade is less than 20 per cent. The comparatively low exposure of services to international competition points to particular impediments to trade that arise from specific properties of services (inherent barriers) or from government interventions in service markets (artificial barriers). Gray's paper is mainly concerned with inherent trade barriers.

Firstly, Gray makes an account of different types of services. International trade in "factor-embodied services" requires the spatial movement of producers or consumers across national borders. In "communication-embodied and other services", by contrast, the spatial movement of people is replaced by transborder flows of information. This terminology is very similar to the approach of embodied and disembodied, or proximity-requiring and long-distance, or non-separated and separated services [Bhagwati, 1984; 1987; Sampson, Snape, 1985].

Gray works out three major consequences of this concept, repeated here in brief:

- Due to rapidly declining information and communication costs the international tradeability of disembodied services is nowadays as high or even higher than the tradeability of goods.
- Since disembodied services mainly consist of information, they may be stored like any other information.
- If services are temporarily embodied in goods for delivery purposes, they continue to be services. The advice of an attorney written on a

letter or the analysis of an economist published in a conference volume are still services, not goods.

The long-standing and still controversial debate on these topics can perhaps be attributed to a mix-up of embodied and disembodied services.

Secondly, Gray stresses the importance of "special delivery systems" like branch offices or communication networks for the international provision of services. They might explain the striking gap between potential and actual trading performance. Of course, trade in goods also requires the availability of specific facilities in importing countries, e. g. harbours, airports or roads. Nevertheless, it seems reasonable that special delivery systems tend to be more important in service industries than in most goods-producing industries. This argument applies in particular to those services that are composite commodities of headquarter services and local inputs, where the physical proximity to customers is essential.

As a result of the dependence on commercial presence in foreign markets, international trade in services is highly sensitive to government regulations. [1] The provision of services from abroad will be hampered or even precluded by restrictions on market entry of foreign-controlled affiliates. Furthermore, operating restrictions are likely to be more inflictive to trade in services than to trade in goods. Their design is often especially convenient to the needs of domestic production. They will in general raise the costs of domestic firms to a lesser extent than the costs of foreign competitors, even if the restrictions are to be observed by domestic and foreign producers as well. Finally, the international provision of factor-embodied services requires the transborder movement of people. Regulations on immigration could, therefore, result in a third category of barriers to trade in services.

In consequence, Gray (p. 95) argues that "the question of the kind of foreign representation may indeed require a separate dimension in... any analysis of liberalization of trade". With regard to the Uruguay Round, a simple extension of existing GATT rules to trade in services would not be sufficient. Issues on liberalising trade in services are inevitably involved in issues on international factor mobility. Negotiations

---

[1] For an analysis of the impact of government regulations on international trade and foreign direct investment in services, cf. Klodt [1988].

should embrace rights of establishment (including the right of non-estab-
lishment) and restrictions on immigration that are not covered by the
GATT treaty as yet. The contracting parties should also strive for a
reduction of operating restrictions in their domestic service markets. [1]

Apart from different treatment in trade talks, services might also
require separate positive models of international trade. Gray presents 13
variables to explain international trade in six different activities, according to which trade in disembodied services shows a similar pattern to
trade in hi-tech manufactures, whereas trade in factor-embodied services
is determined by a rather unique set of variables (cf., Gray's Table 1).
A slight re-condensation of this list might be appropriate in order to
assign these variables to existing trade models.

By and large, two mainstreams of analysing international trade can
be distinguished: models of inter-industry trade and models of intra-industry trade. [2] The former models mainly rest upon a set of variables
related to technology differences (including climate and natural resource
endowments) and another set related to factor proportions (including
human capital). Models of intra-industry trade, on the other hand, are
mainly concerned with scale economies and consumer preferences (differentiated goods, Lancastrian tastes). Most of the remaining variables of
Gray's Table 1 (transportation costs, communication linkages, related
distribution unit, barriers to investment) can be associated with different forms of barriers to trade.

Viewed in this way, different models are not required for different
types of activity but for different types of trade. Trade in services between developing and developed countries is presumably concentrated on
inter-industry trade, whereas trade in services between countries facing
very similar production possibilities could rather be explained by models
of intra-industry trade. Gray has demonstrated elsewhere, how these two
types of analysis could be integrated in a generalised theory [Gray,
1976].

---

[1] The key elements of a proposed international agreement on trade in
services are presented by Jackson [1988].

[2] For an excellent survey of the central implications of different trade
models, cf. Deardorff [1985].

Hence, it may be doubted that the main features of trade in services could not be grasped by traditional trade models. Services deserve special attention, however, with regard to trade barriers. The significance of entry and operating restrictions in service markets should be explicitly considered in each analysis of trade in services. This applies to disembodied services, such as telecommunications with its public monopolies, as well as to embodied services, such as maritime transport with its complex system of cargo preferences.

Gray seems right to argue that autarkic factor prices can hardly explain the actual patterns of trade in services. It might be added that the tension between traditional trade theory and real life primarily results from intense and abundant government regulations of service markets.

Bibliography

BHAGWATI, Jagdish N., "Splintering and Disembodiment of Services and Developing Nations". The World Economy, Vol. 7, 1984, pp. 133-143.

--, "Trade in Services and the Multilateral Trade Negotiations". The World Bank Economic Review, Vol. 1, 1987, pp. 549-569.

DEARDORFF, Alan V., "Major Recent Developments in International Trade Theory". In: Theo PEETERS, Peter PRAET, Paul REDING (Eds.), International Trade and Exchange Rates in the Late Eighties. Amsterdam 1985, pp. 3-27.

GRAY, H. Peter, A Generalized Theory of International Trade. London 1976.

JACKSON, John H., "Constructing a Constitution for Trade in Services". The World Economy, Vol. 11, 1988, pp. 187-202.

KLODT, Henning, "International Trade, Direct Investment, and Regulations in Services". World Competiton, Vol. 12, 1988, pp. 49-67.

SAMPSON, Gary P., Richard H. SNAPE, "Identifying the Issues in Trade in Services". The World Economy, Vol. 8, 1985, pp. 171-181.

John H. Dunning*

Trade and Foreign-Owned Production in Services: Some Conceptual and Theoretical Issues

1. Introduction

Contemporary theories of trade and foreign-owned production are concerned with both the ownership and location of economic activity. The ownership of value added activities, irrespective of where they are located, is of interest, inasmuch as some enterprises, rather than others, seem better able to meet the demands of national and international markets. The location of production is of interest inasmuch as some countries, rather than others, seem better able to offer the necessary producing and transacting facilities to these enterprises to compete in the global market place.

An explanation of both the ownership and the location of economic activity draws upon two strands of economic theory. The first is the theory of the distribution of factor endowments, which is essentially concerned with (although it does not fully explain) the location of production. The second is the theory of economic organisation which is essentially concerned with the ways in which the transactions relating to that production (including those which may impinge on the location of that production) are organised.

In the traditional, e.g. H-S-O, model of trade, only the first issue – the *where* of production – is of interest. No consideration is given to the organisation of transactions relating to that production: this is simply because the market is assumed to be a perfect mechanism of exchange, and to involve zero transaction costs. However, once structural or cognitive imperfections in the goods and/or factor market are brought into the picture, transaction costs become of relevance, as does the organisation of these transactions. Some of the more fruitful advances in

* Part of this paper represents a shortened version of a report on Transnational Enterprises and the Growth of Services, which is to be published by the UNCTC. I am most grateful to the UNCTC for permission to use some of the material.

the theory of both trade and foreign-owned production over the last decade or more have focussed on these issues. These are summarised in Casson [1987], Dunning [1988] and Ethier [1986].

In this paper, we shall argue that a comprehensive explanation of trade and foreign production in the services sector needs to draw upon both strands of economic theory. We shall suggest that the first pre-requisite for firms to engage in trade or foreign production in services is the possession of certain competitive advantages, some of which may reflect the factor endowments of their country of origin, and others may be generated by the firms themselves, independently of their country of origin. Secondly, in considering whether the output of these advantages is embodied in further value-added activities of the firm that owns them, or sold to other firms, we will pay particular attention to the relative production and transaction costs of the two modalities. We shall argue that many of these organisational questions involved are common to trade or foreign production.

Thirdly we shall consider the issue of *where* the value adding activity arising from these competitive advantages is located; and it is here where sometimes trade and foreign production are substitutes for each other, and sometimes complementary to each other. The essential point, however, in examining this and the other two questions is that one needs a similar theoretical underpinning; an amalgam of the theory of the distribution of factor endowments and the theory of economic or-ganisation.

The approach of the paper reflects the author's own particular in-terest in explaining the determinants of foreign-owned production (i.e. the foreign value-adding activities of multinational enterprises) in ser-vices; and especially the extent to which the theories put forward to explain international production in the goods sector need modification when applied to the services sector. Section 2 of the paper rehearses some concepts relating to both the nature of services and that of the multinational enterprise. Section 3 reviews very briefly the main factors affecting the growth of services in recent years, and the role of MNEs in that growth. Sections 4 to 7 comprise the heart of the paper. Section 5 attempts to identify the main competitive or ownership specific advan-tages of firms supplying services to international markets. Section 6 theorises about the location of value-added activities, which embody the

output of these advantages and Section 7 how these two sets of activities
are coordinated which each other. Some conclusions are set out in Section 8.

2. Multinationals, Goods and Services

A multinational enterprise (MNE) is an enterprise which both en-
gages in cross-border transactions and ownes or controls value-adding
activities in two or more countries. Both sets of activities might lead to
production and exchange of tangible goods (e. g. washing machines) or
intangible services (e. g. an audit) or some combination of the two (e. g.
the transmission of data).[1] This output might be sold to other firms or
used by the same firm for further value-adding activities i. e. take the
form of intermediate goods or services; or to final consumers, i. e. take
the form of consumption goods or services; or indeed to both at the
same time (e. g. an automobile or airline journey).

In many respects, the distinction between goods and services is an
artificial one; indeed one observer [Levitan, 1985] claims that it is a
statistical artifact. Firstly, most of the goods purchased are bought for
the services they provide; food is bought to assuage the appetite, for
its nutritional qualities, and for its appeal to the palate; a bicycle is a
form of transport; a TV set is a means of entertainment; shoes are for
walking, and so on. Secondly, there are few "pure" goods or services.
Almost all goods embody non-factor primary or intermediate services,
while most services cannot be produced without some physical assets or
intermediate goods; but *at the point of sale*, most are jointly and simultaneously supplied. Sampson and Snape [1985] refer to these latter types
of services as "separated" services and Bhagwati [1984] prefers the expression "splintered" services. Hirsch [1986] grades services according
to the proportion of their total costs incurred by the producer and user

---

[1] For the purpose of this paper, we define a product as the output of
productive activity, a good as a *tangible* product, and a service as an
intangible product.

during their interaction - what he calls the simultaneity factor.[1] The lower these costs in cross-border transactions, the greater the tradeability of serices is likely to be. Such tradeability also crucially depends on the availability and effectiveness of transportation and communication facilities which, of course, are goods in their own right. Data transmission equipment is to services what ground, sea and air transport facilities are to goods.

In short, the output of economic activity may be considered as ranging from that of pure goods to that of pure services. However, most (and an increasing proportion of) goods embody some non-factor intermediate services, and most services embody some intermediate goods. And, even pure services require people to supply them [Grubel, 1987]. For the purpose of this paper, we shall take a service to mean a product, the *main* purpose of which is to provide a service at the point of sale; where these services also require goods at the point of the sale we shall refer to them as *goods-embodied services*. Likewise, we shall think of a good as a product the main purpose of which is to supply a tangible commodity; where these goods require services (other than factor services) we shall refer to them as *service-embodied goods*. We shall also treat a service as an *output* rather than an input, although many services take the form of intermediate outputs, i.e. those which are subsequently embodied in downstream value-adding activities.

Trade and foreign-owned production in services may be undertaken both by service and non-service companies. For example, in 1982, no less than 82.2 per cent of the assets of US wholesale trading foreign affiliates were owned by parent companies whose main activities were in manufacturing and petroleum production; the corresponding percentages for finance (excluding banking), insurance and real estate activities were 55 per cent and business and other services 53.3 per cent. By contrast, 88.8 per cent of the assets of manufacturing affiliates were owned by parent companies whose main activity was also in manufactur-

---

[1] Where U = total cost of a service to the user, Pi and Ri are costs incurred by the producer and the user independently of each other, and Ps and Rs are the costs incurred by the producer and consumer during their interaction, then the simultaneity factor (S) is equal to (Ps + Rs)/U.

ing.[1] In analysing trade and foreign-owned production, therefore, it may be helpful to distinguish between *service activities* and *service industries or firms*.

3. The Growth of Services in the World Economy

Over the past two decades, the share of services in the gross national product of 54 out of 81 countries which regularly provide data to the World Bank has increased. In 1985, it averaged 61 per cent for developed market economies, compared with 55 per cent in 1965; for developing countries the respective figures were 47 and 42 per cent. However, this increased share has been mainly at the expense of primary, rather than secondary production; indeed, in both developing and developed countries, the rate of growth of manufacturing output has exceeded that of services [UNCTC, 1988]. Moreover, exept for one of the 115 countries providing data, the share of the labour force accounted for the service sector rose between 1965 and 1980 [World Bank, 1987]. The growing importance of services in most national economies has been examined by various scholars in recent years [Daniels, 1982; Shelp, 1981; 1984; 1985; Gershuny, Miles, 1983; Riddle, 1986; 1987]. It reflects a combination of both *demand* and *supply*-led factors. These include:

(i)   The growth of per capital output and the high income elasticity of demand for at least some "discretionary" consumer services;[2]

(ii)   the increasing role of intermediate or producer services in the value-added process. In particular, advances in telematics have helped firms incorporate new information-based services within their own structures and to diversify the services they are able to

---

[1] Further details are set out in UNCTC [1988].

[2] But only some. An unpublished paper by Grubel and Hammes [1987] suggests that in industrial countries the demand for services has remained a constant fraction of real consumption. The authors argue that this demand has been sustained as a result of the increased female participation ratio in the labour force and the monetization of household activities most of which involve the production of services. In some sectors, goods have replaced services (e.g. vacuum cleaners and washing machines for domestic and laundering services, and television and video recorders for cinema entertainment).

offer their customers. One example is the way in which supermarket chains are using data networks originally established for inventory control to support a variety of other service activities (e.g. travel) [UNCTAD, 1985];

(iii)   the increasing tendency of firms in non-service sectors to hive off (i.e. externalise) some of the less productive service activities (e.g. accounting, auditing, legal services, and so on); one recent example is the relinquishment by Exxon of its international transport services;[1]

(iv)   the growing importance of distribution and after sales maintenance and servicing activities to the value of a physical product (e.g. a copying machine, a boiler, an aircraft);

(v)   The increasing role of the State in providing or encouraging the production of both intermediate services (e.g. education and telecommunications) and final services (health); and of services directly related to the functions of Government (e.g. civil service, defence, tax collection, social security, and so on);

(vi)   the growth of finance, banking, legal, insurance, transport, communications and other support services necessary for the efficient functioning of modern society; and

(vii)   the emergence of new intermediate markets for services (e.g. the Euromarket, reinsurance, securitisation, new forms of data transmission, and so forth).

In general, there is some evidence to suggest that, although the quality and variety of services varies more than that of goods, the demand for services, for example as between consumers from different countries at a given level of income, is likely to be less heterogenous. Inter alia, this helps explain the current trend towards the globalisation of some services, such as investment banking, insurance, hotels, advertising, and airlines.

---

[1] On the other hand, technological advances are enabling some firms to internalise functions previously sub-contracted. For example, the introduction of computer-assisted publishing systems has encouraged companies such as GEC (of the UK), McDonnell Douglas (of the US) and Aerospatiale (of France) to produce their own corporate publications, rather than buy these from specific printing firms (Financial Times, 21st June 1988, p. 18, "Publishing Becomes an Inside Job").

The question now arises, what is the role of MNEs in the supply of these services? Data recently published by the UNCTC [1988], indicate that, though not as pronounced as that of goods, the share of MNEs of the total service activities in developed and developing countries is increasing quite rapidly. Moreover, as Table 1 shows, the growth of the FDI stock in most service sectors in industrialised countries has risen much faster than in the primary or secondary sectors. The following sections seek to offer an explanation for these phenomena by drawing upon one of the most widely accepted paradigms of trade and international production. In particular, it argues that the involvement of MNEs in the service sectors has risen over the past two decades, partly because of the *general* demand and supply-led characteristics identified above, and partly because these characteristics have *particularly* favoured foreign-owned production as a modality for utilising the competitive advantages of foreign-based firms and of the transactions associated with these advantages.

Table 1 - Annual Average Growth Rates of the Stock of Inward Direct Investment by Region, 1975-1982 (per cent)

	Europe(a)	North America(b)	Other industrial- ised(c)	Total industrial- ised
Primary	10.8	8.6	18.9	9.7
Secondary	6.7	13.9	13.9	10.0
Tertiary	10.8	22.3	18.4	16.5
Construction	7.4	19.5	7.6	12.8
Transport and communications	4.2	17.8	6.2	11.5
Distributive trade	10.7	22.1	19.0	16.6
Property	9.8	40.2	19.2	17.8
Banking and finance	14.1	18.6	18.9	16.6
Other services	5.1	19.4	23.7	16.1
Total	8.3	15.8	16.6	12.3

(a) Austria, France, West Germany, Italy, Netherlands, Norway, Portugal, Spain, and the UK. - (b) Canada and the US. - (c) Australia and Japan.

Source: Original host-country sources as cited in Dunning and Cantwell [1987] or author's estimates based on these sources.

4. The Theory of Foreign-Owned Production: Its Relevance to the Growth of Services

There is now a general consensus in the literature that the extent and pattern of foreign-owned production, i. e. production undertaken by firms outside their national boundaries is dependent on the strength of, and interaction between, three main factors. These are:

(i)   the extent and nature of the technological, managerial and market- ing assets they possess and can acquire, and the way in which these assets are organised and geographically dispersed. These comprise the *ownership*-specific[1] or *competitive*[2] advantages of firms which will determine their ability to service particular markets, vis-à-vis their competitors[3] whether it be by trade or foreign-owned production;

(ii)   the benefits of combining these advantages with immobile factor endowments in a foreign or the home country to produce further value-adding activities[4] (which reflect the location-specific or comparative advantages of these countries). The configuration of these advantages will determine the *location* of service-producing activities;

(iii) the advantages of internally controlling and coordinating (i) and (ii) with other assets owned by the MNE, rather than licensing the

---

[1] The word "ownership" is preferred to "firm" as it emphasises the gen- eric characteristic of competitive advantages. We accept, of course, that these may vary according to particular attributes of firms (e. g. size, age, management strategy, etc.). We reserve the term firm-spe- cific characteristics (rather than advantages) to embrace these.

[2] Writers such as Porter [1980; 1985; 1986] refer to the advantages which one competitor has over another competitor as competitive advan- tages, but, to the industrial economist, these could well be monopol- istic (in the sense that for some time period at least) the firm pos- sessing the advantages has an exclusive or privileged right to them [Lall, 1980]. But even this latter nomenclature can be misleading when such advantages arise from the superior coordinating advantages which one firm may possess over another [Casson, 1987].

[3] Including "potential" as well as actual competitors. Here the theory of contestable markets is directly relevant.

[4] This may be based on "natural" resources, or "engineered" by econ- omic or political institutions indigenous to the country in question [cf. Scott, Lodge, 1985].

right to use these assets to indigenous firms located in the country of production. The literature suggests that the preferred organisational mode will depend on the relative production and transactional costs involved.

It is further accepted that the configuration of these ownership
location and internalisation (OLI) advantages, and the firms' response to
them will vary according to *industry*, *country* or *region* (or origin and
destination) and *firm*-specific characteristics; this latter incorporating
the perceived competitive positions of firms and their strategies for
growth.

It is also worth observing that while a majority ownership (i.e. a 51
per cent or more equity stake in a foreign affiliate) confers a de jure
right on the MNE to control the use of the ownership advantages it
transfers, and of locally sourced resources, de facto, such control might
be assigned to the buyer by the seller by a contractual agreement. In
consequence, international production should also embrace non-equity
activities, including strategic alliances, wherever the agreement between
the parties allows the non-resident partner some control or influence
over the terms of the agreement, and/or the way in which it is ex-
ecuted.

We now turn to consider the relevances of the three elements of the
eclectic paradigm of foreign-owned production just outlined to the service
sector. In particular, we shall be interested in identifying whether or
not there are distinctive ownership, locational or organisational characteristics of service-producing MNEs, as compared with goods-producing
MNEs. Is there any reason, for example, to suppose that service-based
international companies possess unique competitive advantages, or that
foreign production in services is likely to play a more important role
than trade as a means of supplying markets; or that the transaction
costs of buying or selling intermediate services are likely to be less or
more significant than those of buying or selling intermediate goods?

5. The Factors Making for Trade and Foreign-Owned Production in Services: The Competitive (or Ownership-Specific) Advantages of Enterprises

a. Some General Issues

The concept of corporate competitive advantage refers to the capacity of particular enterprises to satisfy the needs of their customers, or potential customers.[1] Usually, the literature identifies three main groups of needs. These are:

(i)   the characteristics of the services supplied. These characteristics embrace the ingredients of a service which consumers consider as desirable; for example, design, comfort, usefulness, performance, consistency, attention to personal needs, degree of professionalism, attitude, itineraries (as in the case of a shipping cruise);

(ii) price (fewer discounts, but including likely after sales costs, e.g. repairs and maintenance);

(iii) the services complementary with the purchase and use of product, e.g. delivery times, frequency and reliability of services (as in transport services), up-to-dateness (as in news agencies), information and advice on product or service qualities, the number and location of selling outlets, after sales repair and maintenance facilities, the availability of replacements and spares, and so on.

To produce and sell goods and services in international markets more successfully than their foreign competitors, firms must have an exclusive or privileged access to specific assets enabling them to supply a particular good or service at lower cost, and/or to organise more efficiently a set of complementary assets to produce a range of value-adding activities, (so called common governance advantages); and/or be more discerning choosers of *where* to engage in production (so called locational choice advantages). The literature has identified these ownership-specific advantages - primarily from the viewpoint of primary product or manufacturing firms in some detail; these are set out in the appendix. For our purposes, each of the three needs of purchasers identi-

---

[1] For a detailed elaboration of the concept of competitive advantage, see Porter [1980; 1985; 1986] and Dunning [1981, p. 80].

fied in the previous paragraphs rests on the supplying firms' having access to some core technological, managerial, financial or marketing assets so that they can produce and sell specified services at the lowest production costs and on their capacity to coordinate these with other assets so that they can produce the right volume, type and range of products (including intermediate products) in the right locations.

The questions of interest which we seek to answer in the following paragraphs are threefold:

(i)   What are the particular ownership-specific advantages likely to apply in the production and marketing of services?

(ii) In what respects and to what extent do these vary *between* service sectors?

(iii) Under what conditions are MNEs (either generally or from particular countries) better able to supply these services than non-MNEs?

b. The Nature of Competitive Advantages of Firms in Service Sectors

We have already suggested that there are very few "pure" services, in that the consumption of services usually entails, in part at least, the coincident consumption of goods. Where goods and services are jointly supplied, it could be that a firm's competitive advantage rests in its ability to produce goods and/or services, e.g. private medical treatment. Perhaps even more important is the fact that there are many firms (and particularly MNEs) supplying services (whether they be pure or not) which also supply goods (i.e. they are diversified goods and services producers). This would suggest that some of the coordinating advantages of supplying services may arise because of the firm's goods-producing activities; in addition, as we have already observed, a substantial proportion of services are supplied by manufacturing or primary product enterprises. For example, the involvement in the freight shipping business by companies such as Unilever and Royal Dutch Shell arises partly because of the nature of the products transported and partly because of the perceived advantages of logistical management [van Rens, 1982]; while the ability of foreign exchange dealers and new agencies to meet the needs of their clients satisfactorily rest crucially on the availability of sophisticated telecommunications equipment which can transmit information instantaneously to and from any part of the world.

What of the advantages specific to supplying "pure" services? We have seen that the nature of a pure *consumer* service is that it is perishable or near perishable, has little or no storage value and its consumption is coincident with its production. Most *producer* or intermediate services are different in the sense that they are not directly consumed but are embodied in products or other services; moreover, exactly the same service may be used time and time again. A chemical formula may be used to generate $1 million or $100 million of products; a TV advertising commercial can be repeatedly used; the same architecture and interior design can be used to build a hotel in Bangkok or Buenos Aires. Let us now examine some of the competitive or ownership-specific advantages identified in the literature and see how they apply to the service sector.

α. Quality: Product Differentiation

At the end of the day, many services are complex and involve a strong human content. Because of this, their quality is more likely to be variable than that of goods [Grubel, 1986]. Obvious examples include personal, business and professional services, entertainment and retail services, where the service provided is either customer-specific (e.g. a legal consultation or a repair of a car), or collectively idiosyncratic (e.g. a theatre performance or a train journey). The ability to ensure a high consistent quality of service is particularly likely to appeal to business customers whose own reputation may be affected by the service.

Several writers, notably Caves [1982], have suggested that, in consumer goods industries, the ability to create and sustain a successful brand image - and the goodwill attached to it - is one of the key competitive advantages of MNEs. Casson [1982] and some other authors prefer to emphasise the capability of firms to monitor quality and reduce buyer transaction costs by offering services from multiple locations. Likewise, in consumer service sectors, international firms, such as Hilton and Holiday Inn (hotels), American Express and Visa (credit cards), McDonalds and Kentucky Fried Chicken (fast food chains), Avis and

Hertz (car rentals), Saatchi and Saatchi and J. Walter Thompson (advertising agencies), are each recognised for their trademarks or by the kind of markets they seek to serve. Since many of these services are "experience" rather than "inspection" goods, the availability of pre-purchase advice about foreign tours or the experience of related services may guide consumer choice. Similarly, the location and (perceived) quality of after sales and repair and maintenance outlets may affect the selection of durable goods bought by both business and private customers.

β. Economies of Scope

The availability and price of several services rests on the economies of scope of the seller. An obvious example is the services provided by a retail establishment. The larger the range and volume of products stocked is, the better the retailer can bargain for lower prices from the supplier, and therefore he can help reduce the transaction costs of his customers. The greater bargaining power of chain stores and multiples also enables them to exert more control over the quality and prices of the goods they purchase; and they are not always slow to let their customers know about this. The worldwide referral systems of many airlines and hotel chains can also be of major benefit to international business customers. Economies of scope are also widespread in shipping and among business consultants; they are inherent in insurance and many banking activities and, perhaps, are most pronounced of all in brokerage-type services, such as those provided by real estate and travel agents, investment analysts and commodity dealers. They are particularly important in that they help link marketing knowledge with production flexibility and promote a geocentric attitude towards international production.

γ. Economies of Scale and Specialisation

In principle, there is no difference between the economies of *plant* scale and the specialisation enjoyed by firms in manufacturing and those in some service sector. The lower unit costs of providing air transport by a 747 Jumbo compared with a 727, or accommodation by a 500-bed hotel compared with a 30-bed hotel, or medical services by a large compared with a small hospital are directly comparable with the economies of large-scale production of motor vehicles, pharmaceuticals or micro-chips. Similarly, international business consultants, the merchant and investment banks and the hotel chains can profit from the economies of specialisation of personnel, the economies of common governance arising from their ability to move people, money and information between different parts of the same organisation, and from their ability to take advantage of differential factor costs and environmental flexibility. Often, too, large service companies can gain from raising finance on favourable terms and buying goods and services at quantity discounts in exactly the same way as can a manufacturing firm. Shipping is another industry characterised by high fixed costs, with relatively low marginal costs of operation. Nowhere are the advantages of spreading risks, which size and scope confer, better seen than in the insurance and investment banking sectors. Size, indeed, is the main ticket of entry to transnational activities in both these sectors; and without such transnationality each would be smaller than it is.

δ. Technology and Information

The "knowledge" component of production techniques and tangible goods (which is, itself, an intermediate service) varies between industrial sectors and is usually measured by such indices as the proportion of sales accounted for by innovatory (e.g. research and development) activities or the proportion of professional, scientific and engineering personnel in the total labour force. The ability to invent new products and to produce existing products more cheaply, or of a better and more reliable quality is a key competitive advantage in many goods industries.

In the case of some service sectors, it is the capability to acquire, produce, assemble, store, monitor, interpret and analyse information (and to do so at the least possible cost) which is the key intangible asset or core competitive advantage. As one would expect, this is especially so in sectors such as stockbroking, foreign exchange and securities dealing, business consultancy, commodity broking and the various data providing processing and service bureaux (e.g. Extel, Reuters, and so on), and transmitting networks (e.g. Euronet). Here, again, the ability to provide services go hand in hand with the equipment and physical goods and the knowledge of *how* to organise the production and disseminate that information.

ε. Some Special Features of Knowledge as an Asset in the Service Sector

Knowledge as a service has another characteristic: it need not be perishable, and it may be repeatedly used to the benefit of the purchaser at low or zero cost. It is an intangible asset which helps create and sustain the production and sale of a stream of goods which embody that knowledge. Similarly, the production of some services, (e.g. finance and banking, telematics, business and professional services) contain a common pool of codifiable and tacit knowledge, which is specific to the firm (or more particularly to the collective wisdom, intellect and experience and judgment capabilities of the personnel of the firm), plus inherited knowledge (e.g. as contained in documents, tapes, discs, films, and so forth).

The large service firms in information-intensive sectors trade on their name (and sometimes on the specific services they offer) in the way as the large manufacturing companies do. Chase Manhattan Bank, Coopers and Lybrand, A.G. Nielsen, Prudential Insurance Co., McKinsey, Salomon Brothers, Foster Wheeler, Nomura, Extel, Heidrick and Struggles are all as well known and no less valued by their clients for the informational and advisory content of their services, as are ITT, Monsanto, Philips, Texas Instruments, Boeing or Ciba Geigy for their supply of technologically-intensive goods.

In manufacturing industry, the provision of modern process and product technology is becoming increasingly expensive, while its rate of dissemination and/or obsolescence is fast accelerating [Ohmae, 1985]. No less important is the fact that technology requires the possession of, or access to, complementary assets (e.g. modern production facilities, sales and distributing networks) if the good embodying the technology is to be marketed successfully [Teece, 1986].

Two results of these trends are, first, that technology intensive firms are increasingly having to widen their markets in order to absorb the huge fixed costs and reap the economies of scale associated with the production and marketing of technology or technology-intensive goods; and, second, that there is increasing pressure on even the largest MNEs to enter into collaborative arrangements with other firms (including their competitors) to reduce the risks of expensive research and development commitments, to capture the economies of technological synergy, and to broaden the application of technology to different processes, products and markets [Contractor, Lorange, 1988].

ζ. Favoured Access to Inputs or Markets

A secure and privileged access to inputs, distribution outlets and markets afford many manufacturing firms an advantage over their less advantaged rivals. Sometimes (especially where markets are seasonal, uncertain or hazardous) these advantages can only fully be exploited by firms where these markets are internalised; in other cases, an adequate futures market, a comprehensive knowledge about sourcing and market- ing outlets, a satisfactory contractual relationship with suppliers or cus- tomers may achieve the same results. In both cases, however, these ad- vantages can only be sustained by MNEs when some kind of market fail- ure exists. Such failure has, itself, helped create international broker- age or arbitrage-linked service firms whose main purpose is to act on behalf of clients to find an appropriate seller or buyer for their products and services. Security, insurance and commodity broking, estate agencies and travel agents fall into this category. Such competi- tive advantages which they possess rest primarily on their capability to minimise the transaction costs of their clients and advise them of how best to meet their requirements.

In some cases, the competitive advantages of service firms rest in their knowledge of the sourcing of essential inputs, and an ability to reduce the associated search, negotiating and monitoring costs together in the same location. Moreover, some intermediate services need to draw upon each other, and frequently they are jointly demanded by customers (e.g. shipping and insurance, banking and finance). This explains why such services are often located in close proximity to each other; and why, too, mergers and diversifications are common in these sectors. The concentration of globally-oriented business and financial activities in a few major cities of the world (e. g. London, New York, Paris, Tokyo, Hong Kong, and so on) and, within these cities, in a very particular location (e. g. City of London, Wall Street) is explained by the need to gain and sustain this particular form of competitive advantage. In the airline business, the acquisition of rights to particular routes is also an important property right. And the very rationale of executive search agencies rests on their capability to recruit the kind of personnel needed from a world market.

As regards market access, there are numerous examples of firms having advantages over their competitors. The early venturing abroad of multinational insurance, banking, advertising, accounting and executive search companies was prompted by the need to supply migrating individuals or branch firms of MNEs with the services they had previously had at home. However, with the globalisation of markets and production, these firms have found it increasingly desirable to locate their activities near to those of their international clients; and here, advances in telematics have advanced the competitive position of firms best able to offer an integrated package of services, once the necessary data network has been established [Sauvant, 1986]. American and European hotel chains and construction companies, experienced at meeting the needs of domestic customers, know exactly what these customers want when they go abroad (particularly to unfamiliar or uncongenial places). In the mass tourist business, hotels, airlines and tour operators frequently combine to ensure a ready-made market for each others' services. More generally, the growth of international bulk shipping services has followed that of MNE activity, particularly in those sectors (e. g. oil, chemicals and agribusiness) where the propensity for intra-firm trade is high.

A totally different category of service companies are the sales subsidiaries, import and export merchants, the general trading companies and the buying agents of the large retail chains or goods-producing enterprises. These, in fact, acccount for the largest amount of service investments by MNEs. Their function is primarily to promote or sustain markets or to seek out and acquire inputs for their domestic activities. In some cases, notably in the Japanese general trading companies (the

Sogo Shosha), they have developed into huge conglomerates which have integrated backwards or horizontally into a wide range of non-trading activities, or have established long-term and close contractual relationships with manufacturing and/or primary producers. Their main competitive or ownership-specific advantages arise from their control over a global network of activities, their immense bargaining power (particularly in respect of the terms and conditions of trade), their unsurpassed knowledge of market conditions for the products they buy and sell, their ownership of wholesale and retail trading outlets, and their ability to reduce foreign exchange risks and environmental turbulence by diversifying their trading portfolios. In addition, the last two decades or so have seen a growth in specialist multinational buying groups or consortia, representing leading wholesale or retail outlets in Europe and the US (e.g. Sears Roebuck, C & A, Marks & Spencer).

6. The Choice of Trade or Foreign Production in Services: The Comparative or Locational Specific Advantages of Countries

a. Some General Issues

Service firms possessing competitive advantages identified in the previous sections usually have a choice of *where* they (or the firms to which they sell the right to use these advantages) engage in value-adding activities. Sometimes, the nature of the services provided, the technology of production, or government regulations restrict the locational options; and, as we have already stated, it is only possible to transact pure services if they are embodied in goods or people. This would suggest that the tradeability of services is essentially dependent on the transportability of the goods in which they are embodied and on the availability of suitable transport facilities. The behaviour, or anticipated behaviour, of competitors may also affect locational choices in oligopolistic service sectors. This has been observed in the banking, hotel, advertising, construction, car rental and fast food service sectors.

To what extent can the transnationalisation of the service sector be explained by the desire to exploit competitive advantages by way of foreign production rather than by trade? Under what conditions will trade and foreign production complement, rather than substitute for, each other? Are there specific characteristics about services, which make for more or less transnationality of value-adding activities than in the case of goods?

International involvement in services or goods-embodied services usually takes three forms. The first is the exports of final services sold to independent buyers; these may be earned (a) by exporting directly to a foreign country (e. g. Lloyds of London insuring a Norwegian ship, a New York stockbroker buying or selling shares for a German client, or a Canadian telecommunications company paying a Spanish telecommunications company a share of a personal telephone call made by a Canadian to a Spanish citizen), (b) by a foreign customer travelling to the exporting country and buying the service from there (e. g. the main form of export of personal services), or (c) services embodied in material substances which are exported from the home country. The second comprises inter-mediate services sold to independent buyers. These represent the ser-vices of technology, marketing, management skills, and so on, transacted through non-equity licensing or "other" contractual agreements. The goods content of these services varies from virtually zero (e. g. a chemi-cal formulae) to quite a substantial value (a turnkey project). Thirdly, there is foreign-owned production; this embraces the output of services produced by the foreign affiliates of MNEs. In turn, these affiliates may buy intermediate services from their parent company or other affiliates (i. e. intra-firm services), or final goods for resale. They may also earn invisible exports in the form of interest, dividends and fees,[1] while overseas workers (e. g. Korean construction employees employed by Korean constructional MNEs in the Middle East; artists, military person-nel, etc.) might repatriate part of their wages and salaries.

---

[1] While payments for technology, management and administrative services are usually included as "trade in services", profits from FDI are not. This is not really satisfactory as part of the profits (i. e. over and above the opportunity cost of risk capital) should be thought of as a payment for the services of real assets provided by MNEs. For a rea-soned case of why the earnings on FDI should be included as services, see Rugman [1986].

b. The Export versus FDI Alternative

There are two main types of goods which are not normally traded across national boundaries. They are those which involve prohibitively high transport costs - including those for which there are no transport facilities - and those which require a simultaneity of production and con-sumption. Governments, by using a whole range of import restrictions or regulatory regimes, may also make it unprofitable for foreign firms to export products to, or produce products in, their territories. In the service sector, there are six types of services which are not usually tradeable (i. e. they are location bound). These are:

(i)   those the sales of which are dependent upon the presence of people, goods, or other services which are located in the country of use. These include hotel and most local tourist facilities, res-taurants, car hire, construction development, motion picture pro-duction, real estate and news agencies;

(ii)   transportation facilities;

(iii)   telecommunication and public utility services, though some services (e. g. water, electricity) in one country my be part of a grid lo-cation in another country, and TV programmes can be "exported" by satellite;

(iv)   warehousing, wholesaling, and retailing services, including repair and maintenance services;

(v)   most forms of public administration and social and community-re-lated services (e. g. libraries);

(vi)   services which require "on the spot" customisation or "face to face" contact between the buyer and seller.

In addition, education, health services and most personal and household services are traded only to a limited extent - inasmuch as the foreign purchaser may avail himself of such services at the location of production.

Next, there are other services where the international transaction (including transport) costs (either to the buyer or seller, or to both) are, in practice, too high to allow much trade; these include most busi-ness consultancy services, professional services, and commercial bank-ing.

Finally, there are services which are widely traded. These include most intermediate services but, most notably, all kinds of codifiable information and technology, investment banking, insurance, commodity broking, advertising, services, and a variety of property rights (e.g. firms, broadcasting, patents, architectual drawings, tape recordings). A large proportion of these services are transferred *within* MNEs; that is to say, direct investment is a necessary prerequisite for such trade to occur. It is this group of services, the tradeability of which, over the last decade or more, has been revolutionised by advances in data transmitting devices and techniques [UNCTC, 1988].

Since the opportunities for trade in services are generally more restricted than those for goods, it might be reasonably supposed that the relative involvement of foreign production in the former sector would be that much greater. In fact, this is not the case, simply because in many sectors (e.g. the social services, public utilities, some professional and many personal (and personalised) services, and much of wholesaling, warehousing, and retailing, building and construction, and ground transportation services) the competitive advantages of foreign-owned companies are not as pronounced as those of domestic companies, or are insufficient to outweigh for the additional organisational costs of foreign production [Hirsch, 1976]. Another reason is that governments tend to set strict limits on the extent of foreign-owned involvement in strategically sensitive service sectors, such as air transport, communications, banking, community services, (e.g. education, health and public utilities) and, by a variety of non-tariff barriers (e.g. procurement and standards policies), favour indigenous companies.

At the same time, as the information and knowledge component of other services (e.g. banking, finance, insurance, advertising and tour operators) has intensified so has the presence of foreign-owned producers. Moreover, as firms seek to globalise their supply of services in order to meet the needs of their multinational customers and/or to promote a distinctive brand image, the tendency for competitive advantages to become more firm-specific increases. This explains the growth of US, European and Japanese MNE involvement in the "up-market" sectors of many professional services, some education and health services, real estate, and in those consumer services where "branded" names or "trademarks" are important (e.g. hotels, fast food chains and some retail stores).

As we have described, the main reasons for the increase in trade and foreign production in services over the last two decades has been the growth in demand for consumer services, resulting from a rise in real income; technological advances which have increased the demand for and supply of services and their tradeability; the expansion of telecommunication and other service support facilities as goods have become technically more complicated; the expansion of trade in goods associated with increased geographical process or product specialisation; the increasing complexity and uncertainty of modern society leading to the need for insurance and professional advisory services; the increasing specialisation and round-aboutness in production, and the increasing role of government. We have also suggested that MNEs, relative to other firms, have been well placed to benefit from these developments.

c. Which Particular Locational Variables Influence FDI in Services?

Recent technological advances in data transmitting facilities have confirmed that the transportability of services can be an important influence on the location of their production as it can in the case of goods. At the same time, both being in close proximity to the customer and adapting the service to his special needs probably play a more important role. The size and character of the market, and the level of real wage costs, are also significant in influencing the siting of business and professional services as they are of tourist-related activities.

In other sectors, the location of human and/or natural assets is the key variable affecting the location of production. The siting of tourist hotels depends on the scenery, climate and physical amenities which the visitors are seeking; that of financial and insurance institutions, particularly when intended to serve a region or when they are part of a global network of activities, rests on an adequate supply of premises, communication facilities and suitably trained labour. There are also agglomerative economies of being close to competitors, suppliers and customers. More generally, the provision of most industrial and high income consumer service activities tends to be concentrated in the larger and wealthier countries, and in the leading cities within these countries. Where these activities supply a regional or global market, they are likely to be footloose between alternative locations. Indeed, it is worth noting that the fastest growing service sectors are currently those which (a) are subject to increasing economies of scale and scope, (b) tend to be geographically concentrated, (c) are regionally or globally oriented, and (d) which generate a substantial amount of intra-firm trade.

The role of government in influencing the location of service activities is of particular significance. The same kind of incentives, controls, and regulations which affect trade and foreign direct investment in goods also abound in services; indeed, it is generally agreed that both the production and consumption of services are more closely regulated than that of goods. Though there has been a strong movement towards the deregulation and liberalisation of some services (e.g. airlines, telecommunications, banking, finance and insurance) in recent years, many others remain strongly under government control or surveillance. In addition, foreign MNEs may face a gamut of non-tariff barriers and are sometimes treated less favourably than indigenous companies. These issues are currently the subject of much debate in the EEC, OECD, GATT and other international fora.

On the other hand, some governments are making deliberate attempts to attract inward investment in services, particularly in infrastructure projects. Examples include Chile's efforts to attract US MNEs in the health care and sanitation sectors; Brazil's invitation to foreign MNEs to participate in some of the multi-billion highway, port and railroad construction schemes; Greece's decision to invite bids from foreign investors to build a new international airport and subway system in Athens and an expressway linking Athens with Thessalonika. Other governments are seeking to attract financial and business services. For example, Curaçao and Luxembourg are making a bid to develop offshore financial facilities; Barbados, Jamaica and Ireland are trying to create a comparative advantage for themselves in the supply of well-trained and motivated labour for business services; while China, India, Jamaica, Mexico and the Philippines are attempting to attract offshore data entry services for MNEs [Riddle, 1986; 1987].

d. Summary of Forces Influencing the Location of MNE Activity

Some 84 per cent of the stock of FDI by service MNEs is located in developed countries, compared with 75 per cent of all kinds of investment. But the *structure* of service activity in developed market economies is very different from that in developing countries. In the former, purchases of intermediate services by capital or technologically-advanced industrial sectors, financial, business and professional services, and services competing for the discretionary income of consumers play a much more important role. In the latter, there is a higher proportion of investment in trade and distribution, building and construction, public utilities, tourism, and some basic financial services.[1] The variation *within* developing countries is no less marked. The pattern of service activity in Singapore and Hong Kong is totally different from that in most other developing countries. In these latter countries, the structure of markets and resources, and the role played by government are crucial factors influencing the level and pattern of service output. To give one or two obvious examples: MNEs in tourist-related activities dominate the service sectors in island economies like the Seychelles, Barbados and Fiji; Singapore and Hong Kong are becoming the leading international financial and business centres in Asia, while the larger populated developing countries (e.g. India, Brazil and Indonesia) have attracted a wider and more balanced composition of service activities. Regulations and controls on service activities also differ widely between developing countries. In general they are most relaxed in East Asia and most stringent in Latin America.[2]

The most significant features affecting the changing balance between trade and foreign-owned production activity by international companies in recent years have undoubtedly been:

---

[1] As Riddle [1986; 1987] points out the role of services in economic development has been inaccurately described as an adjunct to industrialisation rather than as an engine of growth in themselves. The classification of economies into pre-industrial, industrial, and post-industrial is then unhelpful; services - and particularly producer services - act as a crucial part of a country's infrastructure whatever its level of development. What varies is *which* services are provided and *the way* in which these services are provided.

[2] But, as Riddle [1987, p. 57] observes, the Andean Pact nations have recently "reversed their conservative stance on FDI in services".

(i) changes in regulatory patterns, including the deregulation and liberalisation of the financial and telecommunications sectors in some countries; and

(ii) advances in the technology of transborder data flows.

As far as developing countries are concerned, one of the reasons for a more liberal attitude towards inward investment in services is the growing realisation that without such investment (e. g. in infrastructure projects such as hydro-electric power, telecommunications and roads) national development goals could be stunted. At the same time, by assisting trade in goods-embodied services, technical advances in data collection, assembly, processing and transmission may help bring about a relocation and reorganisation of service activities by MNEs [UNCTAD, 1985; Sauvant, 1986]. While, on the one hand, they may lead to more decentralisation of routine service activities, on the other, by reducing the transaction costs of cross-border activities, they may pave the way for more economic integration among service (as well as manufacturing) MNEs, and more intra-firm trade between different parts of the MNE network. [1]

7. The Factors Making for the Internationalisation of Services: The Organisation of Transactions through MNE Hierarchies (Internalisation Advantages)

a. Some General Issues

Why should firms of a particular nationality of ownership wish to exploit their competitive advantages in another country by engaging in vertical or horizontal integration, rather than lease the rights to those advantages to indigenous firms in a foreign country? For service firms to become MNEs in the traditional sense of the word, they must engage in FDI. Such investment is assumed to be necessary for firms to exercise

---

[1] The question of the extent to which the recent expansion of output of services has led to a centralisation or decentralisation of the location of these services has received scant attention in the literature. Neither is there any literature on the comparative locational economics of high value cf. low value service activities or of innovatory cf. mature services, as there is in the case of the manufacturing sector.

authority over the way in which their ownership advantages are organised and deployed across national boundaries, or, in some cases, to acquire these advantages in the first place. The fact that they choose this route of foreign entry rather than make use of non-equity cooperative arrangements suggests that they perceive there are costs associated with the latter modality of exchange which impede them from securing the full economic rent on their assets. By internalising the market (i.e. coordinating the use of its assets with other value-adding activities), the firm believes it can best advance its strategic goals, and, in so doing, it becomes an MNE,[1] or increases the extent of its multinationality.

The literature suggests that the mode of organising cross-border exchanges of services will depend firstly on the relative transaction and production costs involved, and secondly on the extent and pattern of government intervention. The transaction costs include:

(i)   those relating to the transaction *per se*, e.g. search (for the right buyer or seller), identification and negotiating costs;

(ii)   those relating to the *terms* of the contract; these include: (a) price - as information is often asymmetrical, the buyer may be prepared to pay the seller less than the good or service is worth - (b) specification of the good or service to be supplied, (c) control over use made of the good or service supplied, and (d) frequency and timing of deliveries (including inventory and warehousing costs);

(iii)   those relating to the *monitoring of the performance* of the contractee;

(iv)   those relating to the *uncertainty* of whether the terms of the contract will be adhered to, and the costs of (a) their being broken (e.g. disruption to the production process through untimely or

---

[1] One definition of an MNE is that it is a firm which internalises intermediate product markets across national boundaries [Casson et al., 1986]. These products might take the form of goods or services. Strictly speaking, *cross-border* internalisation can only take place when a firm adds value-creating activities in a foreign country to those it undertakes in its home economy; in this case, FDI automatically leads to intra-firm trade in goods or services. In fact, an MNE may sometimes achieve the same effects of internalisation without ownership, in the sense that some contractual agreements assign control over the use of intermediate products to one or other of the contracting parties.

irregular delivery, loss of competitiveness through dissipation or abuse of property rights and (b) litigation to recoup the costs associated with (a); and

(iv)   those relating to the *external costs (and benefits)* of the transaction (i. e. which accrue to parties other than those directly involved in the exchange).

As to the role of governments, this may vary between outright control over the form of foreign involvement (e. g. no FDI is usually allowed in broadcasting or airlines, while only franchise agreements might be permitted between domestic hoteliers and foreign hotel chains) to various fiscal and other devices designed to tilt the balance of advantage away from one organisational form to that of another. For example, deregulation of financial markets might be expected to lead to more equity investment by financial institutions and fewer contractual agreements; while, by aiding intra-firm transactions, improvements in information mining and monitoring and communications technology might lead to the reverse situation (e. g. in advertising and commodity broking). Tariff and non-tariff barriers, including labour union and other restrictions on the employment of foreign workers, might lessen the ability of firms to exploit the economies of common governance.

The literature further identifies the types of situation in which firms are likely to wish to internalise market transactions. Some of these are set out in the Appendix. They vary between the nature of the activity (i. e. good or service being exchanged), the firms organising the transaction, and the market conditions specific to the countries engaged in the transaction. Competitive advantages which are idiosyncratic, non-codifiable and comprise the core assets of firms, and/or which are used to produce goods and services, the quality and reputation of which are of special appeal to consumers, are not likely to be traded externally; while the more volatile and hazardous the international environment in which they are produced and traded, the more likely firms will prefer to internalise transactions.

The question now arises: how important are transaction costs as a factor in explaining the growth of multinational service activities? Moreover, to what extent do different services incur different kinds of transactions costs?

Such fragmentary evidence as is available on the significance of the various vehicles of cross-border transactions among services suggests that not only have all forms of transactions increased in the last 20 years, but that the modalities vary as much as - and perhaps even more than - those within the primary and secondary sectors.[1] In Table 2 we summarise some of the main variables affecting transactional modes and how they affect different service sectors.

There are three groups of services the cross-border supply of which tends to be organised via foreign-owned production rather than by contractual relationships. The first comprises banking and financial services and most kinds of information-intensive business and professional services (e.g. management and engineering consultancies, computer related and data-based services, travel agents and airlines). Here, there are three main reasons for integrating either vertically along the value added chain or horizontally across value added chains:

(i)   much of the proprietary knowledge and information is tacit, expensive to produce, complex and idiosyncratic, but easy to replicate;

(ii)   there are substantial synergistic advantages to be gained from the geographical diversification of productive activities (e.g. those which arise from risk spreading and the arbitraging of people, goods, money and information) which can best be accomplished within MNE hierarchies; and

(iii)   the use of crucial assets, notably financial assets and information will help to gain access or control.

The second group comprises firms which engage in forward integration to ensure productive efficiency and/or the quality of the end product (and hence the customers' goodwill). Very often such companies are known by their brand name or image. Advertising, market research, executive search, international construction companies, some business consultants and some consumer-oriented services (e.g. fast food chains) and car rentals (where FDI does take place) and some goods-related

---

[1] Riddle [1987] makes the interesting point that "service companies have mor legal options regarding their forms of foreign investment than do manufacturing companies, as the latter by the very nature of their services are forced to establish manufacturing plants and distribution centres abroad". By contrast she adds "service companies may establish more outposts of the corporation managed by a small number of skilled employees, operate joint ventures or set up subsidiaries".

Table 2 - Illustrations of Ownership (O), Location (L) and Internalisation (I) Advantages Relevant to MNE Activity in Selected Service Sectors

	Ownership (competitive advantages)	Location (configuration advantages)	Internalisation (coordinating advantages)	Foreign Presence Index (a) (US data) (b)	Organisational form
Accounting/ auditing	· Access to multinational clients · Experience of standards required · Professional expertise · Branded image of leading accounting firms	· On-the-spot contact with clients · Accounting tends to be culture-sensitive · Adaptation to local reporting standards and procedures · Oligopolistic interaction	· Limited inter-firm linkages · Quality control over (international) standards · Government insistence on local participation	· High (92 per cent) · Little intra-firm trade	· Mostly partnerships or individual proprietorships · Overseas subsidiaries loosely organised, little centralised control · Few joint ventures
Advertising	· Favoured access to markets (subsidiaries of clients in home markets) · Creative ability; image and philosophy · Goodwill · Full range of services · Some economies of co-ordination · Financial strength	· On-the-spot contact with clients · Adaptation to local tastes, languages · Needs to be close to mass media	· Quality control over advertising copy · Need for local inputs · National regulations · Globalisation of advertising-intensive products · To reduce transaction costs with foreign agencies	· High (85 per cent) · Some intra-firm trade	· Mainly 100 per cent; some joint ventures; limited non-equity arrangements
Commercial banking	· Access to multinational clients, foreigners abroad · Professional expertise · Access to capital · Effective distribution networks · Intrinsic value of reserve currencies	· Person-to-person contact required · Government regulations · High value activities often centralised · Lower costs of foreign operations · Psychic distance (Islamic banks)	· Quality control · Economies of scope · Economies of coordinating capital flows · Importance of international arbitraging · Some consortia	· High (virtually 100 per cent) · Some intra-firm trade in information and finance capital	· Mostly branches or subsidiaries, some agencies · Some joint ventures - notably, where governments insist
Computer software/ data processing	· Linked to computer hardware · Highly technology/information intensive · Economies of scope · Government support	· Location of high skills and agglomerative economies often favours home country	· Idiosyncratic knowhow: need for protection against dissipation · Quality control · Coordinating gains		
Construction management	· Size, experience and reputation · Government assistance · Low labour costs (developing country MNEs)	· Economies of concentrating technology-intensive activities · On-the-spot interaction with clients and/or building firms	· Need for complementary local assets, risk spreading on large projects · Quality control · Good deal of subcontracting	· Favours exports (39 per cent) (but often foreign receipts include local subcontracting element)	· Mixture; joint ventures favoured to gain access to markets, or where partner(s) bring complementary assets to the venture

Table 2 (continued)

Service					
Educational services	· Country-specific, related to stage of economic development and role of government · Experience of client needs (Japanese schools in London)	· Largely invisible exports through students visiting supplying countries · Some foreign affiliates of private schools to cater for citizens of home country living abroad · Need to expose students to foreign cultures	· Quality control · Integration with curricula in home country · Exposure to foreign curricula/teaching methods	· Low (2 per cent) · Little intra-firm trade	· Originally 100 per cent subsidiaries, but increasingly more joint ventures with foreign educational establishments
Engineering architecture surveying services	· Experience in home and other foreign markets · Economies of size and specialisation · Economies of scope/coordination	· Customisation to local tastes and needs · Need for on-the-spot contact with customers and related producers	· Joint ventures, to gain local experience expertise · Quality control · Knowledge often very idiosyncratic and tacit	· Fairly high (75 per cent) · Substantial intra-firm trade (in technology and management skills)	· Mixture, but often professional partnerships · Some licensing
Information services: data transmission	· Highly capital and human skill intensive · Sometimes "tied" to provision of hardware · Considerable economies of scope and scale · Quality of end product/services provided	· Varies according to type of information being sold and transmission facilities between countries · Where "people-based", clients may visit home country or firms may supply services in clients' countries · News agencies are location-bound, i.e. where the news is!	· In case of "core" assets, need for protection from dissipation · Quality control · Substantial gains from internalising markets, to capture externalities of information transactions · Cognitive market failure, asymmetry of knowledge	· Balanced (50 per cent) · Some intra-firm trade	· Mixture, but 100 per cent where market failure pronounced
Insurance	· Reputation of insurer; image (Lloyds of London) · Economies of scale and scope: and, sometimes, specialised expertise (e.g. marine insurance) · Access to multinational clients	· Need to be in close touch with insured (e.g. life insurance and related services (shipping finance)) · Oligopolistic strategies among larger insurers · Governments prohibit direct imports; extent to which there is freedom to trade · Economies of concentration (in reinsurance)	· Economies of portfolio risk spreading · Tacit knowledge · Need for sharing of large-scale risks (reinsurance syndication) · Government requirements for local equity participation	· High (78 per cent) · Some intra-firm trade	· Mixture; strongly influenced by governments, types of insurance and strategy of insurance companies
Investment banking (brokerage)	· Reputation and professional skills (I.B. is an "experience" service) · Substantial capital base · Knowledge of and interaction with international capital markets · Finanical innovations	· Need to be close to clients · Need to be close to international capital/finance markets, and also main competitors · Availability of skilled labour	· Complex and organic character of services provided · Protection against exchange/political risks · Need to pursue global investment strategy · Quality control	· High (84 per cent) · A lot of intra-firm trade in form of control/coordination from headquarters	· Mainly via 100 per cent subsidiaries

Table 2 (continued)

Hotels	· Experience in home countries in supply up-market services · Experience with training key personnel · Quality control · Referral systems · Economies of geographical specialisation, access to inputs	· Location-bound when selling a "foreign" service · Exports through tourists, businessmen visiting home country	· Investment in hotels is capital intensive · Quality control can generally be ensured through contractual relationships (e.g. a purchase or management contract) · Governments usually prefer non-equity arrangements · Referral systems can be centrally-coordinated without equity control	· Favours non-equity involvement, but exports of knowledge/management	· Vary, but mainly through minority ventures or contractual relationships
Legal services	· Access to multinational clients and knowledge of their particular needs · Experience and reputation	· Need for face-to-face contact with clients · Foreign customers may purchase services in home country · Need to interact with other local services · Restrictions on use of foreign barristers in courts · Extent of local infrastructure	· Many transactions are highly idiosyncratic and customer-specific · Quality control · Need for understanding of local customers and legal procedures	· Low (2 per cent) (mainly because trade in legal services is "people-embodied")	· Some overseas partnerships, but often services are provided via movement of people (clients to home country lawyers or vice versa)
Licensing	· (By definition) ability to supply technology; but most technology supplied by non-service firms	· All exported	· To protect licensor and to exploit economies of scope · Quality control	· All exports (100 per cent) · Largely intra-firm, 70 per cent in US cases	
Management, consultants and public relations	· Access to market · Reputation, image, experience · Economies of specialisation, in particular, leveld of expertise, etc. skills, countries	· Close contact with client; the provision is usually highly customer-specific · MNE clients might deal with headquarters · Mobility of personnel	· Quality control, fear of underperformance by licensee · Knowledge sometimes very confidential and usually idiosyncratic · Personnel coordinating advantages	· Balanced (55 per cent) · Some intra-firm trade, headquarters often co-ordinates assignments	· Mostly partnerships or 100 per cent subsidiaries · A lot of movement of people
Medical services	· Experience with advanced/specialised medicine; high quality hospitalisation · Modern management practices · Supportive role of government	· Usually consumers travel to place of production; but some foreign-owned hospitals or medical facilities are mobile	· Quality control	· Favours exports (39 per cent) · Little intra-firm trade	· A people-oriented sector; overseas operations, mainly 100 per cent owned subsidiaries
Motion pictures (production and rental receipts); live entertainment (theatre)	· Experience in home markets, good domestic communication (e.g. broadcasting) facilities · Government subsidies of arts	· Location-bound (motion picture production) · Sometimes customers visit place of production and sometimes vice versa	· Quality of film production and TV programmes · Theatre production usually involves non-equity contracts	· Balanced (50 per cent) · Little intra-firm trade	· Mixed · Again services embodied in people or bought by people who are internationally mobile

Table 2 (continued)

Service	Ownership advantages	Location advantages	Internalization advantages	Form of FDI/trade	Ownership pattern
Regional offices (RO)	• Part of MNE network; needs and functions of office vary according to nature of MNE's business and extent of foreign operations	• Depends on labour, office, communication costs where R.O.s are located • Work permits, taxes, etc. • Location of goods-producing units of MNEs	• All advantages relate to economies of coordination, and acting as agent on part of parent company	• Entirely via FDI • Virtually all intra-firm trade	• All 100 per cent owned
Restaurants, car rentals	• Brand name, image of product (service) • Reputation and experience • Referral systems • Economies of scale and scope • Tie up deals with airlines and hotels	• Location-bound • Foreign earnings through tourists and businessmen visiting exporting countries	• Franchising can protect quality control	• As with hotels	• As with hotels
Telecommunication	• Knowledge-intensive • Technology, capital, scale economies (e.g. ability to operate an international communications network) • Government support	• Government regulation of trade and production • Sometimes location-bound (telephone communications)	• Large costs often require consortia of firms • Quality of "goods" part of service often needs hierarchical control (e.g. by companies like AT&T); otherwise service usually provided on leasing basis, or exported	• Balanced (50 per cent) • Some intra-firm trade	• Mixture, but a good deal of leasing
Tourism	• Reputation in providing satisfactory experience goods • Economies of scope (kind of travel portfolio offered) • Bargaining power • Quality of deals made with airlines, hotels, shipping companies, etc.	• Need for local tour agents and support facilities • Customers initially originate from home country • Costs of supplying local facilities usually lower	• Coordination of itineraries, need for quality control of ancillary services for tourists • Preferences of host governments for local support facilities • Economies of transaction costs from vertical integration	• 90 per cent plus exports either of final or intermediate services	• Large tour operators have local offices; others may use agents
Transportation shipping and airlines	• Highly capital intensive • Government support measures, and/or control over routes of foreign carriers • Economies of scope and co-ordination • Linkages with producing goods firms (in shipping)	• Essentially location-linking • Need for local sales office, terminal maintenance and support facilities (at airports and docks)	• Logistical management • Advantages of vertical integration • Quality control	• Favours exports (39 per cent) • A lot of intra-firm trade involving non-service companies	• Mostly 100 per cent owned subsidiaries • Some consortia of TNCs

(a) The per cent in brackets represents proportion of sales of US foreign affiliates to US exports plus sales of foreign affiliates. – (b) From US Office of Technology Assessment [1986].

personal services (e.g. motor vehicle maintenance and repair facilities) fall into this category.

The third group consists of trade-related services affiliates which are often owned by non-service MNEs, and whose purpose is to obtain inputs for the parent companies (or as in the case of Japanese trading companies for other home-based companies) at the best possible terms, or to attain or develop markets for goods produced and exported by parent (and/or home-based) companies. In the first case, the protection of the supply position of the importing company and the assurance of the right quality at the right price is the dominant motive; in the second, the belief that fully or majority-owned subsidiaries are likely to be more efficient and better motivated to serve the exporting company's interests than independent sales agents is the main reason for internalisation [Nicholas, 1983]. Included in this group might be real estate companies whose function it is to advise and act as brokers to foreign clients in the purchase of real estate.

By contrast to the above sectors, there are others where minority joint ventures or non-equity collaborative arrangements tend to be the preferred route of foreign participation. We might identify four groups of service companies which typify this entry or expansionary mode of MNE activity.

The first comprises hotels, fast food restaurants, and car rental companies. In these cases, the performance requirements of the contractor can often be satisfactorily codified in a management contract or franchising agreement. A UNCTC study on tourism [UNCTC, 1981] also emphasised that synergistic advantages of global reservation and referral systems could also be otained without an equity capital stake, which in the hotel business could be both substantial, and in some parts of the world, highly risky. Moreover, although the customers for hotel, restaurant, and car rental companies were often from the investing countries, local knowledge of such things as food preferences, accommodation needs, decor and ancillary services made it desirable for there to be a substantial local managerial input.

The second group typifies the need for local specialised knowledge even more, and the fact that products require specific customisation. These activities include a range of business services (e.g. engineering, architectural and technical services, and some types of advertising where local tastes and product images may be very different from those of the investing country), recreational activities, and accounting and legal services (where, again, knowledge of local standards and procedures may be acquired). Consulting engineers and industrial construction companies who engage in turnkey projects also fall in this group. Although sometimes the larger of these companies may have permanent offices in the countries they serve, for the most part, their foreign business will be of a transitory nature.

Thirdly, to reduce marketing and distribution costs, newly established or smaller manufacturing MNEs may wish to join forces with, or use as licensees, local selling agents or after-sales service firms. The presence of a local partner both reduces capital risk of the foreign investor and helps buy complementary competitive assets or advantages necessary to exploit those of the foreign company. In other sectors (e.g. engineering and construction) a joint venture with a local firm can help an MNE win contracts from the host government and/or lessen the risks of expropriation. [1]

Lastly, in some sectors (e.g. investment banking and property/casualty insurance) the risks borne in providing particular services are such that they have to be shared by, or syndicated among, a consortium of firms. Sometimes these consortia may involve firms from only one country, and, in other cases, from several countries.

b. *Recent Changes in Organisational Form*

There have been several forces making for more cross-border hierarchical activity in services, and several which have operated in the opposite direction over the last decade or so. Of the former, two deserve special mention. The first force has been the liberalisation of the attitudes and policies of several developed and developing country governments towards inward direct investment; and the movement towards

---

[1] For example, the US Department of State study [1971] reported that the financial sector, and notably banking and insurance, was second only to the extractive industry in the incidence of expropriation. More recently evidence by Kobrin [1984] suggests that this incidence has not declined [Enderwick, 1986].

deregulated markets in the finance-related and insurance sectors. The second force has comprised advances in the technology and management of information collecting, handling and storage (e.g. sophisticated computing monitoring systems), data processing (e.g. system integration services, facilities management, remote computing services), and of data transmission (e.g. satellite and optic cables). Both these developments, by reducing the cost of coordinating decision making across national boundaries, have tended to increase the value of centralised control. It is seen in service sectors such as engineering and project control through computer-aided design and graphic systems, and in the operations of such services as those conducted in series, such as banking services, insurance sales, airline reservations, and hotel room bookings [UNCTAD, 1985]. Some excellent examples of the ways in which this is being achieved are given by Feteketuky and Hauser [1985]. [1]

On the other hand, there have been forces making for an increase in minority ventures or contractual arrangements. We might identify four of these. The first is the increasing specialisation among suppliers of finance capital, information and people-related services (e.g. employment agencies). When considered alongside the maturation of some kinds of intermediate services and the increasing ability of sellers to exercise control over their property rights through an appropriately worded contract, firms in such diverse sectors as hotels, telecommunications, and construction are increasingly opting for the technical service agreement, management contract, or franchise as a modality of operation. Secondly, as economic development proceeds, so will the necessary indigenous supply capabilities required by foreign MNEs in the service sector to conclude joint ventures or non-equity agreements to become available. Thirdly, the assets required to provide some services, particularly those which are information intensive, are either too costly or require different skills and technology for any one firm to possess. In consequence, some

---

[1] In banking, for example, modern information technology has made it possible for managers to centralise information resources in areas such as foreign currency and economic forecasting on a global scale. In computing, IBM's worldwide communications network allows it to introduce design changes in all its manufacturing facilities around the world in a single day. Similarly, the Bechtel Group has set up a computer and communications network, which enables it to coordinate the activities of engineers in India, project managers in San Francisco and construction supervisors on site in Saudi Arabia.

service firms are either merging or collaborating on particular projects. Cross-border acquisitions and mergers have been particularly marked in the communications, banking, insurance and advertising sectors [Contractor, Lorange, 1988; Porter, 1986]. Such cooperative arrangements help their participants to reduce the risks but capture the advantages of joint information and technical synergies. The fourth reason (and this is the same as the second reason for making for more direct investment) is the reduction in market failure brought about by improved information and data flows. The hypothesis here is that this could ease the possibility of non-equity arrangements for specific projects, even though making for more equity involvement by large and diversified MNEs pursuing a global strategy.

c. Summary of Points about Organisational Form

MNE activity, as well as depending on competitive advantages of the investing companies and locational advantages of producing in two or more countries, is dependent on the extent to which it is beneficial to exploit these two advantages by using internalised markets. *Indeed, the way in which firms organise and coordinate their proprietary assets may itself be a crucial competitive advantage.*

As a broad generalisation, there is some reason to suppose that the exchange of intangible services through the market is likely to involve higher transaction costs (relative to total costs of production and transaction) than that of goods. There are six reasons for this.

(i)   Most services contain a larger element of customer tailoring than do goods, and services are more idiosyncratic.

(ii)   Since there is generally a greater human element in the production of services, their quality is likely to vary more than those of many goods. For example, it may be easy to control the quality of refined oil, or the right mixture of a group of materials, or the tolerance of an electronic component by machine, but it is very difficult to control the quality of the pure service element attached to a legal consultation, a restaurant meal, or a shipping cruise.

(iii) Until very recently, at least, a major proportion of the information provided and the certain knowledge and experience connected with interpreting and evaluating the information was tacit and non-codi-fiable.

(iv) Partly because of (iii) and the fact that information or knowledge related to service activities may be inexpensive to replicate, the possibility of abuse or dissipation of that knowledge is a real threat to the firm possessing it.

(v) Since markets for many services are highly segmented, the oppor-tunities for price discrimination (which can be best exploited via hierarchies) other than markets are considerable.

(vi) The control of some service activities may be perceived to be a crucial element in the success of non-service producing companies; for example, some shipping lines may be owned by manufacturers to ensure delivery of goods on time, while the prosperity of large retail outlets may be dependent on their expertise and goodwill of their buyers of foreign goods.

Together with the fact that many services are impossible or difficult to transport, the above reasons explain both the presence and the rapid growth of MNE activity in this sector. As suggested earlier, both people and firms tend to spend more on services as incomes rise; technology, information and software services are becoming increasingly significant in the value-added process of all types of goods and services; non-service firms are becoming increasingly involved in service activities (examples include the large MNE petroleum companies diversifying into banking, and the computer hardware companies into the provision of software); and new and specialised service companies are being set up as the pro-vision of some services becomes more complex.[1] All these trends are making for an intensification of international activity in its varied forms.

Table 2 sets out the main competitive advantages of MNEs in various service sectors; the more important characteristics which favour a home or foreign location for the value-adding activities using such advantages; and the leading considerations affecting the modality by which MNEs ex-

---

[1] An example, quoted by Fetetekuty and Hauser [1985], is that of the McDonnell Douglas Corporation, a manufacturing firm that developed a data base for its internal research and development activities, and now has a separate subsidiary that provides on-line data services to the general public both in the US and abroad.

ploit their competitive advantages. The final columns of the table give some indication of the way in which foreign markets are penetrated; and also the extent to which the organisation of cross-border transactions differs between service sectors.

8. Some Concluding Remarks

In this paper, we have sought to identify the main competitive advantages of firms in providing services to international markets; the way in which these advantages are used to advance best the strategic goals of the companies in question; and the reasons why, at least some of the value-added activities which these advantages generate are undertaken outside the home country of the MNE.

The paper has also identified some of the reasons for the growth of MNE involvement in the service sector over the last two decades and, in particular, why FDI has been the preferred route for organising cross-border activities involving some services and not others. Special attention has been paid to the increasing need of firms, both in service and non-service sectors, to integrate their domestic activities vertically or horizontally with services obtained from, or sold to, foreign countries; and the fact that, over recent years, both demand and supply-led forces have intensified the advantages from the common governance of interrelated activities involving services. Moreover, new opportunities for industrial and geographical diversification have created their own locational and ownership advantages which have strengthened the position of MNEs in an increasing number of service sectors. At the same time, we have suggested that both the liberalisation of some service sectors, and the growing tradeability of services made possible by improvements in transport facilities may lead to a relocation of some service activities. Whether this will lead to more centralisation of such activities (and particularly high value activities) or more decentralisation remains to be seen. But it does suggest a widening of the opportunities for rationalised foreign production and intra-firm trade in services and for MNEs in the service sector to be able to exploit the advantages common governance now enjoyed by MNEs in the primary and secondary goods services.

Currently, the internationalisation of the service sector is less pronounced than that of the goods sector. We suspect that over the next
decade or so, the increase in both trade and foreign-owned production
in services will outpace that of goods.

Appendix - The Eclectic Paradigm of International Production[1]

1. *Ownership-Specific Advantages* (of enterprises of one nationality (or
   affiliates of same) over those of another)
   a. Property right and/or intangible asset advantages
      Product innovations, production management, organisational and
      marketing systems, innovatory capacity; non-codifiable knowledge;
      "bank" of human capital experience; marketing, finance, know-
      how, etc.
   b. Advantages of common governance
      i. Which those branch plants of established enterprises may enjoy
          over *de novo* firms. Those due mainly to size and established
          position of enterprise, e. g. economies of scope and specialisa-
          tion; monopoly power, better resource capacity and usage. Ex-
          clusive or favoured access to inputs, e. g. labour, natural re-
          sources, finance, information. Ability to obtain inputs on
          favoured terms (due e. g. to size or monopsonistic influence).
          Exclusive or favoured access to product markets. Access to
          resources of parent company at marginal cost. Economies of
          joint supply (not only in production, but in purchasing, mar-
          keting, finance, etc., arrangements).
      ii. Which specifically arise because of multinationality. Multination-
          ality enhances above advantages by offering wider opportuni-
          ties. More favoured access to and/or better knowledge about
          international markets, e. g. for information, finance, labour,
          etc. Ability to take advantage of geographic differences in
          factor endowments, markets. Ability to diversify or reduce
          risks, e. g. in different currency areas, and/or political
          scenarios.

---

[1] Dunning [1988].

2. *Internalisation Incentive Advantages* (i.e. to protect against or exploit market failure)

Avoidance of search and negotiating costs. To avoid costs of enforcing property rights. Buyer uncertainty (about nature and value of inputs (e.g. technology) being sold). Where market does not permit price discrimination. Need of seller to protect quality of intermediate or final products. To capture economies of interdependent activities (see b. above). To compensate for absence of future markets. To avoid or exploit government intervention (e.g. quotas, tariffs, price controls, tax differences, etc.). To control supplies and conditions of sale of inputs (including technology). To control market outlets (including those which might be used by competitors). To be able to engage in practices, e.g. cross-subsidisation, predatory pricing, leads and lags, transfer pricing, etc., as a competitive (or anti-competitive) strategy.

3. *Location-Specific Variables* (these may favour home or host countries)

Spacial distribution of natural and created resource endowments and markets. Input prices, quality and productivity, e.g. labour, energy, materials, components, semi-finished goods. International transport and communications costs. Investment incentives and disincentives (including performance requirements, etc.). Artificial barriers (e.g. import controls) to trade in goods. Infrastructure provisions (commercial, legal, educational, transport and communication). Psychic distance (language, cultural, business, customs, etc., differences). Economies of centralisation of R & D production and marketing. Economic system and policies of government; the institutional framework for resource allocation.

Bibliography

CASSON, Mark C., "Transaction Costs and the Theory of Multinational Enterprise". In: Alan M. RUGMAN (Ed.), New Theories of the Multinational Enterprise. New York 1982, pp. 24-43.

--, The Firm and the Market. Oxford 1987.

-- et al., Multinationals and World Trade. London 1986.

CAVES, Richard E., Multinational Enterprise and Economic Analysis. Cambridge 1982.

CONTRACTOR, Farok J., Peter LORANGE, Cooperative Strategies in International Business. Lexington, Mass., 1988.

DANIELS, Peter W., Service Industries: Growth and Location. Cambridge 1982.

DUNNING, John H., International Production and the International Enterprise. London 1981.

--, "The Eclectic Paradigm of International Production: A Restatement and Some Possible Extension". Journal of International Business Studies, Vol. 19, 1988, pp. 1-31.

--, John A. CANTWELL, The IRM Directory of Statistics of International Investment and Production. London 1987.

ENDERWICK, Peter, Some Economics of Service-Sector Multinational Enterprises. Belfast 1986, mimeo.

ETHIER, Wilfried J., "The Multinational Firm". Quarterly Journal of Economics, Vol. 101, 1986, pp. 805-833.

FEKETEKUTY, Geza, G. HAUSER, "Information Technology and Trade in Services". Economic Impact, Vol. 52, 1985, pp. 22-28.

GERSHUNY, Jonathan I., Ian D. MILES, The New Service Economy: The Transformation of Employment in Industrial Societies. London 1983.

GRUBEL, Herbert, Direct and Embodied Trade in Services. Fraser Institute, Service Project Discussion Papers, 86-1. Vancouver 1986.

--, "Traded Services Are Embodied in Materials or People". The World Economy, Vol. 10, 1987.

--, David L. HAMMES, Household Service Consumption and Monetization. 1987, mimeo.

HIRSCH, Seev, "An International Trade and Investment Theory of the Firm". Oxford Economic Papers, Vol. 28, 1976, pp. 258-269.

--, International Transactions in Services and in Service Intensive Goods. Tel Aviv University, Jerusalem, 1986, mimeo.

KOBRIN, Stephen T., Expropriation as an Attempt to Control Foreign Firms in LDCs: Trends from 1960 to 1979". International Studies Quarterly, Vol. 28, 1984, pp. 329-348.

NICHOLAS, Stephen T., "Agency Contract, Institutional Modes, and the Transaction of Foreign Direct Investment by British Manufacturing Multinationals before 1939". Journal of Economic History, Vol. 43, 1983, pp. 675-686.

OHMAE, Kenichi, Triad Power. New York 1985.

PORTER, Michael E., Competitive Strategy: Techniques for Analyzing Industries and Competitors. New York 1980.

--, Competitive Advantage: Creating and Sustaining Superior Performance. New York 1985.

-- (Ed.), Competition in Global Industries. Boston 1986.

van RENS, J. H. P., Multinationals in the Transport Industry. Paper presented at the IRM Conference on Multinationals in Transition, 15-16 November. Paris 1982.

RIDDLE, Dorothy I., Service-Led Growth: The Role of the Service Sector in World Development. New York 1986.

--, The Role of Service Transnational Corporations in the Development Process. 1987, mimeo.

RUGMAN, Alan M., A Transaction Cost Approach to Trade in Services. University of Toronto 1986, mimeo.

SAMPSON, Anthony, The Money Leaders. New York 1982.

SAMPSON, Gary P., Richard H. SNAPE, "Identifying the Issues in Trade in Services". The World Economy, Vol. 8, 1985, pp. 171-182.

SAUVANT, Karl P., International Transactions in Services. Boulder, Col., 1986.

SCOTT, Bruce R., George C. LODGE (Eds.), U.S. Competitiveness in the World Economy. Boston 1985.

SHELP, Ronald K., Beyond Industrialization: Ascendancy of the Global Service Economy. New York 1981.

--, Service Industries and Economic Development. New York 1984.

--, "Service Technology and Economic Development". Economic Impact, Vol. 52, 1985.

TEECE, David J., "Profiting from Technological Innovation: Implications for Integration, Collaboration, Licensing and Public Policy". Research Policy, Vol. 15, 1986, pp. 285-305.

UNITED NATIONS CONFERENCE ON TRADE AND DEVELOPMENT (UNCTAD), Services and the Development Process. UN E. 85. II, D. 13, New York 1985.

UNITED NATIONS CENTER ON TRANSNATIONAL COOPORATIONS (UNCTC), Transnational Corporations in World Development. New York 1988.

US DEPARTMENT OF COMMERCE, US Direct Investment Abroad: 1982 Benchmark Survey Data. Washington 1985.

US DEPARTMENT OF STATE, Nationalization, Expropriation and Other Takings of US and Certain Foreign Property since 1960. Washington 1971.

US OFFICE OF TECHNOLOGY ASSESSMENT, Trade in Services: Exports and Foreign Revenues. Washington 1986.

VAITSOS, Constantine V., Transnational Activities in Services, National Development and the Role of TNCs. Paper prepared for the UNDP/ UNCTAD/ECLA Project RLA/82/02. New York 1986.

WORLD BANK, World Development Report. New York 1987.

Comment on John H. Dunning, "Trade and Foreign-Owned Production in Services: Some Conceptual and Theoretical Issues"

Pan A. Yotopoulos

1. Introduction

Dunning's paper is detailed, painstaking and methodical. The wealth of information he presents, especially concerning the type of services which enter international trade, and the mode in which they enter it, is invaluable. I have no quarrel with it; I am only confused. Why should there be so many gradients of tradability in services as opposed to goods? And how is this fact reconciled with the underlying precept of Dunning's paper - indeed the precept of the entire conference - that free trade in services is a good thing?

As a footnote to Dunning's paper, and to the conference, I would like to suggest an alternative view: services belong in fragmented markets, and people free-trade in fragmented markets at their own peril. In relation to the former point, I will do some classificatory housecleaning to suggest that services are inherently nonhomogeneous commodities. This has implications regarding the role of multinational corporations (MNCs) in the production of services as well as with regard to issues of trade liberalization and the tradability of services.

2. The Roots of Heterogeneity in Services

The taxonomic discussion that took place at the beginning of the conference [Siniscalco, 1988] highlighted two alternative definitions of services. Fuchs [1968] defines services as "the commodities which are intangible, instantaneous (in that they perish in the very instant of production) and are purchased next to the consumer and with its own participation; they cannot be stored, nor transported, nor accumulated". This seems to be the definition implicit in Dunning's typologies. Hill [1977], on the other hand, sets the differentia specifica between goods and services on appropriability. Transactions in goods establish *rights* over objects, while services, being changes that affect the user, can only become the object of *obligations*. I happen to believe that this definition is more useful in clearing the taxonomical thicket. Why is the distinction important?

An obligation is contingent on one's intention to deliver according to certain specifications. Normally, there can be a great variety of specifications, which means that ordinarily services are more customized than goods. Moreover, it usually is impossible to establish a priori with certainty the intentions of a party to deliver, which means that services are ordinarily more subject to asymmetric information (and conceivably adverse selection of risk) than are goods. For example, while the butcher would be happy to clear the market by auctioning off his beef at whatever price the market will bear, the banker would be nervous with a loan portfolio which specializes on the debtors willing to outbid all others for his funds. Similarly, while I may settle for the cheapest apples in the market, I will certainly not go to the cheapest surgeon to have my appendix removed. Intentions to deliver enter services in a crucial manner since more attributes are unobservable pre-purchase as compared to goods. As a consequence, the issue of trust (or reputation) becomes germane in the case of services.

Both factors mentioned above, customization and trust (or reputation), imply that services are generally more heterogeneous than goods. I say "generally" because in fact there is a continuum between the two, which is reflected in the type of markets in which they normally trade, ranging from perfect markets to (extremely) fragmented markets: I will call the two extremes of the continuum "pure goods" (markets) and "pure services" (markets) respectively. Whether a commodity is transacted in a market that is closer to the one or the other extreme depends largely on the inherent characteristics of the commodity itself which determine whether an "arms-length" transaction is possible (pure goods) or instead a personalistic relationship between the transacting parties, involving trust and reputation, is required (services). Within that continuum, in turn, there are some goods that are more "pure goods" than others (an apple versus an automobile), and some services, e.g., a "sneak-preview" movie ticket, that are closer to "lemons" [Akerlof, 1970] than are the Pension (Providence) Funds, which are closer to goods.

Since services are heterogeneous, detailed typologies are inevitable. Dunning's paper is rich - and presumably exhaustive - in typologies. He lists six attributes which explain the increase in the share of services in GNP; and another seven factors which reflect the combination of both demand and supply. Most sound plausible, but I doubt he would have put them all in a regression equation, and I doubt that I do (or I should) remember them all in the absence of an organizational (filing) rule. Such a rule is customization plus trust, as I mentioned above.

3. The Role of Multinational Corporations

MNCs are important players in services, and their share has been rapidly increasing. So has the foreign direct investment in the service sector. What explains the increasing propensity of MNCs to enter the production of services?

Dunning lists a number of factors which account for a competitive advantage for MNCs in producing services and he traces them to principles of economic organization. Most revolve around economies of scale which arise from the indivisibility of certain inputs. The size of the plant is a classical form of such indivisibility. Its modern-day counterpart is indivisibility in technology and in information. I will call this aspect of the size advantage of MNCs "tangible size advantage". Size affords also some "intangible advantages" which favor MNCs in the production of a broad variety of services. The name recognition of a big international corporation, along with trademarks, reputation, and good will that it might control, are all important to the buyer of services who is dealing with "experience goods" as opposed to "inspection goods".

The location of a commodity in the continuum between goods and services once again matters in deciding the relative importance of the tangible versus the intangible size advantage on a case-by-case basis. It could provide the organizing principle for Dunning's Table 2, which is rich in detail but rather unmanageable. What, for example, makes MNCs less successful at selling education services and more successful at selling life insurance? Is education closer to a "pure good" which is produced with tangible diseconomies of scale, while the intangible size advantage of MNCs becomes more important in life insurance which is closer to "pure services"? Small private universities, like mine, obviously believe this is so for education - and scale their tuition fees accordingly.

4. Trade Liberalization and the Degree of Tradability in Services

The issue of the continuum between pure goods and pure services becomes also important in determining the extent of international tradability in services, and as such it may pertain to the current Uruguay Round discussions of trade liberalization. One important hint about those discussions emerges from Dunning's very detailed classification of services: the huge variety of services listed is likely to make for long, laborious and tedious negotiations, conducted on a case-by-case basis. Are there any organizing principles for such negotiations? I would venture some guesses.

It is fair to assume that countries, and especially the LDCs, are likely to be interested in liberalizing trade in services that they are more likely to export - or least likely to import. Therefore, looking at the DC-LDC negotiating interests, one could guess:

(i)   Following Ricardo's insightful observation, it is expected that the DC-LDC productivity differential is greater in goods than in services. As a result, LDCs are likely to be interested in increasing the international tradability of services with an eye to increasing exports. An important caveat should be noted, however. If the intangible size advantages favor mostly the rich (DCs/MNCs), and to the extent that in a fragmented market such advantages are reflected in higher prices of services (with "international" reputation, as opposed to without), the productivity-differential advantage of LDCs may disappear. As an example, LDCs are more likely to be interested in the liberalization of air transport services as opposed to financial services.

(ii)   The traditional tangible size advantage can probably be better mustered by LDCs, as compared to the intangible size advantage. The closer a service is to the goods-end of the continuum, the more likely it is to attract the interest of LDCs for liberalization.

(iii)   The income elasticity of demand for each specific type of services should be carefully considered. It becomes important both for considerations of "unequal exchange" (terms of trade) and for issues of dynamic comparative advantage.

5. Conclusion

Dunning's paper is good, and it is rich. Not unlike good food, one can best enjoy it in small portions - and by carefully organizing the sequence of courses. On this last point the discussion is less than fully successful. It often runs the risk of having more categories than data points.

Bibliography

AKERLOF, George A., "The Market for 'Lemons': Quality Uncertainty and the Market Mechanism". The Quarterly Journal of Economics, Vol. 89, 1970, pp. 488-500.

FUCHS, Victor R., The Service Economy. New York 1968.

HILL, T.P., "On Goods and Services". The Review of Income and Wealth, Vol. 23, 1977, pp. 315-338.

SINISCALCO, Domenico, "Defining and Measuring Output and Productivity in the Service Sector". In this volume.

III. SECTORAL ANALYSIS

Gerald R. Faulhaber*

Telecommunications and the Scope of the Market in Services

1. Introduction

The promised liberalization within the European Economic Community in 1992 is likely to be the most significant economic event of the coming decade. Should this transformation actually occur, it will at last create a market, the world's largest, appropriate to the economic potential of the region. The free movement of goods, people, and information among 325 million consumers, workers, and stockholders promises to create enormous wealth for Europeans, and enormous opportunities for the rest of us. I would like to focus on the role of telecommunications services in this transformation, which I believe is far more vital than is generally recognized. Note I use the word "services". Much has been written and said about the market for telecommunications *equipment*, including the "threat" of the Japanese and American manufacturers. I am going to ignore completely the trade in telecommunications equipment problem; I view this market as mature, in which transactions are few in number but large in value, very highly politicized, and well-studied by others. What I find of far greater interest is the role of telecommunications services in defining the *scope of the market* of services, which after all is what 1992 is all about.

2. Market Scope in Services

The free movement of goods, people, services, and information has long been viewed as an important factor in creating wealth within a mar-

---

* This paper was also presented at the Conference on Innovation in Europe 1992 in Spoleto, Italy, in July 1988.

ket. The US, the world's largest market, is also its richest. Workers within the market can seek employment anywhere he or she is in demand; highly specialized firms have a very large pool of consumers from which to draw; firms that depend upon scale economies have a market whose scale matches their needs. And all this without trade barriers, without barriers to the movement of people.

And also with the world's largest, most reliable, and most ubiquitous and diverse telecommunications system. For a manufacturing or agriculture-based economy, the benefits from access to a large market depend upon the ability to move one's product to market quickly, reliably, and cheaply. For a services-based economy, these benefits depend upon the ability to move *information* to market quickly, reliably, and cheaply.

Traditionally, economists and others have seen trade restrictions against the goods of foreigners as the chauvinistically short-sighted barrier to achieving the efficiencies of large markets. The fact that goods moving from New York to New Jersey pay no duty, and goods moving from Germany to France pay duty, if they are permitted to move at all, is argued to be an important contributor to the relatively greater per capita wealth of the US. Less well-recognized is the growing importance of moving people and information freely from New York to New Jersey. There has been some attention paid within the EEC to the free movement of people within the Community post-1992, so that British accountants can easily do business in France or Italy. However, there has been less attention paid to the problems and prospects of the unrestricted and inexpensive movement of information across borders.

Currently, European telecommunications remains in a traditional public monopoly mode; state-run or state-regulated, focused on its protected monopoly position, unresponsive to market needs. Even British Telecom, usually held up as a model to the rest of Europe, is still a regulated monopolist. How can this fragmented, insular industry hope to cope with the demands that service firms, anxious to expand into new markets, will place upon it for new, expanded service at low cost? Where are the competitors that will offer expanding service firms the diverse array of telecommunications they will need to capture new markets?

I would like to concentrate on two service industries which are apparently becoming more telecommunications-intensive at the same time as their geographic market scope has been increasing: financial services and retail trade. You will not be surprised to hear about the first, although I suspect you will be surprised to hear about the second. In each industry, I make three points: (i) the changing scope of the market; (ii) the importance of telecommunications as an enabling technology for this change; and (iii) the forces that have been or will be brought to bear from within and without the telecommunications industry to meet the needs of these industries.

The point of this exercise is to sketch how the market forces attendant to the liberalization within the EEC in 1992 may play out in the market for telecommunications during a period of long-run disequilibrium, both in the telecommunications market as well as in downstream markets.

3. Telecommunications and the Scope of Financial Services

The fundamental changes taking place in the financial services industry have been well-documented elsewhere. At base, these changes have been about increasing the geographic scope of the market, as well as a merging of markets; in fact, the term "financial service industry" is a very recent one, suggesting that the old industry distinctions of commercial banks, investment banks, insurance and brokerage are irrelevant today.

Prior to 1970, banking was almost exclusively a local industry; the local banker knew his credit risks as well as his deposit base and interactions with other banks and other parts of financial services was minimal. Apart from a few New York banks, so-called "money center" banks, US banking was nearly a cottage industry. This tendency was reinforced by Federal restrictions on interstate banking, rules which protected local banks from competition, but forced them to hold relatively undiversified portfolios of assets.

Today, US banking is at least multistate and more likely global, tightly linked with other financial service firms, and seeking to expand into related product and geographic markets. The scope of the market, therefore, has gone from local to global in under two decades.

What were the causes of this transformation?

- This transformation *could* not have happened without fundamental changes in technology; the two key technologies involved are information processing and telecommunications. Money, after all, is an electrical phenomenon.

- This transformation *would* not have happened unless profits were to be earned in doing so. In fact, the economic agents primarily responsible for forcing this transformation were not banks, but customers of banks and non-bank institutions.

- *Financial regulations,* far from inhibiting these changes were in fact the *cause* of the changes. During the 1960s, banks' large customers learned to function in overseas capital markets on their own and earn higher returns than they could with their bankers' help. An important necessary condition was the ability to transfer information quickly and cheaply. During the 1970s, US banks learned that, although they were prohibited from investment banking in the US, they were not so constrained in other markets, so that much of their activity moved offshore. Again, an important necessary condition was the ability to maintain management control of global operations quickly and cheaply. Finally, in the 1980s, the London Exchange showed that deregulation and going totally electronic would attract business from around the world. Screen-based trading by brokers around the world 24 hours a day seems to be where this industry wants to go. Again, the information and telecommunications technology is the necessary condition. One might wonder why banks and other financial institutions were so anxious to go global. What was it about foreign markets that made them so attractive? Financial services went offshore principally to avoid home-country regulation; if commercial banks could not engage in investment banking at home, they could (and did) in London. If non financial firms were limited in their access to domestic markets by regulation, they would enter foreign markets to achieve higher returns. It was the new electronic technology which allowed this to happen [cf. Kane, 1981].

On the US domestic front, similar things were happening. States that passed stringent laws regarding consumer credit found that banks established their credit card centers in Delaware and other "safe haven" states with less stringent laws. One of the more striking trends in US banking has been the development of regional banking, the most profitable segment of the industry. Through aggressive acquisition strategies, these banks have brought together the knowledge of local bankers with a large bank's sophisticated products. However, this trend also depends upon the availability of high-speed data links to tie together local banks' processing needs into large computer centers. Nor is this need just for transactions processing; regional banks use this market information, such as customer financial profiles, to develop and market new products through their distribution networks.

The hypothesis, then, is that the scope of the market in financial services vastly expanded with the advent of cheap telecommunications and information technology. That expansion is still going on, and is transforming this industry dramatically. Just as this revolution was fueled by the dizzying array of products and services available in the computer industry, so also has it thrived on (i) the uniformity and ubiquity of the basic US telecommunications network, and (ii) the wide availability of multiple telecommunications vendors, including self-supply. Big firms do not have to wait for the telecommunications utility; they can, and will, do it themselves.

Our hypothesis is that telecommunications has been an enabling technology for these market scope changes in financial services. Do the data support this hypothesis? As measured by assets, international banking by US banks has grown both absolutely and as a fraction of domestic banking, as shown in Figure 1. Although our data on the presence of foreign banks in the US is more sparse, Figure 2 suggests that the growth of offshore banks in our domestic market has been substantial as well. In Figure 3, we show the growth of international telephone traffic over a similar period, and we again note a quite rapid increase.

We do not have industry-specific numbers for international telecommunications traffic, so our comparison here is suggestive rather than compelling. Yet, the contemporaneous rapid growth of both international banking and international telecommunications is consistent with our hypothesis. The European Community, faced with the uncertainty of 1992, especially needs to understand this link between banking and telecommunications.

What are the potential consequences of liberalization of services trade within the EEC in 1992 on telecommunications services? There are two:

Figure 1 - Assets of Foreign Branches of US Banks

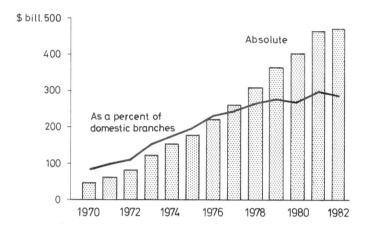

Source: Federal Reserve System [1970-1982].

Figure 2 - Number of Banking Families with US Branches

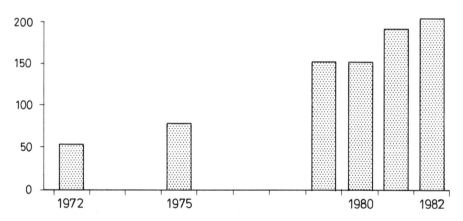

Source: Kane [1988, Fig. 4].

- Germany and other countries will be pushed toward the most liberal standard in the EEC, which now appears to be Britain's. Previously insular national systems will be opened up to competitive challenge by other firms; those most responsive to markets will be the most successful. The process of transforming European telecommunications into a more competitive industry will be quite long, difficult, and sub-ject to much political debate. The damage to both the capital and the

Figure 3 - International Messages to Europe and Asia (millions of calls)

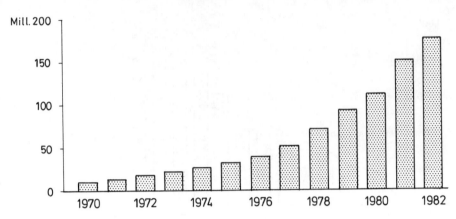

Source: FCC [1983, T. 13].

the employees of the traditional PTTs could be most serious, as the American experience has shown us.

- Large financial service firms, and consortia of such firms, will ener- getically turn to self-supply. This will lead to the development of private networks to carry commercial traffic. This solution may be in- efficient from an economic point of view, but clearly necessary for such firms to avoid the anticompetitive local telephone monopolies. It will also lead to entry by others into this market, especially American financial service firms which possess a high level of competence in information/telecommunication technology.

4. Telecommunications and the Scope of Retailing

Retailing is in many ways the quintessential low-technology indus- try: highly labor-intensive, and dependent upon face-to-face transac- tions that resist technical change. Of course, various innovations such as point-of-sale terminals and their attendant communication nets have brought electronic technology to this market in the recent past. But a quite dramatic change in retailing has been wrought in the last decade by the twin "innovations" of credit cards and "800 Service", a telecom- munications service in which a firm can purchase an incoming line over which their customers may call them free of charge. Since 800 Service became nationwide in 1977, a whole retail sub-industry has grown up, dependent upon their customers reaching them by telephone to place orders.

Of course, the so-called mail order business is not new. It was pioneered by Sears, Roebuck in the US, aimed at a market segment that was unable to visit ordinary retail outlets because of their rural remoteness. The business depended upon the ubiquity and reliability of the US mail service, a paper technology. In recent years, such firms have generally been in decline.

By contrast, today's mail order business depends on the speed of electronic communication. Its market segment is not those with too much space (rural America) but those with too little time (upwardly mobile, two-income America). It is a very rapidly expanding sector, whose growth seems to parallel that of the growth of 800 Service revenues. Anyone who has lived in the US and found their mailbox stuffed daily with such catalogs will need little convincing of this trend.

In Figure 4, we show the growth of mail order sales as a fraction of total general merchandise. By comparison, we also show the evolution of sales for mail order department stores, of the more traditional variety. Against the backdrop of the decline of traditional mail order, the growth of the new mail order is most impressive. Included in this figure is the growth of 800 Service revenues over the same period of time. Again, we have no industry-specific numbers regarding 800 Service, but the contemporaneous growth of the two is suggestive, to say the least.

The US telecommunications industry, with its larger market and more competitive market structure, has moved far in front of their European colleagues with this service, and have done much more to help their domestic retail industry. Even with the US experience as a model, European PTTs have not aggressively pursued this market, and European retailing as well as telecommunications and ultimately the consuming public has been the worse for it.

What are the prospects for the EEC in 1992? If more competition comes to the telecommunications market, we can expect that retailers will demand this type of service to be available throughout Europe. If the national PTT monopolies drag their heels, we can expect that the retailers themselves will adopt private systems which access consumers through the PTT's distribution network, and bring political pressure to

Figure 4 – Mail Order Sales as a Percent of General Merchandise and "800 Service" Revenues

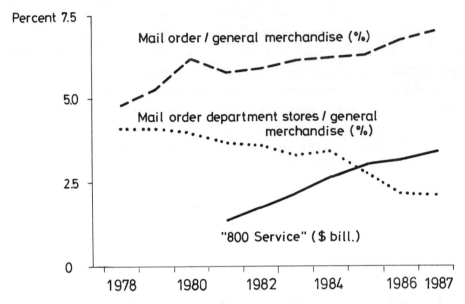

Source: Bureau of the Census [various issues]; FCC [1981-1986].

bear should the PTTs resist. Again, the process will most likely be a long and difficult one.

The opening up of the Common Market to this type of retail trade will be even more dramatic than in the US. For example, Britons spend twice as much on mail order (of the traditional variety) than do Americans. What might we expect when they can shop by phone around Europe? As the market opens up, we should expect that the firms that will do best, at least initially, will be American. It is the L.L. Beans and the Lands Ends that have the experience in this business, and they will have an initial advantage over the Ikeas and the Carrefours. In fact, the date that L.L. Bean establishes their first 800 Service number in Europe will mark the real dawn of pan-European retailing.

Bibliography

BUREAU OF THE CENSUS, Monthly Retail Trade Survey. Washington 1978-1986.

FEDERAL COMMUNICATIONS COMMISSION (FCC), Statistics of Communications Common Carriers. Washington 1983.

--, Monthly Revenue Report 0004 (MR-4). 1981-1986.

FEDERAL RESERVE SYSTEM, BOARD OF GOVERNORS, Federal Reserve Bulletin. Washington 1970-1982.

KANE, Edward J., "Accelerating Inflation, Technological Innovation, and the Decreasing Effectiveness of Banking Regulation". Journal of Finance, Vol. 36, 1981, pp. 355-367.

--, How Market Forces Influence the Structure of Financial Regulation. AEI Financial Markets Project and Ohio State University. Columbus 1988, mimeo.

6352

Comment on Gerald R. Faulhaber, "Telecommunications and the Scope of the Market in Services"

6350

166 - 72

Axel Busch

For several years, the services sector has belonged to the main subjects of economic studies. In this context, telecommunications and data processing have become more and more of especial interest. Nearly every discussion on technical progress and its implications for growth and employment usually leads to new information and communications technologies. Completing Gerald Faulhaber's statements, I would like to make some general remarks on these subjects. What are the reasons for this increasing public interest in telecommunications and data processing and what kind of impact on trade and investment has to be expected?

Due to constant or increasing unemployment in many countries, suitable action has to be taken in order to create new jobs. According to experience in the US and Great Britain, the services sector seems to be one of the main fields for this purpose and thereby information-intensive services obviously play a major role.

Based on increasing internationalization, diversification and specialization, the demand for information and communications has been growing rapidly over the last decades. This phenomena measured by a growing share of information-related jobs in overall employment relates not only to industrialized but also to developing countries [OECD, 1986]. The demand for information and communications is accompanied by very fast progress in both the information and communication technologies [Sauvant, 1986]. Technological developments related mainly to integrated circuits or microelectronics have dramatically decreased the physical size and the price of electronic data processing and transmission equipment and increased the range of their applications in both manufacturing and service industries.

According to existing industries, the increasing application of telecommunications and data processing has several implications. First of all, this development leads to a growing volume of information-related inputs used to produce traditional goods and services. That means that the production process becomes more information-intensive. Another fact is that the boundaries between information or communications industries on the one hand and traditional industries on the other become less distinct by increasing diversification. General Motors, for example, a well-known automobile corporation, bought an important electronics supplier and satellite producer 1985. In West Germany something similar happened when Daimler Benz aquired two firms: Dornier, an important aerospace company and AEG, a company producing electronics. A further example for the increasing diversification is the banking industry. The Deutsche Bank, the biggest German banking company, entered the market for electronic databanks offering information on a commercial basis that was formerly intended only for internal use. The same company is planning a joint venture with British Telecom, the main supplier of telecommunications services in Great Britain, in order to install a mobile radio system in West Germany. For a few years, General Motors has been offering special computer services to third parties in order to use its own computer capacities more efficiently.

But new information and communications technology doesn't have an impact on traditional industries alone. It even leads to new information service industries. Not only do the production and selling of computer software or the establishing of computer consulting firms belong to that, but also several telecommunications services such as Electronic Mail or Telefax-Service. In this context, also a small, but growing industry, the electronic databank industry, has to be mentioned. By using electronic information, storage and retrieval time and money can be saved when compared with traditional information sources like books and journals. Information contained in electronic databanks are maschine-readable and can be transferred via telecommunications lines from one computer to another for further processing or for final use. The attractiveness of this information technique has increased in such a way that nowadays nearly 3800 databanks have been produced and provided by 550 firms on a commercial basis worldwide [Busch, 1988].

Besides the described effects on the volume of applications and the changing character of industries and corporations, the international implications of new information and communications technology are of growing interest. In this context, one important fact is the impact on trade and foreign direct investment (FDI). On, the one hand, due to modern telecommunications systems, there will now be trade in regions or industries in which FDI alone was practicable in the past. It means that services, for example, that were not tradable in the past now become tradable. In this way, as Gerald Faulhaber described, banking, insurance or retail companies have an instrument to widen their international market activities making them better than before.

But there may be not only a substitution between trade and FDI due to new information and communications technology. It is also possible for trade in services or goods initiated by the described technological developments also to speed up FDI, for example, special information-service investment for maintenance or general service. For instance, electronic telephone-switching equipment or complicated software require continuous servicing [Sauvant, 1986]. If it cannot be done by using telecommunications systems, FDI in special information-service activities may be necessary.

Even Gerald Faulhaber made it clear that, for several industries competing in international markets, communications and data processing facilities are necessary because these firms require extensive information flows. Not only banking or retail firms belong to this group, but also international air transport, insurance and the credit-card industry. All of these need modern telecommunications and data processing systems, not in order to create new information services, but in order to offer their traditional services more effiently. To the same extent as international competition is increasing modern telecommunications and data processing systems are playing a more important role.

I agree with Gerald Faulhaber that, in this context, it is of crucial importance whether the underlying telecommunications infrastructure guarantees the frictionless production and exchange of computer-based information within a country and especially across the borders. Focusing on Europe the situation is not always satisfactory. Compared with the US, Japan or Great Britain in most European countries the telecommunications sector is regulated. Firms and private users cannot provide their own telecommunications networks. Like in Germany, they can only use public lines in order to transmit computer-based information.

Several recent studies show that in West Germany, for example, telecommunications charges are the highest compared with other industrialized countries [McKinsey, 1988]. Firms established in the most indus-

trialized regions of Germany also complain of inefficient telecommunications lines. Due to high rates and inefficient communications facilities,
companies acting in international markets run the risk of losing their
competitive advantage. Furthermore, a country would probably lose the
advantage of location under such restrictive telecommunications conditions. This means that a company would probably change its place of
residence and invest in foreign countries if no efficient and cheap telecommunications infrastructure existed. For these reasons, Japanese and
US firms dealing with information-intensive goods and services have
already removed their computer centres from Germany to Great Britain
[Busch, 1988]. This fact, for example, underlines Faulhaber's mention of
the unattractiveness of Frankfurt as a banking centre of Europe.

Focusing on the evidence of a cheap and efficient telecommunications
infrastructure for economic growth and the completion of the European
Common Market in 1992, several European countries are planning to
deregulate the telecommunications sector (France, the Netherlands,
Belgium, West Germany). Attempts are in progress to liberalize market
entry for terminal equipment and several telecommunications services.
But I question whether these plans will be sufficient to optimize the
telecommunications infrastructure as a whole or to stay in touch with the
development in the countries that have already liberalized (US, Great
Britain, Japan).

In Germany, for example, the government recently published its
proposals based on the report of a special commission [BMPF, 1988].
Following these plans that, however, still need to be passed by parlia-
ment, more competition by private firms will be established in the market
for telecommunications services and equipment except for the basic
telephone service. As a contrast to these plans, it is characteristic not
only for West Germany but also for the other countries that, with some
exceptions, the telecommunications networks will remain monopolized by
the state-owned or state-controlled firms.

From the economic point of view, this fact is for different reasons
more important than the liberalization of the equipment or service markets [Busch, 1989]. The network monopoly means first of all that private
companies planning or already making provision for telecommunications
services in liberalized markets will have to rent line capacities from the
PTT. Without alternatives they will have to accept the tariffs required

and the quality of the leased lines. Network monopoly secondly means that investment and innovations in network capacities will be further under government control. In West Germany, for example, nearly 80 per cent of all investments in the public telecommunications sector refers to transmitting and switching equipment.

For that reason the Deutsche Bundespost as a monopolist will be able to influence further the technological progress in telecommunications in a crucial way. It also has to be considered that, according to the situation in West Germany, nearly 90 per cent of all the PTT's revenues come from the monopolized services, especially from the basic telephone service. Under the described conditions, this is not expected to be changed in the near future. Furthermore, it is planned to use these revenues from the monopolized services in order to finance services that involve losses. This cross-subsidization, which is often justified by infrastructure objectives and equity considerations, in addition raises the price of telecommunications.

Therefore, not only the absence of competition in main telecommunications fields but also the network and telephone service as main source of revenues call into doubt whether the planned reforms will optimize the telecommunications supply in West Germany as well as in other European countries. Furthermore, since private firms are not competing in this field, the PTT has no incentive to provide telecommunications services or install a telecommunications network in the most efficient way.

The situation in most European countries show that plans for deregulating special parts of the telecommunications sector do exist, but, in spite of these plans, the network and telephone monopoly will still remain. Even the Commission of the European Communities agrees on this opinion. Based on the remaining monopoly, the present plans for reforming the telecommunications sector are less advanced than those used before in the US, Great Britain and Japan. I would like to say that the plans for reorganizing the European telecommunications markets therefore seem to be only the first step in the right direction. But others have to follow to provide companies and consumers with telecommunications services and equipment for the most effient transfer of information within countries and across the borders.

On the one hand, I am optimistic and I agree with Faulhaber that this will happen. It is especially the situation of the EC after 1992 that will push Germany and other European countries to the most liberal telecommunications standard in the EC which was recently formulated by Great Britain. On the other hand, I think that even these measures are not enough, because there are other legal factors which additionally influence the transfer and usage of information worldwide and which have to be mentioned if you are speaking about telecommunications, data processing and their impact on trade and investment. To these factors belong, for example, rules enacted by countries in order to prevent an abuse of personal data by unauthorized persons or institutions [Busch, 1988].

According to interviews with representatives of firms dealing with data processing and data transfer, the indistinct legal situation on data protection law which differs from country to country obstructs the collection, production and trade in information. In this way, those companies that are producing information-intensive goods and services are likely to be impeded. For this reason, in 1974, for example, a German company being afraid of restrictive protection law moved its computer centre from Germany to Luxemburg.

According to the international aspects of telecommunications and data processing, two other points are of interest. Not only in less developed but also in industrialized countries trade in services and especially trade in information-intensive services, telecommunications and data processing are restricted by non-tariff trade barriers. Companies in Brasilia, for example, that want to install a computer system for data transfer across the borders have to be authorized by the government. Some years ago, the Europeans Community installed an international aggregate called EURONET/DIANE to make European countries more competitive in the databank industry as compared with American companies. For this reason, firms from America were not allowed to participate in this aggregate. Even Eastern European countries have suffered from barriers to information-related goods and services that are contained in the COCOM List and which are allowed to be exported to Eastern European countries.

My considerations show that when discussing telecommunications and data processing and their impact on trade and investment, different points have to be paid attention to. The most important thing is that, today, many industries need an increasing amount of information for different purposes.

For that reason, they are depending on an efficient telecommunications infrastructure and a legal frame that allows a frictionless information transfer worldwide. As described by Gerald Faulhaber, it is especially the European countries which have to do a lot of things to stay in touch with the development in other industrialized countries.

Bibliography

BUSCH, Axel, "Mehr Wettbewerb in der Telekommunikation - Traum oder Wirklichkeit? Kritische Anmerkungen zu den Reformplänen der Bundesregierung zur Neuordnung des Fernmeldewesens". In: Wirtschaftsdienst, Vol. 69, January 1989, pp. 36-42.

--, "Electronic Databank Services, Problems and Prospects on Creating an Industry of Increasing Importance on World Economic Growth". In: Posta Kisérleti Intézet (PKI), Scientific Days '88 of the Research Institute of the Hungarian Posts and Telecommunications - Telecommunications, Economy, Society. Budapest 1988, pp. 81-88.

DER BUNDESMINISTER FÜR DAS POST- UND FERNMELDEWESEN (BMPF), Reform des Post- und Fernmeldewesens in der Bundesrepublik Deutschland. Heidelberg 1988.

McKINSEY & COMPANY Inc., Leistungsstand, Tarife und Innovationsförderung im Fernmeldewesen. Frankfurt 1987.

ORGANIZATION FOR ECONOMIC COOPERATION AND DEVELOPMENT (OECD), The Trends in the Information Economy, Information Computer Communications Policy Papers, 11, Paris 1986.

SAUVANT, Karl P., International Trade in Services. Boulder, Col., 1986.

Günter Knieps

6352
4233

Telecommunications Policy - Assessing Recent Experience in the US, Japan and Europe and Its Implications for the Completion of the Internal Common Market

6350

173 - 189

1. Introduction

In recent years a new trend in European telecommunications policy towards more competition has emerged. A cornerstone of this new development was the Commission of the European Communities' British Telecom decision in 1982 and its confirmation by the European Court of Justice in 1985. According to this decision, British Telecom should no longer be allowed to forbid the high-speed forwarding of telex messages between foreign countries by competitive agencies in Great Britain. The procedural setting of this case was most unusual because the Italian government and not British Telecom appealed against the Commission's decision. Moreover, the British government intervened, taking sides not with the Italian government, but with the Commission. The important message of the British Telecom case is that the Commission of the European Communities is able to apply the Treaty of Rome's competition rules in the European telecommunications sector too, in spite of the strong role of national telecommunications administration based on the public law of the different member countries.[1]

Since then, the Commission has initiated a wide-ranging discussion on the possibilities of completing the common internal market for telecommunications in the European Community. Obviously, this effort is strongly related to the Commission's endeavour to complete the common market by 1992. The "Green Paper on the Development of the Common Market for Telecommunication Services and Equipment" - issued by the Commission in June 1987 - proposes that the provision of terminal equipment as well as enhanced telecommunication services should be liberalized within

---

[1] For a detailed explanation of this case, see Schulte-Braucks [1986].

and between the member countries.[1] Basic services (mainly telephone) could still be monopolized by the national telecommunications administration; however, arguments concerning the public interest of such a monopoly should periodically be investigated. Moreover, the monopoly of public telecommunications networks would also be accepted in future.

With these proposals, the Commission of the European Communities tolerates, at least to some extent, the rather conservative attitude of most of its member countries with respect to deregulating telecommunications. There are, for example, several similarities to the proposals of the Report which the Government Commission for Telecommunications in Germany issued in September 1987 [Witte, 1987] and which currently is the basis for changing the in German telecommunications law from 1928.

In this paper I shall analyse the deregulation experiences in the telecommunication sectors of the US, Japan and Great Britain in order to evaluate the current telecommunications policy in Europe. These countries have undertaken the most progressive steps towards deregulation, which also have particular influence on the liberalization of the international telecommunications markets.

The first lesson is that the large innovation potential of the European telecommunications sectors can only be exhausted rapidly if market entry is guaranteed into all subparts, including public networks and basic services. The second lesson is that the strategies of partial entry deregulation and remaining entry restrictions typically become unstable over time. As a consequence, the third lesson is that the traditional cross-subsidizations within telecommunication systems also become unstable, when legal entry barriers disappear. To the extent that infrastructure objectives are politically desired but not lucrative, alternative methods of finance have to be designed which are compatible with free entry into telecommunications.

---

[1] In addition, the Commission pleaded for a liberalization of the procurement policy of the national telecommunications administration as well as for an introduction of European-wide telecommunication standards.

2. Market Entry into Public Networks: The Experience of the US, Japan and Great Britain

The US, Japan and Great Britain are at present the most progressive countries in respect to deregulating telecommunications because entry has become possible not only in the market for terminal equipment and telecommunication services, but also in the area of public networks.

It is interesting to remember that the deregulation of telecommunications in the US started on the level of interstate networks rather than on the services or equipment level. The "Above 890" decision of the Federal Communication Commission (FCC) in 1959 granted firms with high communication demand the right to build their own microwave systems. Applications to provide specialized common carrier services with microwave systems in competition to the traditional monopolistic carrier AT&T started being granted in 1970. Market entry with the establishment to domestic communication satellites became possible in 1972. The resale and shared usage of AT&T's private line services were only allowed four years later in 1976. Since 1980, free entry has been possible into all parts of interstate telecommunications, including the construction of network facilities to provide a public telephone service. Local networks are still monopolies in many states and include such parts of intrastate long-distance telecommunication networks which belong to the same Local Access and Transport Area (LATA)[1] [Knieps, 1983; 1985, Ch. III. A; OECD, 1987; Wieland, 1985].

In Japan, a new telecommunications law was introduced in 1985. As a consequence several Japanese firms have become active as new network suppliers, competing with the traditional monopolist Nippon Telegraph and Telephone (NNT). Since then, several suppliers of public telecommunication networks have started business, including traditional electricity and highway companies. Market entry took place by means of microwave systems, satellites and fibre-optic networks.

Already in 1984 Japan National Railways had founded the subsidiary Japan Telecom to become a network carrier with a fibre-optic network. The state-owned highway company together with several automobile firms

---

[1] LATAs were defined in 1982 during the Antitrust Case between AT&T and the Department of Justice. LATAs are much larger than a local network. The size of a LATA may even cover a whole state [FCC, 1983, p. 12].

founded Teleway Japan, which also became active with a fibre-optic network. In addition, electricity companies started to found subsidiary companies in order to build their own regional fibre-optic telecommunications
networks. Three private consortiums active in trade, banking and production entered the market with communication satellites. Market entry
with microwave systems was undertaken by one of the leading producers
of ceramic components for integrated circuits. Of course, market entry
into the Japanese telecommunication sector not only took place with alternative networks, but also with new services on the basis of public networks [Ito, Iwata, 1986; Müller, 1987; Neumann, 1987; OECD, 1987].

The most progressive country as far as deregulating telecommunications in Europe today is concerned is Great Britain. Until 1981, British
Telecom was operating as part of the Post Office as the monopolistic supplier of the whole British telecommunication sector. With the passing of
the Telecommunication Act in October 1981 the statutory monopoly of
British Telecom to run the British telecommunications network ended. In
February 1982 the Mercury consortium (Cable and Wireless, Barclay's
Merchant Bank and British Petroleum) received a licence to operate a
private digital network with fibre-optic cables for voice and data in competition with British Telecom. Since 1984, Mercury has been wholly
owned by Cable and Wireless. In addition, the market entry of private
suppliers of value-added network carriers on the basis of public networks has been allowed [Commission, 1987, Appendix A; Heuermann,
Neumann, 1985; Müller 1986; OECD, 1987].

The major advantage of this extensive entry deregulation is that
rapid and exhaustive exploration of the increasing innovation potential of
the telecommunications sector is possible.[1] The development of new
transmission technologies (e.g. microwave systems, satellites, fibre-optic
cables) together with the digital transmission and switching technologies
strongly increase the possibility of different network architectures as
well as the potential of new network services and the spectrum of terminal equipment.

---

[1] It is well-known that in a dynamic environment it is more important for
competition to be a social mechanism by which innovations are stimulated. The competition process can be seen as a "discovery procedure"
[von Hayek, 1968] which dominates the centralized monopolistic process
if the purpose is to try out better problem solutions compared to those
available in the past.

The market entrants into the public networks of the US, Japan and Great Britain have typically pursued a strategy of providing new services (product innovations) together with new network architecture. For example, in the US the firm DATRAN was founded in 1973 to construct a digital communications network for business users. The introduction of new switching technologies and the optimization of the network for data transmission made possible a more accurate and high speed data transmission, which traditional telephone companies had been unable to offer until that time. Market entry with satellites was allowed in the US in 1972 and very recently has also been permitted in Japan. In these countries, the supply of new innovative services plays a central role. This became possible because the cost characteristics of satellite systems differ from those of terrestrial systems. Satellite transmission costs are nearly independent of distance allowing a high-speed transmission; they also make possible the multiple distribution of communications signals. Thus, satellite systems are particularly suitable for long-distance, high-speed transmission of large data quantities. One example is the transmission of newspaper articles from one composing room to different printing offices in different places. The construction of a high quality digital fibre-optic network by Mercury in Great Britain also led to a better quality of network services. Since the transmission is more accurate and more rapid than those of British Telecom, the service offered by Mercury has been of particular use for business data communication.

In those countries where market entry in public networks has been granted (US, Japan and Great Britain), the question whether inefficient cost-duplications would result is not currently important.[1] Firstly, it is widely recognized that the growing demand for telecommunications reduces the importance of economies of scale in long-distance telecommunications. Secondly, it becomes obvious, that entry may lead to a more efficient utilization of existing network capacities (if networks can be used for public telecommunications previously reserved for the internal usage by train systems, highways or pipeline companies). Thirdly, the importance of different network qualities, due to different usage characteristics of alternative transmission systems (e.g. terrestrial versus non-

---

[1] In contrast, the major question is to what extent the distributional objectives could still be fulfilled under competition conditions (cf. Section 3).

terrestrial) becomes increasingly important, especially for business users.

As a consequence of the progressive entry deregulation in the US, Japan and Great Britain, competition in the international telecommunication markets has also increased. For many years AT&T was the only supplier of international voice communication for the US in co-operation with the PTTs abroad. The international message and data transfer was handled by ITT World Communication, RCA Global Communications and Western Union International. Since then, other suppliers of international voice and data services (for example MCI, US Sprint and Graphnet) have entered the market. Since 1986 suppliers of value-added network services have been able to be registered as recognized private operating agencies and are therefore entitled to bargain with foreign telecommunications administrations over the right to use oversea-cables. At the same time, the FCC asked two US firms to set up private oversea-cables. The purpose of this cable system was to sell gros transmission capacities for non-common carrier users [Commission, 1987, p. 158].

Since 1952 KDD (Kokusai Denstrin Denwa) has been the only Japanese international network carrier and service supplier. Since the new telecommunications law in 1985 two new firms have applied for a licence. International Telecom Japan Inc. (ITJ), a consortium of Japanese firms, applied to offer a world-wide service network for Japanese enterprises on the basis of lines leased from Intelsat or the national telecommunications administrations. The second consortium, International Digital Communications (IDJ), consists of the Japanese Warehouse Ito, the British firm Cable and Wireless and the US regional carriers Nynex and Pacific Telesis as well as Merill Lynch. IDJ applied for a licence as network carrier in order to use a world-wide fibre-optics network planned under the direction of Cable and Wireless.

In August 1983, the British government decided that Mercury could also enter the market for services on international networks. Mercury now has the licence to provide all telecommunication services nationally as well as internationally. Several services between Great Britain and the US have already started. In order to increase international competitiveness, Cable and Wireless, the owner of Mercury, has been allowed to build a transatlantic fibre-optics cable.

It is obvious that those countries which are most progressive in deregulating their national telecommunications sector are also the most active in liberalizing international telecommunications. In particular there is pressure from new firms already active in the national market in the US, Japan and Great Britain to enter the international market.

The liberalization of national and international telecommunications markets not only increases the spectrum of available telecommunication services but also reduces the long-distance telecommunications tariffs (especially on "high-density routes"). Although these reductions of long-distance tariffs are partly due to the rebalancing of tariffs thereby burdening local users (see Section 3.b), they also reveal increasing efficiency due to entry into long-distance telecommunications.

3. Entry Restrictions due to Infrastructure Objectives: The Experience of the US, Japan and Great Britain

a. The Instability of Partial Entry Deregulation

Although the US, Japan and Great Britain are the most progressive countries as far as deregulating their telecommunications sector is concerned, they have pursued a strategy of partial entry deregulation in the past. Even nowadays, some regulations of market entry do exist.

In the US during the first two decades of deregulation of interstate telecommunications, entry was only allowed in the area of private line services, and the monopoly of public telephone services was reserved for the traditional network carrier AT&T.[1] This strategy of partial deregulation was only given up by the FCC in 1980 (F.C.C. Docket 78-72) when it became obvious during the "Execunet Case" that the borderlines between private lines and public telephone services were blurring.[2] Since

---

[1] "Only Private Line Service, however, was opened to competition, basic public telephone service (MTS and WATS) remains a telephone monopoly" [FCC, 1976, p. 99].

[2] For example, electronic private branch exchanges made it possible to route a telephone call automatically either over a private line or the public telephone service depending on the available capacities at a given time.

the divestiture of AT&T in 1984 based on the AT&T settlement,[1] free entry into inter-LATA telecommunications is possible whereas in many states intra-LATA basic telecommunications is still provided under monopoly (by the newly founded regional holding companies). Nevertheless, one can observe some tendencies to weaken these regional monopolies. Firstly, since the FCC's Computer Inquiry III [FCC, 1986, p. 252], competition has been allowed in enhanced local services. As has already been realized on the long-distance level [FCC, 1980] technical progress makes it increasingly difficult to differentiate between basic communication and enhanced communication. Secondly, the introduction of microwave systems is becoming increasingly attractive, especially in rural areas, due to the high cost-saving potential compared with cables [Kahn, 1987]. Thirdly, the possibilities of bypassing local networks for long-distance telecommunications are increasing due to technical progress in satellite and microwave systems.

In Japan, entrants are classified into different categories according to their activities. Whether the Ministry of Posts and Telecommunications (MPT) will provide a licence to set up a network (Type I telecommunication business) depends on "economic" criteria, such as sufficient demand in the underlying area or the avoidance of overcapacity [Ito, Iwata, 1986]. Furthermore, foreign capital investment is restricted to a maximum of one third. Although, in general, the entry policy seems quite generous, the application of a third satellite enterprise was denied [Müller, 1987, p. 313] and market entry into international telecommunications was hampered by the MPT's intention to restrict the influence of foreign countries. Suppliers of services which rent network capacities from firms of category I either serve the demand of a large number of unspecified users ("Special Type II Telecommunications Business") or small-scale value-added network services ("General Type II Telecommunications Business"). General Type II suppliers are regulated to a very small extent. In contrast, Special Type II suppliers have to be registered by the MPT.

The traditional network carrier NTT originally tried to exclude the resale of leased lines by forbidding access to its public telephone

---

[1] United States versus AT&T, Modification of Final Judgement, District Court for the District of New Jersey, Civil Action, 17-49, 8 January 1982.

network. It soon became obvious that this would restrict the scope of service suppliers' products unnecessarily. Since 1985, the resale of leased lines only for data communication has been granted [Neumann, 1987, p. 150]. The resale of leased lines for voice communication connected with the public telephone network is still restricted. Although NTT still intends continuing with these restrictions a certain instability has occurred due to the increasing tendency to mix voice and data communications services. In addition, new network carriers have been allowed to resell leased lines from NTT to become active in geographical areas where they do not have their own networks. Moreover, the alternative of using the network capacities of NTT's competitors (including the local network capacities of the electricity companies) exists as well as the possibility for large customers to bypass NTT's local networks by using microwave systems or cable TV networks.

In Great Britain, the entry of only one alternative network carrier (Mercury) has been granted. All value-added network services (VANS) using leased lines from British Telecom or Mercury have to be licenced by the Department of Industry. These licences run for a period from 10 to 25 years. British Telecom defines VANS as services by which private firms rent circuits, add either special equipment or transform them such that specific services become possible [Beesley, 1981, para. 10]. It is the purpose of the licencing procedure for VANS that only more advanced services should be supplied through competition, whereas the resale and shared usage of leased lines would remain prohibited. There are obviously large enforcement problems due to difficulties in distinguishing between pure resale and VANS (similar to the problem in the US in distinguishing basic and enhanced services). There are, for example, services which, on the one hand, satisfy typical characteristics of value-added services, and, on the other hand, also include the resale of transmission services. Therefore the registration procedure has been adopted such that shared usage as well as resale for limited user groups has been permitted. Simple resale remains prohibited (at least) until July 1989 [Heuermann, Neumann, 1985, p. 123].

Mercury can compete with British Telecom on all levels of telecommunications, including the local networks. Competition occurs in large towns between British Telecom and Mercury to provide data communication. A further threat to British Telecom's monopoly on the local level may occur through the bypass activities of Mercury's business customers when using the services of cellular radio companies or CATV networks.

The experience of the US, Japan and Great Britain demonstrates that the separation into monopolistic and liberalized submarkets is likely to become unstable over time. As soon as a specific submarket is reserved for a monopoly (for example, the public telephone service) incentives arise for entrants to extend the borderlines of the competitive submarket. Great Britain and Japan could have learned this from the US's deregulation experience. Nevertheless they have tried the strategy of partial entry deregulation, although with different criteria for splitting a market.

b. The Instability of Cross-Subsidizations

In the US, the policy of *partial* entry deregulation was justified by infrastructure objectives and equity considerations. As long as a relevant subpart of telecommunications was monopolized, enough revenue could be earned there to cross-subsidize the supply of unlucrative telecommunication services in rural areas or local telephone services. For example, AT&T's monopoly of public telephone services until 1980 has been justified by the FCC: "entry in the Private Line Market will not require any significant adjustments in the rates charged for local telephone services" [FCC, 1976, p. 162]. In fact, the political aim of the Communications Act from 1934, Section 1 "to make available, so far as possible, to all the people of the United States a rapid, efficient, nationwide, and world-wide wire and radio communication service with adequate facilities a reasonable charges" was still not abandoned.

However, free entry into interstate public telephone services, which started through the unexpected instability of partial deregulation, initiated a trend away from rate-averaging towards cost-oriented tariffs. The cross-subsidy in favour of rural areas decreased because elements of traffic density became important in telecommunication tariffs as a reaction to the price-setting of market entrants.

Furthermore, the cross-subsidizations between interstate public telephone services and local networks became unstable.[1] Traditionally, the interstate public telephone traffic had according to its actual usage of the local networks to contribute to those network access costs not dependent on the actual traffic. The intense (business) users of interstate communications strongly subsidized local networks because they paid much more than the costs of their network access. As a consequence, incentives occurred for entrants to bypass local networks, especially in areas with a high concentration of interstate business customers. In order to avoid such an "uneconomic" bypass, the FCC immediately changed the traditional contribution system such "that a substantial portion of fixed exchange plant costs ... assigned to interstate services should ultimately be recovered through flat per line charges that are assessed upon end users" [FCC, 1983, p. 3]. Since then, local tariffs have been increasing towards cost-oriented network access and usage charges.

In Japan, too, the principle of nationwide universal service at uniform tariffs has a long tradition. NTT's tariffs for long-distance telecommunications are typically independent of traffic-density. Moreover, local networks are heavily subsidized by long-distance traffic [Ozawa, 1984].

The new telecommunications law is pursuing a continuation of these possibilities of cross-subsidization by means of asymmetric regulations between the NTT and its competitors. In contrast to its competitors, the NTT is obliged to provide a nationwide telephone system, and is also responsible for local networks. In exchange, the NTT has been allowed to forbid the resale of its leased lines (partial deregulation). In the last few years, these resale restrictions have become increasingly difficult to enforce. It can be expected that intense market entry on all levels of telecommunications in Japan will soon end the NTT's possibilities of cross-subsidization within its network by rate-averaging.

There is little possibility that cost-independent access charges to the NTT's local networks can avoid the expected increase in local tariffs. On the one hand, the new network carriers owned by electricity companies can rely on their own local networks. For example, the Tokyo

---

[1] The possibility of cross-subsidy between (monopolized) intra-LATA long-distance and local networks still exists.

Power Company can use its local network in the area of Tokyo and serve their regional customers under a bypass of the NTT's local network. Furthermore, some of the new network carriers provide their own local lines to larger customers in particular. Experience in the US demonstrates that bypass technologies exist (e.g. small satellite antenna, shared leased lines), which makes bypassing local monopolies cost-effective even for smaller users, if access-charges are not cost-oriented. Although the access-charge debate is still continuing in Japan, serious doubts exist as to whether entry may be controlled through excessive access-charges and the traditional subsidy of local networks can be continued. Finally, it remains unclear to what extent the infrastructure objectives reflected in the traditional tariff structure of the NTT are still socially or politically desired in the future.

In Great Britain, the principle of a universal nationwide telephone system with uniform tariffs has also played an important role in the past. There has been cross-subsidization between high-density and low-density routes and between long-distance and local networks. The new telecommunications law still assigns to British Telecom some infrastructure obligations which are not lucrative. In contrast to Mercury, British Telecom has to provide the existing pay-telephones and the emergency call system independent of its rentability; some services (e.g. telegrams) have to be continued even when they are not lucrative. Furthermore, British Telecom is obliged to provide a nationwide network.

Although the tariffs of British telecom are regulated with respect to price increases, they are also allowed to vary according to traffic density in order to compete with Mercury. British Telecom's possibilities for cross-subsidization will decrease further when simple resale is allowed in the near future. Although Mercury has to bear the costs of using British Telecom's local networks, this seems not to be an adequate source from which to finance British Telecom's unlucrative service obligations. In the past, Mercury's business strategy has been to provide services mainly for business customers, who usually have easy access to bypass technologies, for example by using cellular mobile telephone or cable TV networks. The quality of British Telecom's local networks is moreover for Mercury's digital services not always sufficient. In order to achieve a cost-effective, high-quality local network access Mercury is currently building a fibre-optics cable network in the city of London on the basis of the old water-pipes from the hydraulic system of Victorian times [Heuermann, Neumann, 1985, p. 133].

4. Implications for the Liberalization of the European Telecommunications Market

Experiences in the US, Japan and Great Britain demonstrate that the large innovation potential of the telecommunications sector can only be rapidly exhausted when market entry is possible not only in the area of terminal equipment and VANS, but also in the area of basic services and networks. Although many entrants may only want to compete in the terminal equipment or VANS markets the possibility of free entry into a basic network infrastructure has the additional advantage of disciplining the incumbent carriers. Only then is it guaranteed that leased lines can be provided at cost-oriented tariffs and a large variety of services can be offered with optimal designed network architectures. Moreover, the necessity of differentiating between basic networks and VANS disappears.

Furthermore, it has become obvious, that the strategy of partial entry deregulations to guarantee unprofitable infrastructure objectives does not provide a stable solution. In spite of the high enforcement and control efforts in the US, Japan and Great Britain the split into monopolized and liberalized subparts became unstable. It is therefore unrealistic to expect that the market-split approach of the current European telecommunications policy (PTT monopoly of public network and telephone services and liberalized VANS and terminal equipment market) would turn out stable in the future. As soon as the Integrated Service Digital Networks (ISDN) are introduced in Europe, the differentiation between voice and data communication will even become more difficult. The recent proposals (e. g. in Germany) to liberalize non-terrestrial networks (e. g. satellites, cellular mobile telephone) will also challenge the monopoly of terrestrial networks, due to the possibilities of substitution between the two.

Since a partial deregulation strategy in Europe cannot be expected to be stable it is not possible to expect that the traditional cross-subsidization will continue of local networks or rural areas, even if this were intended. Entrants would simply concentrate on the lucrative sub-parts and leave the unlucrative subparts to the telecommunications administrations. Already the process of entry deregulation in the US has demonstrate that the cross-subsidization of local networks by long-distance traffic (depending on the actual usage of the local networks) is becoming unstable due to the possibility of bypassing local networks. [1] This is the reason why the infrastructure problems in the US, Japan and Great Britain still remain unsolved.

A more promising approach for the European telecommunications policy seems to be to allow free entry into all subparts (including public networks and telephone service) and to finance the socially desired, but unlucrative infrastructure objectives with alternative methods, instead of cross-subsidizations. A basic prerequisite would be to remove the asymmetric burden of providing unlucrative services from the national PTTs. [2]

All companies, regardless whether public or private, should be able to supply the unlucrative but socially desired services by competing for a subsidy. The competition for subsidies would also reveal how high the infrastructure burden really is and what the minimal costs of traditionally cross-subsidized services are [Blankart, Knieps, 1988, pp. 20 ff.]. For example, in the area of local telephone networks, the PTT's need not necessarily be the most cost-effective suppliers, if new firms with cost-saving technologies like mobile telephone and microwave systems entered the market [Kahn, 1987]. It can be expected that the competition for subsidies will strongly reduce the volume of required subsidies.

From an allocative point of view, the best alternative to financing the required subsidies may be the public budget. Nowadays, however, a strong political resistance may occur to such increases. Therefore a more realistic approach would be the introduction of an entry tax, which all suppliers of lucrative telecommunications activities (PTTs and its com-

---

[1] This should not be confused with the requirement, that long-distance carriers have to pay the costs of using the local networks. Such necessity is stable and does not create incentives for any uneconomic bypass of local networks.

[2] A more detailed version of this can be found in Knieps [1987] and Blankart and Knieps [1988].

petitors) would have to pay, independent of the actual usage of the local networks [Knieps, 1987].

The entry tax should be designed in such a way that entrants and national enterprises would have to make the same contribution to finance the required subsidies. The payment should be measured so that firms which are more efficient or more flexible than the PTT would be able to work profitably even under such burdens. On the other hand, a less efficient firm should not enter this market. The entry tax should therefore be raised in analogy to the value-added tax.[1]

Experience in the US, Japan and Great Britain demonstrates that equity considerations in the form of socially desired infrastructure objectives may strongly influence the course of deregulation processes in the telecommunications sector. Although, finally, those objectives could not be stabilized through cross-subsidizations financed by monopolistic subparts, similar considerations can currently be observed in the rest of Europe. Nevertheless, in order to exhaust the benefits of free entry into European telecommunication sectors rapidly, it is necessary to find an early political consensus as to which unlucrative infrastructure functions (if at all) should be provided in the future and how they should be financed without having to restrict entry into telecommunications. It seems to be important for the European telecommunications policy to learn from foreign experience, but not to imitate their errors.[2]

Bibliography

BEESLY, Michael E., Liberalization of the Use of British Telecommunications Network. London 1981.

BLANKART, Charles B., Günter KNIEPS, Grenzen der Deregulierung im Telekommunikationsbereich? Die Frage des Netzwettbewerbs. Vortrag vor dem wirtschaftspolitischen Ausschuß des Vereins für Sozialpolitik in Münster, 23 March 1988.

---

[1] Of course, from an efficiency point of view, cost-based tariffs in all subparts of a telecommunications system would be desirable.

[2] Another, rather cynical, approach would be to consider the current proposals of the European Commission's Green Paper as a necessary step of an unavoidable dynamic adjustment process. Why should European policy makers be more capable to avoid the strategy of partial deregulation than their colleagues in the US and Japan?

COMMISSION OF THE EUROPEAN COMMUNITIES, Green Paper on the Development of the Common Market for Telecommunications Services and Equipment. Brussels 1987.

FEDERAL COMMUNICATION COMMISSION (FCC), Report 20640. Washington 1976.

--, First Report. Docket 20003. Washington 1976.

--, Second Computer Inquiry, Rules and Regulations. Docket 20828, Final Decision. Washington 1980.

--, In the Matter of MTS and WATS, Docket 78-72, Phase III. Washington 31 May 1983.

--, Third Computer Inquiry, Report and Order. Docket 85-229, Phase II. Washington 1986.

FOREMAN-PECK, James, Jürgen MÜLLER (Eds.), European Telecommunications Organisation. Baden-Baden 1988.

von HAYEK, Friedrich A., Der Wettbewerb als Entdeckungsverfahren. Kieler Vorträge, N.F., 56, Tübingen 1968.

HEUERMANN, Arnulf, Karl-Heinz NEUMANN, Die Liberalisierung des britischen Telekommunikationsmarktes. Berlin 1985.

ITO, Youichi, Atsushi IWATA, Deregulation and the Change of Telecommunications Market in Japan. Paper presentend at the Malente Symposium, Max Plank Institute, Hamburg, 2-6 March 1986.

KAHN, Alfred E., The Future of Local Telephone Service: Technology and Public Policy. Fishman-Davidson Center, Discussion Papers, 22, Wharton, April 1987.

KNIEPS, Günter, "Is Technological Revolution a Sufficient Reason for Changing Regulations? - The Case of Telecommunications". Zeitschrift für die gesamten Staatswissenschaften, Vol. 139, 1983, pp. 578-597.

--, Entstaatlichung im Telekommunikationsbereich. Eine theoretische und empirische Analyse der technologischen, ökonomischen und institutionellen Einflußfaktoren. Tübingen 1985.

--, "Zur Problematik der internen Subventionierung in öffentlichen Unternehmen". Finanzarchiv, N.F., Vol. 45, 1987, pp. 268-283.

MÜLLER, Jürgen, Competition in the British Telecommunications Market: The Impact of Recent Privatization Deregulation Decisions. Paper presented at the Malente Symposium, Max Plank Institute, Hamburg, 2-6 March 1986.

--, "Liberalisierung des japanischen Fernmeldewesens: Ein mögliches Modell für die Bundesrepublik?" Deutsches Institut für Wirtschaftsforschung (DIW), Wochenbericht, Vol. 54, 1987, No. 23, pp. 312-317.

NEUMANN, Karl-Heinz, Die Neuorganisation der Telekommunikation in Japan. Berlin 1987.

ORGANIZATION FOR ECONOMIC COOPERATION AND DEVELOPMENT (OECD) (Ed.), Trends of Change in Telecommunications Policy. Amsterdam 1987.

OZAWA, Tikira, The Study on Access Charges, Paper presented at the 6th International Congress IDATA: The New Communications Business. Montpellier, 24-26 October 1984.

SCHULTE-BRAUCKS, Reinhard, "Das 'British Telecom'-Urteil: Eckstein für ein europäisches Fernmelderecht?". Wirtschaft und Wettbewerb, Vol. 3, 1986, pp. 202-215.

von WEIZSÄCKER, Carl C., "Free Entry into Telecommunications?" In: Herbert GIERSCH (Ed.), New Opportunities for Entrepreneurship. Symposium 1983. Tübingen 1984, pp. 107-128.

--, The Economics of Value Added Network Services. Cologne 1987.

WIELAND, Bernhard, Die Entflechtung des amerikanischen Fernmelde-monopols. Berlin 1985.

WITTE, Eberhard (Ed.), Neuordnung der Telekommunikation. Bericht der Regierungskommission Fernmeldewesen. Heidelberg 1987.

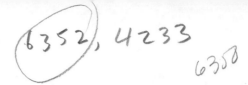

Comments on Günter Knieps, "Telecommunications Policy - Assessing Recent Experience in the US, Japan and Europe and Its Implications for the Completion of the Internal Common Market"

Tyll Necker   190 - 97

The German Government Commission for restructuring our telecommunications system consisted of 12 people of whom I was one. I voted for the recommendations provided but filed with three other members a minority report. Let me quote our key-message from this minority report: "The authors of this minority report agree with most of the proposals for reform made in the report of the Commission. They are however convinced that some important recommendations do not go far enough and thus do not promote the rapid creation of a general setting permitting the optimum and future-oriented development of telecommunications as a key sector of the economy. If the networks and the telephone service remain a public monopoly, as has been proposed by the Commission, 90 per cent of the telecommunications sector - in terms of the Deutsche Bundespost's proceeds - will continue to be protected from competition. This would have far-reaching repercussions on the entire telecommunications sectors and on the competitiveness of the Federal Republic of Germany as an industrial location".

Without competition also on the network-level, the outcome of the restructuring will be limited. Our position in favour of competition in all sectors of telecommunications, including the network, is mainly based on the positive results which we think will come from competition in all sectors of telecommunications:

- Prices and services rendered would be determined demand and competition.
- Customers would be able to choose from different suppliers and sources.
- Innovations and investments would be considerably stimulated and preferably made in those fields where they proved to be profitable for the economy as a whole.

- Political influence would be largely limited to sovereign functions and to supervising competition.
- Cost in the telecommunications sector would tend to be minimized.

This concept of competition has been chosen by the United States, Japan and the United Kingdom, whose share in the telecommunications' market amounts to over 50 per cent of the world market. These countries are making definite progress with regard to innovations, investments and cost effectiveness.

In defence of the state monopoly with regard to the network, we were confronted especially with the postworkers' unions, politicians, and part of the telecommunications industry.

The Postworkers' Unions

They want to protect their members against competitive pressure and lay-offs. A special resistance to the curtailing of subsidies from telecommunications to the "Yellow Post" (post office) was obvious. They further claim to be protecting the interest of the customers.

The influence of the Unions in the Deutsche Bundespost is strong since they are highly organized.

Politicians

They argue in favour of the state monopoly to guarantee high surpluses which could be used for the development of the infrastructure but also to subsidise other political goals and tasks.

They are also interested in protecting the government's opportunities to influence the development of communication requirements in the private and business sectors.

A special argument was to grant everybody access to telecommunications on equal terms, including those living in remote areas.

Part of the Telecommunications Industry

Some of the major "Amtsbaufirmen" feel worried that their close relations to the Deutsche Bundespost could deteriorate and that the security of planning and orders might diminish. Some smaller and medium-sized companies without a sales organization are extremely afraid of losing their only customer.

All three groups claimed that without a monopoly and its profits, financial support for the development of the infrastructure would be lacking.

There was no discussion on the privatisation of German telecommunications because this would not have been in line with the German Constitution and the mandate of the Commission. The German Minister of Finance was and is a strong defender of the present system which favours his revenues and traditional rules for civil servants.

In order to summarize, let me say that economic arguments conflicted with political and emotional standpoints, and that the outcome of the restructuring of the telecommunications system in Germany will be somewhat a diluted compromise of the proposals made by our Commission, a step in the right direction, but a small one.

Herbert Ungerer

I would like to concentrate in my comments on the conclusions drawn by Knieps from an analysis of Telecommunications Policy in the US, Japan and Europe, concerning the future options for telecommunications policy in the European Community.

A few preceding remarks on current policy seem necessary concerning the overall context and major thrust of current European Community telecommunications policy, and the boundary conditions to be kept in mind. The policy proposed in the Green Paper on the common market for telecommunications services and equipment cited by Knieps, which has developed over recent months into a kind of broad discussion platform for the developing of telecommunications reforms in Europe, concentrates on one major goal: achieving a Europe-wide market by 1992. It is in this overall context that telecommunications policy gains its crucial importance for the Commission of the European Communities:

- the establishment of a common European market for services is a major component of the overall 1992 objective for the implementation of a common market for services: financial services, insurance, the capital market, transport *and* telecommunications, given the growing role of services in the economy - the overall topic of this conference;
- services are, for the same reason, becoming one of the central topics in the global negotiations on world trade now under way in the GATT negotiations - the Uruguay Round.

Telecommunications in volume terms is still a minor part of the total service sector, even if steeply rising in absolute terms. World-wide, the annual turn-over in telecommunications is now reaching 400 billion ECUs (roughly US$ 400 billion), out of which roughly 300 billion is in tele-communications services. In the European Community, the total market corresponds to 80 billion ECUs, out of which 60 billion are for services. But beyond the sheer volume, telecommunications services are essential in general for the tradability of services.

It is these basic facts which determine the main thrust of the European policy option for the sector. Given its importance, the European Community must take a political approach which takes account of *market realities* and economic *and* social considerations. It is in this light that I would like to comment on Knieps' conclusions for the liber-alisation of the European telecommunications market. The paper briefly summarises the EC Green Paper on telecommunications which set out to address the regulatory questions in the sector for the European Com-munity in a global way.

In the Green Paper, the European Commission has basically chosen a two-pronged approach:

- on the basis of the EC Treaty, it strongly urges the liberalisation of everything which is clearly tradable in the sector - telecommunications equipment and value-added services;
- it accepts, at the current stage of technological development, main-tenance of monopoly rights on items which are essentially not tradable - the network infrastructure. It also accepts the continuation of monopoly for the services closely connected to the network and in-

dispensable for national emergency situations - voice telephony for the general public.

As far as satellite services, which are considered as having both infrastructure and service function, are concerned, the Green Paper calls for competition, insofar as there is no interference with the operation of the basic network infrastructure.

It should be noted that the EC Commission accepts the continuation of monopoly. It leaves the actual decision on monopoly or competition in the network area to the member states. This approach corresponds, according to the Green Paper, to the limits set for the Commission by the Treaty of Rome. These positions are supposed to be reviewed periodically with regard to the impact of technological change. For the liberalisation of European telecommunications, the Commission focuses with this strategy on those areas which are essential for the future functioning of Europe's international service economy. Is is only in this context that telecommunications liberalisation aquires any macro-economic importance.

Let me comment from this angle to some of the points raised in Knieps' paper. The paper makes a strong point concerning the instability of partial entry deregulation or, in more general terms, partial liberalisation of the telecommunications sector. I would be inclined to consider what is called "instability" in the paper as a necessary "adjustment process", which unavoidably must stretch over a certain period of time. I believe that, for real economic systems, we should accept the notion of regulation as a framework for a dynamic process which allows economic and social forces to evolve.

The paper sets out in a very clear way the basic *economic* issues involved. It does, however, not always go into the same level of detail with regard to the market realities of the situations reviewed. I believe that, with regard to the issue of network competition which is at the centre of the arguments in the paper, solutions cannot be defined in the abstract but must be defined in the concrete market setting.

I may recall some of these market realities which play a substantial role in the discussion in European countries concerning the issue of free entry into the network area - network competition. As is well known, operation of the bulk telecommunications network infrastructure is highly capital-intensive. The total sunk in investments in Europe's public telecommunications network infrastructure is near 200 billion ECUs. Given

the enormous value of this asset (at replacement value likely to be substantially larger if inherent externalities such as environmental effects
are included), I believe the duplication argument, which plays a major
role in European discussions, is dismissed somewhat lightheartedly.

In fact, in all the countries reviewed in the paper, these features
have led to oligopolistic structures where open entry has been allowed
into the bulk network infrastructure. Up to now- apparently because of
high duplication costs - in no country has the general local network
distribution structure (in the European Community 120 million con-
nections) been duplicated by the new entrants - not in the United
States, nor in Japan, nor in the United Kingdom, even when so allowed
by regulation. As a consequence, in all countries concerned, the access
arrangements to the local network infrastructure have become a crucial
issue. Effectively, network competition is largely determined by the
complex regulation of the access arrangements. Unfortunately, the paper
does not discuss this major aspect of the current regulation process in
these countries.

In the United States, AT&T pays more than 50 per cent of its costs
in the form of access charges to the Bell Operating Companies, under
strict regulation by the US Federal Communications Commission, to obtain
access to, and to compensate distribution of its services via the local
network infrastructure. Regulation has remained (and even increased) in
all countries reviewed in order to manage access arrangements and to
maintain network competition.

While the paper makes a number of arguments concerning the role
of network competition in accelerating cost adjustment and innovation -
even if regulation has remained an important element in price-setting
processes in all countries cited and the network infrastructure is as advanced in a number of countries where network infrastructure has continued to be operated under monopoly given the pressure for lowering
costs also at work in these countries - I would have liked to see an in-
depth discussion of another argument which is often advanced in
European countries concerning competition in the network - enhanced
transaction costs resulting from a multiplication of networks. Clearly,
there is a trade-off between the dynamism created by free entry competition and the increase in transaction costs caused by duplication in
this area. Impact on transaction costs could be particularly high in

Europe given its inherited different national network structures - very different from the US environment, which is still largely chracterised by the homogenous AT&T technology.

Finally, I believe, more discussion is needed concerning the specificity of the national situations of the countries reviewed in order to come to final conclusions:

- the deregulation process in the United States must be seen against the size of a continental market which corresponds to more than 35 per cent of the world market. Deregulation in a market, where total turn-over in telecommunications services alone is US$ 120 billion and is shared basically between ten major actors: the seven Regional Holding Companies, AT&T, GTE, and MCI and must be compared with caution with deregulation in Europe, where total turnover in telecommunications services varies between 90 million (Luxembourg) to 1.5 billion (Belgium) for the smaller countries and 9.3 billion (Italy) to 16.5 billion (Federal Republic of Germany) for the larger countries;

- current entry in Japan of additional network providers must be seen against the specific geography of the country and the concentration of the population on the Tokyo/Osaka line which facilitates low cost entry of additional carriers. All these additional terrestrial carriers are in fact concentrated in this area;

- with Cable and Wireless the United Kingdom had traditionally a second carrier active in Hongkong and the Carribean area and the available experience has without doubt facilitated the return of Cable and Wireless, as the owner of Mercury to its home country.

Summarising, the regulatory discussion in Europe seems to emphasise as the main issue in Europe the emergence, out of the telephone network, of the multi-purpose digital network. The major regulatory issue in Europe will be that of open entry to this emerging network infrastructure, and not so much the issue of additional network providers - though satellite communications will be an important European issue, as suggested in the Green Paper. Competition in the basic terrestrial network infrastructure must be looked at taking account in the specific national situations and is unlikely to be resolved definitely in abstract terms. The discussions in Europe (as expressed also in the EC Green Paper) concentrate on the liberalisation of the use of the network. An approach for the liberalisation of the European Telecommunications market should not be built on the assumption of perfectly functioning markets which do not correspond to the market reality nor to the economic and social environment. Liberalisation should concentrate, with priority, on those areas where, according to general perception, possible economic gains are highest and possible economic and social losses are lowest.

In the transformation of our economies towards a service-based world economy, efforts should therefore be concentrated on liberalising the provision of services via the telecommunications network, instead of engaging in a prolonged theoretical debate on the opening of the network infrastructure which, at this stage of the technological development, cannot have a conclusive outcome at the European level because the different national market factors can lead to a different outcome of the national discussions.

The EC Green Paper focuses on telecommunications in the broader context of the future role of services in the economy. It tries to avoid a sterile debate on free entry into the network area, where a European consensus is not possible at this stage. Instead, it aims at a procedural approach, with the necessary minimum of regulatory controls and built-in check points, essentially provided by EC competition law and regulation to enforce open network access and fair technical usage and tariff conditions.

Robert Z. Aliber*

3120

4320

Protection and the Structure of the Banking Industry in an International Context

1. Introduction $198 - 218$

The international banking industry is characterized by several stylized facts. The first stylized fact is that the industrial structure of banking differs sharply among the major countries. In most industrial countries five or six banks account for 90 percent of total bank deposits. In contrast, in the United States, the ten largest banks account for less than 50 percent of total bank deposits – and there are 15,000 banks, more than in all other countries combined. A second stylized fact is that the banks are extensively regulated compared with firms in most other industries; banks are subject to constraints on the mix of assets and on their maximum loan to any one borrower. Banks must hold reserves at the central bank, their deposits are subject to interest rate ceilings, and their deposits are limited as a multiple of their capital. Entry into new markets is constrained and requires approval. Similarly, the types of products or services they can sell is limited. Moreover, bank regulation differs by country. A third stylized fact is that the returns earned by firms in the banking industry do not seem inconsistent with the competitive model, perhaps because there are few if any monopoly elements in banking. The profits of banks headquartered in countries characterized by a small number of firms in the industry do not appear higher than the profits of banks in countries with more banks. Nothing a bank produces is patentable – indeed, the products of individual banks within a country are nearly perfect substitutes for each other, and hence "commodities". The fourth stylized fact is that a very large number of firms in the industry have brand-name recognition – Citibank, Bank of America, Chase, Morgan Guaranty, Deutsche Bank, Société Générale, Banque Nationale de Paris, Barclays, Bank of Tokyo,

---

* Joe Vencil has been of special assistance in developing data on the costs of capital to banks.

National Westminster, Bank of Montreal, Dai-Ichi Kangyo, Fuji - an average businessman might be able to recall the names of 25 to 50 banks headquartered in one of ten or twelve countries. That there are so many well-known firms in a "commodity business" is a paradox - typically commodity businesses are characterized by small anonymous firms. The fifth stylized fact is that the relationships among firms in the banking industry are complex - banks compete with each other for deposits and for loans, they participate jointly in loan syndications and in service bureau activities. Moreover, banks borrow from and lend to each other in extensive interbank transactions, which appear to have no good counterpart in any other industry (except perhaps petroleum). The sixth stylized fact is that international trade in banking is modest; most residents of most countries purchase their bank deposits from a banking office located in their neighborhood, and virtually all of these banking offices are branches of banks headquartered within that country.[1] Indeed, international trade in banking is significantly less extensive than international trade in most consumer goods and many service industries, such as airline travel, shipping, and movie rentals. The seventh stylized fact is wholesale banking, which involves the extension of credit or purchase of loans from business firms. Wholesale banking is much more international than retail banking. The eighth stylized fact is that the share of foreign banks in the several domestic markets appears to be negatively related to concentration in these markets; the larger the share of foreign banks in the several national markets, the smaller the concentration.

That consumers in most countries buy their banking services from offices (e.g. plants) in their neighborhood, just as they buy their groceries and their gasoline in their neighborhood, suggests that

---

[1] International banking is a broad term that comprehends three or four distinct activities. The largest is offshore banking - banks sell deposits and make loans in a currency other than that of the country in which the banking office is located. Export banking involves the extension of credit to customers based in countries other than those of the country in which the bank is located; export banking and whole-sale banking are somewhat overlapping sets. Foreign banking involves sale of deposits in a domestic currency by banks headquartered in a foreign country; the sale of British pound deposits in London by US banks, Swiss banks, and German banks. This is an example of foreign banking.

proximity is important in the relationship between the buyers of bank deposits and the banks that produce these deposits. Bank customers are involved in many transactions in a year. Distance is a form of trans-actions costs and explains why the buyers of the various products or services from banks transact with a nearby office; the greater the distance from the customer to the banking office, the higher these costs - especially when deposits and currency are exchanged. Economic intui-tion suggests that banks establish plants which are close to their customers as a way to minimize the costs of economic distance - the customers of banks are reluctant to deal with banking offices that are located at some distance. [1] Proximity does not explain why the banking offices in each country are almost always owned by a domestic firm.

The number of firms and the number of plants in the banking industry reflect both economic factors and regulatory factors. The economic factors that affect the size and structure of the industry include economies of scale in production, economies of scale in market-ing, synergies among various types of bank products on both the de-mand and the supply sides, and capital market advantages of firms headquartered in countries with low costs of capital. The regulatory factors that affect the structure of the industry include limitations both on entry and on takeovers, and a large number of portfolio mix require-ments and interest rate ceilings. One question is whether these portfolio regulations have a major impact on the size and structure of the in-dustry, and the national identity of the firms that produce banking services in various countries.

Contemplate the structure of the banking industry in a unified world - in a world with one uniform set of national banking regulations and one national currency. The number of firms in the industry would be smaller than now; some of marginal banks, especially in the smaller countries would have merged either with each other or with smaller banks headquartered in other countries. The number of plants in the industry would be smaller. Each firm would have more plants; the de-

---

[1] Changes in technology - the rapid expansion of automatic teller ma-chines (ATMs) - will reduce the significance of the proximity argu-ment. The ATMs will be owned by a service bureau, and will be used by the customers of many different banks. As a result, proximity to a plant will become less significant in the choice of the bank.

cline in the number of firms would be larger in percentage terms than the decline in the number of plants. The spatial distribution of plants would differ. Most consumers, especially those in smaller industrial countries, would have access to a larger number of plants within a given market area; however, a few consumers would have access to fewer plants, because cross-subsidization from large city-plants to small city-plants would be less extensive, a result of the more competitive structure of the industry. Competition in the larger "national" markets would be more extensive, and firms not previously extensively involved in these markets would enter them as a way to increase size; obtaining any particular volume of activity is easier in a large market than in a small one. The costs of some banks would be lower; a larger number of banks would have achieved scale economies. Moreover, in most national markets competition among banks would be more extensive. However, moves to a uniform type of regulation could lead to higher or to lower costs, depending on whether the new regulations are more or less restrictive than the current regulations.

The structure of the banking industry might differ from the structure contemplated in a unified world because of regulation. Or, alternatively, the differences might reflect the way the industry has developed in individual countries. The basic question of this paper is whether protection explains why most of the banking offices in each country are owned by domestic firms.[1] The structure of the banking industry might reflect that the banks fail to expand their plants in various foreign countries because there is no financial incentive to do so. The lack of financial incentive might reflect that costs of banks are similar, and that few if any banks have a cost advantage that would enable them to compensate for the costs of economic distance. Formal or informal barriers limiting the entry of foreign banks into national markets would be redundant; even in the absence of these barriers, banks would not expand

---

[1] The proximity argument suggests that, with the existing payments technology, most customers will buy their banking services and products from nearby banking offices. As a result, the thrust of this paper is with "the right of establishment" of foreign firms rather than with the ability of residents of individual countries to buy services and products from banking offices located in other countries. A study of the regulations that limit the purchase of products of banks located in other countries would involve a compilation of exchange controls along the lines of the *Exchange Restrictions Yearbook*.

abroad. Banks headquartered in one country are likely to expand abroad
only if they have an economic advantage relative to their host-country
competitors; this is the necessary condition. But these banks will expand
abroad only if entry into the foreign market is not restricted or constrained; nonrestricted entry is the sufficient condition.

Economic factors set the preconditions for the ability of banks
headquartered in one country to expand into other countries; whether
the firms expand into the foreign market depends on whether the economic incentives are constrained or frustrated by regulation. One of the
major concerns is whether the industry structure in particular countries
is now stabilized - whether the economies of scale have been so fully
realized that new entrants into individual national markets are forestalled
either because the initial cost disadvantage is so large, or because the
probability of achieving scale economies comparable to those of domestic
banks is low.

The second section of this paper reviews the structure of the
banking industry, and especially the impact of regulation on domestic
and international structure. The third section evaluates several theories
of international banking, and seeks to establish the implication of each
theory for the structure of the industry. The fourth section examines
some financial data in an effort to predict or forecast how the international bank structure will evolve. The fifth section summarizes the data
on protection in international banking. The concluding sections discuss
the implication of protection in banking, and the impacts of financial
liberalization on the structure of the banking industry.

2. The Structure of Banking and Financial Services

The typical textbook suggests a hierarchical structure of banking
and the financial services industry in each country. Each type of institution is ranked within this structure by the moneyness of its liabilities.
The central bank is at the apex of the structure; it produces high-
powered money from the view point of the monetary analyst and a risk-
free asset from the view point of individual investors - or, at least, an
asset which is free of default risk. Commercial banks are at the next
rank in this hierarchy, and produce demand deposits, which are trans-

ferred as part of the money payments process; the investor is concerned (modestly) with the default sensitivity of the liabilities of each bank and with any differential in default sensitivity. Nonbank financial intermediaries produce near-monies, which have the liquidity of money but are not directly transferable as means of payment.

The ability of a bank to expand its size to acquire more assets is determined by its skill in marketing its liabilities; in this sense, banks sell deposits and buy money, or more precisely, they buy high-powered money in the form of currency and deposits at the central bank. In effect, banks exchange their own, newly-produced deposit liabilities for high-powered money. Banks pay interest on their liabilities as a way to induce investors to buy these liabilities - in effect they seek to obtain high-powered money so they can buy more income-earning assets.[1] (For many banks, buying more assets and selling more liabilities occur almost simultaneously.) Once an individual bank has acquired high-powered money in excess of its required reserves, the bank can then acquire additional assets. By limiting the supply of high-powered money, the central bank limits the size of the banking system for a given supply of high-powered money (although the size of the system depends on investor demand for different types of deposits).

A bank can increase its share of the total market for bank deposits by increasing its marketing expenditures - by selling its liabilities at a lower price (e.g. paying a higher interest rate on its deposit liabilities), by improving the perceived quality of its product (e.g., the safety of its deposits), by enhancing the convenience and reducing the costs of using its deposit liabilities in payments, and by atmospheric advertising. Just as a drug company seeks to optimize its marketing expenditures by choosing between nonprice advertising and various price-cutting promotions, so a bank seeks to optimize its marketing expenditures between reliance on price and on nonprice promotions - the key question is whether, for a given cost, an increase in the interest rate paid on deposits or an increase in marketing expenditures has a larger impact in

---

[1] The terminology in this paragraph is unconventional. Thus the unique product of a bank - one that carries the bank's own brand-name - is its liabilities. Each bank produces or sells deposits, just as drug companies produce aspirins, vitamins, and Valium. All of the bank's assets are identified with someone else's brandname.

increasing the volume of deposits. The ability of a bank to increase its marketing expenditures depends on its success both as a investor, which comprises several arguments - its ability to acquire an portfolio of assets whose total return is high relative to their risk, its ability to cope with transformation risk (e.g., managing the yield curve) and hence in integrating its liability management activities with its asset management activities, and its ability in managing the institution at a low cost.

The liability management activities of a bank are conceptually distinct from the asset management activities. The liability management activities primarily involve marketing and promotion; the bank's "brandname" is important, especially to large depositors. In contrast, the asset management activity primarily involves risk appraisal - although marketing credit is important to the extent that nonprice credit rationing is important. The liability management and the asset management activities are linked in several ways: the transformation risk question about the shape of the yield curve and changes in the yield curve is relevant; since the maturity of assets is longer than the maturity of liabilities, an unanticipated increase in interest rates may lead to a more rapid increase in interest rates on deposits than on loans. The two sides of the bank's balance sheet can be viewed as being aspects of a vertically-integrated form, with the sale of deposits the upstream activity and the purchase of loans the downsteam activity. And, while many customers are both buyers of deposits and sellers of loans, households are primarily depositors, and business firms are the primary borrowers. Price competition in the wholesale market is likely to be much more extensive than on the liability side. [1] Hence, the deposit business is more of a retail business.

Residents of each country can choose among a very large number of monies and near-monies; the choice involves at least four dimensions. One dimension involves the liquidity or moneyness of the assets they

---

[1] One implication is that the return or profit rate on capital committed to the wholesale credit activity might be lower than the return on the less competitive national activity of selling deposits. The dilemma may be more apparent than real; theory suggests that the firm might reallocate resources from the less profitable activity to the more profitable activity as a way to enhance total return. The complication is that, if the deposit market is oligopolistic, then any firm which increases its investment in this activity may induce a response from other firms, so that total returns will decline.

might acquire, a second involves the default sensitivity of the firm that produces these assets, the third involves the currency of denomination of these assets, and the fourth involves the venue of issue of these assets. A particular type of risk is identified with each of these dimensions; in some cases, the risk is institution-specific and in other cases, investor-specific. For example, the currency denomination risk is investor risk. Each of these differences affects the risk attached to particular assets, and some of these differences affect the cost of producing these liabilities. Investors choose among the wide array of assets on the basis of currency preferences, the return on the liabilities offered by particular institutions, the default-sensitivity risk associated with liabilities of different institutions, and where they wish to hold their funds. Despite the range of choice, residents of most countries buy assets denominated in their domestic currency produced in a domestic center; in some cases, investors buy assets produced in an offshore center.

The received wisdom is that the economies of scale in banking are modest, and achieved at a reasonably small sized institution; small banks coexist with large banks. The idea of scale economies are associated with production, and with efficient utilization of an indivisible unit of capital equipment or an indivisible factor. However, the economies of scale in marketing may only be achieved at a substantially larger scale; indeed, unit costs may continue to decline for very large increases in marketing expenditures.

Banks are extensively involved with other banks, both in management activities and in a variety of credit activities. Banks participate with other banks in ownership of service bureaus, which provide a large number of them with a service or product; one is the ownership of ATMs and others are the ownership of a clearing house and the provision of research. Thus, many banks participate in loans as part of a syndicate; loan syndicates are a low-cost way for banks to reduce both the costs of diversification and the cost of negotiating loans. Banks hold deposits in other banks to facilitate the settlement of imbalances. And banks provide credit to other banks in the interbank market; these interbank transactions may reflect that individual banks differ in the location of their offices, or in their capital and perceived strength to depositors, or in the relative strength of their marketing skills and their investment

skills. Perhaps the single most important factor in explaining the per-
sistent pattern of interbank transactions is that banks differ in their
ability to sell deposits, because their credit standing differs. Thus,
banks with the highest credit standing sell deposits at the lowest interest rates, and, in turn, lend funds to banks that are considered
somewhat riskier. These banks borrow - on the margin - from the banks
with the superior credit standing rather than from the public, as a way
to reduce their own interest costs. In turn, the banks with the superior
credit rankings lend to other banks because the returns are high relative to the risks. One implication from the pattern of interbank transactions is that the banks most likely to establish plants abroad will be
those with the strongest ability to sell deposits.

Banks are affected by a large number of portfolio regulations,
including reserve requirements, capital deposit regulations, interest rate
ceilings, loan limits, and portfolio mix requirements. To the extent that
these regulations, like reserve requirements and portfolio mix requirements, limit the income of banks, the size of the banking industry is
smaller than it would otherwise be; similarly, the higher the capital
deposit requirements, the lower the profitability of banks, and the
smaller the size of banking industry. To the extent that these regulations limit (price) competition among banks, the size of the average bank
is smaller, and there are more firms in the industry.

Domestic portfolio regulations may handicap the ability of a bank
based in one country to expand its plants in other countries, and especially its ability to establish plants to sell deposits. The source-country
bank will need a share sufficiently large so that scale economies can be
obtained, especially in marketing. And this type of argument may be
especially important for entry into those national markets characterized
by a small number of banks. And in many countries, the bank may find
it necessary to establish a significant number of plants to get these
economies. [1] Portfolio regulations may limit the ability of the source-
country firm to exploit its advantage by cutting price.

---

[1] The problem of entry into a foreign market is affected by whether the
media markets within a country are national or regional. The more
national these markets, the more powerful the economies of scale
argument in deterring the entry of foreign firms.

The demarcation of the world into multiple currency areas also may affect the structure of the industry. Thus, exchange controls or exchange rate policy may have the indirect consequence of protecting domestic producers. And domestic banks may have a marketing advantage in the sale of their liabilities because they have preferred access to their central bank for liquidity.

3. The Theory of International Banking

The theory of international banking seeks to explain the ownership structure in the banking industry – and why banks headquartered in one country establish offices in other countries. Most of the approaches to the theory of international banking are extensions of the theory of direct foreign investment [Aliber, 1984]. Two approaches to the theory of international banking can be identified. One approach, sometimes called the gravitational pull approach, is that banks establish foreign offices to follow the movement of domestic firms into foreign countries. One motive is that the banks want to reduce the likelihood that the foreign banks will begin to gain a share of the foreign business of these firms, which might be the "thin entering wedge" in a new business relationship; another motive is that they have a valuable set of information on their clients and can satisfy the needs of these clients at a lower cost than the host-country banks can.

The second approach toward the theory of international banking is that banks will expand abroad when they have a capital market advantage relative to their host-country competitors. There are two aspects of this advantage: one is why this advantage exists; and the second involves the implications of this advantage for the structure of the industry. The advantage reflects that national capital markets are partially segmented. As a result, the costs of capital of firms and of banks headquartered in various countries differ. This advantage means that source-country banks will pay a higher price than host-country banks will for a particular host-country income stream, because the source-country firms place a higher value on this income stream than host-country banks. Hence, the factors which make it possible for source-country firms to pay a higher price for host-country income streams also explain why source-country banks expand abroad. This capital market view relies on perfect market assumptions, in that source-country firms compete with most-country firms on comparable terms in both product markets and in factor markets, with the exception that source-country firms have a cost-of-capital advantage. The implication of the perfect market assumption is that source-country firms expand abroad only because they have an advantage which compensates for their unique costs of economic distance. This advantage is an equity market advantage.

The gravitational pull approach focuses on the asset side of the bank's balance sheet; banks that wish to make loans to their clients who are investing abroad can source the funds necessary for these loans in the interbank market or they can establish offices to sell deposits.[1] In contrast, the capital market advantage centers on the liability side of the bank's balance sheet; other things being equal, the capital market advantage means that the source-country bank will be able to pay a higher interest rate on deposits than the host-country bank.

The implication of the capital market view is that the necessary condition for entry of a bank into the foreign market with the establishment of offices to sell deposits is that the cost of capital of the source-country bank is below the costs of capital for host-country banks, and by more than enough to compensate for the costs of economic distance. Moreover, because banking is so highly leveraged, this cost-of-capital advantage must be substantial, since high leverage means that the capital has a modest weight in the total supply of funds to banks. Nevertheless, a cost of capital advantage of two to three percentage points could translate into a nontrivial difference in an average weighted cost of funds.[2]

---

[1] The stylized fact is that a large part of international banking loans are funded in the interbank market. Most of the foreign banks in London do not have a significant volume of British pound deposits; similarly most of the foreign banks in New York do not have a significant volume of US dollar deposits.

[2] Consider the combination of the impacts of a capital-deposit ratio of ten percent and a cost of capital advantage of three percentage points. If the deposit interest rate averages five percent, then the source-country banks might be able to pay an interest rate 30 basis points higher than the host-country banks. These examples are sensitive to

4. The Investor Evaluation of Banks

One financial aspect of the theory of the firm is that firms expand when their cost of capital is below the anticipated profitability on a potential new investment. This capital-budgeting proposition has several implications - one is that the firm within an industry that is most likely to expand is the one with the lowest cost of capital. The rationale for this implication is that firms compete in many of the same factor markets, and a firm which has a cost-of-capital advantage is favorably positioned relative to its competitors. Another implication is that firms are agents of their shareholders, and the signals about whether a firm should expand are given to the firm's managers by investors.

The cost-of-capital argument for the banking industry is that the lower the cost of capital to an individual bank, the more rapid the rate at which this bank will expand. This cost-of-capital argument is linked to the credit reputation of the bank; in the absence of regulation, each bank would choose the ratio of capital to total deposits that would minimize the total cash outflows associated with maintenance of a particular level of loans. The more attractive a bank's liabilities are to depositors, the lower the interest rate that the bank will pay on these liabilities, and the greater the profitability. Thus, some banks trade on their name, and act to protect the value of their name. [1]

One unique aspect of banking is that the industry is highly leveraged, more so than almost any other industry; leverage is measured by the reciprocal of the ratio of capital to deposits. However, a higher level of capital deposit ratio may lead to higher total costs. Those banks with the higher *levels* of capital/deposit ratios may be able to sell their deposits at a lower interest rate, since the "buffer" between the losses a bank might incur and the losses to a depositor is larger, the higher the level of the capital/deposit ratio; hence, the risk to the holder of deposits is lower. Those banks with a *lower cost* of capital will be able to increase their market share because they will be able to pay a higher

---

the spread between the deposit interest rate in the host country and the cost of capital to host-country banks.

[1] These banks also use their name advantage to sell "lines-of-credit" - a source of fee income which does not affect reserves or their interest payments.

interest rate on their deposits, or to increase their expenditures associated with the marketing of deposits. A major difference among banks headquartered in various countries is their cost of capital, which is country-specific. Moreover, within individual countries, there may be industry-specific costs of capital, which could reflect differences in anticipated growth rates of particular industries or differences in the variability of their earnings.

Banks headquartered in countries identified with low costs of capital are in an advantageous position to enter the domestic markets of banks headquartered identified with a high cost of capital. The first group of banks have a competitive advantage not shared by the second group of banks. The differences among banks headquartered in the various countries in their cost of capital may be country-specific - thus, the relationship among the costs of capital for firms headquartered in different countries might differ systematically by country.

One approach to comparing the cost of capital to banks headquartered in various countries is to compare their price/earnings ratio - the lower this ratio, the lower the cost of capital. An alternative approach is to compare the dividend yields; this alternative is less compelling because dividend/payout ratios may differ across countries.

Estimates of the cost of capital of banks headquartered in seven large industrial countries are summarized in Tables 1 and 2 for the 1975-1987 period. Summary data also are shown for the price/earnings ratios for all firms in each of these countries. One inference from the data is that national differences in price/earnings ratios are substantial. A second is that the ranking of price/earnings ratios for banks in each country and for each country are similar but not identical. A third is that the range of price/earnings ratios for banks is larger than the range for all firms - with the implication that there is a significant bank industry effect; in general, however, the price/earnings ratios for banks within each country are lower than those of the country as a whole.[1]

---

[1] The price/earnings ratio for each country includes the price/earnings ratio for the banks headquartered in each country. The more appropriate approach would involve adjusting the price/earnings ratio for each country to exclude the price/earnings ratios for banks. The weights of banks in each country's price/earnings ratio differ; the smaller the country, the larger the weight.

Table 1 - The Cost of Capital to Banks by Country, 1975-1988

		Bank P/E	Country P/E
1987	Japan	74.04	45.70
	Italy	20.48	21.00
	Switzerland	11.27	14.30
	Canada	8.60	17.60
	Great Britain	7.25	13.40
	United States	7.16	14.10
	Germany	NA	14.70
	WORLD	19.90	18.20
1986	Japan	58.71	25.90
	Italy	21.45	26.20
	Switzerland	12.87	14.40
	Great Britain	10.33	12.10
	Canada	8.00	15.30
	United States	7.46	13.70
	Germany	NA	16.70
	WORLD	17.30	15.00
1985	Japan	51.04	25.90
	Switzerland	9.43	11.40
	United States	8.14	9.90
	Italy	7.98	18.10
	Canada	7.10	17.80
	Great Britain	6.45	11.10
	Germany	NA	13.50
	WORLD	13.70	11.90
1984	Japan	25.01	25.10
	Switzerland	9.97	12.60
	Italy	8.48	NA
	United States	6.26	12.20
	Canada	6.23	27.50
	Great Britain	4.43	10.40
	Germany	NA	15.00
	WORLD	9.30	13.90
1983	Japan	27.00	22.20
	Germany	15.40	11.20
	Great Britain	10.38	9.80
	Switzerland	9.73	10.90
	Canada	6.73	10.90
	United States	5.80	10.10
	Italy	3.95	NA
	WORLD	9.10	11.50
1982	Japan	33.91	18.20
	Germany	15.40	8.50
	Italy	12.53	NA
	Switzerland	10.00	10.70

Table 1 - continued

		Bank P/E	Country P/E
1982	United States	6.15	7.70
	Canada	5.13	8.60
	Great Britain	3.48	8.30
	WORLD	9.40	9.20
1981	Japan	30.60	16.10
	Switzerland	13.83	12.50
	Germany	10.63	7.40
	Italy	9.45	NA
	Canada	7.50	8.60
	United States	5.78	9.10
	Great Britain	2.70	6.20
	WORLD	8.90	9.10
1980	Japan	23.50	19.20
	Switzerland	14.23	13.20
	Germany	9.40	9.00
	Canada	6.48	8.70
	United States	5.24	7.40
	Italy	3.45	NA
	Great Britain	3.35	5.40
	WORLD	8.30	8.40
1975	Italy	21.20	NA
	Japan	19.03	14.00
	Germany	14.27	9.70
	Switzerland	6.60	6.30
	Great Britain	2.10	3.10
	United States	NA	8.10
	Canada	NA	6.80
	WORLD	9.80	7.70

Note: (a) The date of each ranking is the first day of the year in the heading (or the last day of the previous year). - (b) The 1975 edition does not include North American Companies. - (c) Banks used in bank P/E ratios are for the *United States*: Citicorp, Bank of America, Chase Manhattan, Bankers Trust, JP Morgan, Chemical Bank, First Chicago Corp., Security Pacific Corp.; *Canada*: Royal Bank of Canada, Bank of Nova Scotia, Bank of Montreal, Canadian Imperial Bank; *Germany*: Commerzbank, Deutsche Bank, Dresdner Bank; *Switzerland*: Schweizerischer Bankverein SBS, Schweizerische Bankgesell. UBS, Schweizerische Kreditanstalt; *Italy*: Banca Commerciale Italiana, Credito Italiano, Medico-Banca, Banca di Roma; *Great Britain*: National Westminster, Lloyds Bank, Barclays Bank, Midland Bank; *Japan*: Dai-Ichi Kangyo Bank, Fuji Bank, Mitsubishi Bank, Mitsui Bank, Industrial Bank of Japan, Daiwa Bank, Bank of Tokyo, Sanwa Bank, Sumitomo Bank.

Source: Morgan Stanley Capital International [various issues].

Table 2 - Dividend Yields of Banks by Country, 1975-1987

		Bank yield	Country yield
1987	Japan	0.05	0.70
	Switzerland	2.43	1.90
	Italy	2.45	1.70
	Germany	3.53	2.80
	United States	4.05	3.60
	Great Britain	5.30	4.20
	Canada	5.40	2.90
	WORLD	1.90	2.60
1986	Japan	0.63	1.00
	Switzerland	2.37	1.90
	Germany	2.40	2.70
	Italy	2.63	2.10
	United States	4.61	3.80
	Canada	5.35	3.10
	Great Britain	6.03	4.40
	WORLD	2.30	3.20
1985	Japan	0.74	1.00
	Italy	2.40	3.60
	Switzerland	3.40	2.70
	Germany	5.10	3.90
	United States	6.19	4.70
	Canada	6.55	3.60
	Great Britain	7.10	4.50
	WORLD	2.80	3.80
1984	Japan	1.65	1.30
	Italy	2.85	3.10
	Switzerland	3.17	2.50
	Germany	4.73	3.70
	United States	6.05	4.50
	Canada	6.05	3.20
	Great Britain	7.65	4.80
	WORLD	3.90	3.80
1983	Japan	1.66	1.70
	Italy	2.30	2.50
	Switzerland	2.57	2.90
	Germany	3.30	4.90
	United States	6.26	5.00
	Great Britain	6.48	5.50
	Canada	6.53	3.90
	WORLD	4.20	4.50
1982	Italy	0.98	1.60
	Japan	1.45	1.70
	Switzerland	3.60	3.50
	Germany	4.17	6.30

Table 2 - continued

		Bank yield	Country yield
1982	United States	6.28	5.80
	Canada	7.13	4.60
	Great Britain	7.25	6.10
	WORLD	3.90	5.00
1981	Italy	1.48	1.90
	Japan	1.74	2.00
	Switzerland	2.83	2.90
	Canada	5.20	3.90
	United States	6.28	4.90
	Great Britain	7.02	6.40
	Germany	7.83	6.40
	WORLD	4.00	4.70
1980	Japan	1.89	2.00
	Switzerland	2.93	2.80
	Italy	3.93	2.60
	Canada	5.93	3.80
	Great Britain	6.13	6.70
	Germany	6.67	5.90
	United States	6.70	5.70
	WORLD	4.20	5.10
1975	Japan	2.05	2.90
	Italy	2.68	2.70
	Switzerland	4.13	4.40
	Germany	4.50	4.80
	Great Britain	10.08	11.60
	United States	NA	5.10
	Canada	NA	5.40
	WORLD	3.90	5.40

Note: (a) The date of each ranking is the first day of the year in the heading (or the last day of the previous year). - (b) The 1975 edition does not include North American Companies. - (c) Banks used in bank P/E ratios are for the *United States*: Citicorp, Bank of America, Chase Manhattan, Bankers Trust, JP Morgan, Chemical Bank, First Chicago Corp., Security Pacific Corp.; *Canada*: Royal Bank of Canada, Bank of Nova Scotia, Bank of Montreal, Canadian Imperial Bank; *Germany*: Commerzbank, Deutsche Bank, Dresdner Bank; *Switzerland*: Schweizerischer Bankverein SBS, Schweizerische Bankgesell. UBS, Schweizerische Kreditanstalt; *Italy*: Banca Commerciale Italiana, Credito Italiano, Medico-Banca, Banca di Roma; *Great Britain*: National Westminster, Lloyds Bank, Barclays Bank, Midland Bank; *Japan*: Dai-Ichi Kangyo Bank, Fuji Bank, Mitsubishi Bank, Mitsui Bank, Industrial Bank of Japan, Daiwa Bank, Bank of Tokyo, Sanwa Bank, Sumitomo Bank.

Source: As for Table 1.

The ranking of banks by country by dividend yield is generally inverse to the ranking by price/earnings ratio. The dividend yields for banks headquartered within a country are generally higher than those for all firms headquartered within that country. From the viewpoint of any one bank, a low dividend yield is an advantage, for the cash flow requirements of meeting the needs of shareholders are minimal. Earnings can be used to finance expansion.

Banks headquartered in Japan, Italy, and Switzerland consistently appear toward the top of the price/earnings ratios and the (low) dividend/yield ratios. The price-earnings of banks headquartered in all countries have increased; however, the increase in the price/earnings ratios for banks headquartered in other industrial countries is smaller than for banks in these three countries. The implication from both the comparisons of the levels of price/earnings ratios and the rate of increase in the price/earnings ratios is that banks headquartered in Japan should be expanding their offices abroad. One extension of this argument is that banks headquartered in the United States might have been at the forefront of foreign expansion in the 1960s because these banks then had a cost-of-capital advantage. And another is that US banks will be selling foreign offices.

5. Restrictions on Entry into National Banking Markets

A number of lists are available on the national treatment of foreign banks. Some countries prohibit or formerly prohibited the entry of foreign banks. Other countries restrict foreign banks to entry on a joint venture basis, where the partner to the foreign bank is a national firm, which effectively blunts the brand-name advantage of the foreign bank. Many countries do not restrict entry of foreign banks; however, they constrain the activities or the market share. In some countries, entry is not formally restricted; nevertheless, informal guidance may limit the entry of foreign banks. And in some countries the domestic banks are government-owned firms, and thus have a remarkable advantage in the sale of deposits.

The presence of restrictions on entry of foreign banks should be distinguished from the effectiveness of this regulation; the implication is that the restrictions were adopted as a precautionary device to keep foreign banks from "knocking at the door" rather than implying that they were already at the door [Dale, 1984].

If the cost-of-capital argument is the necessary condition for entry into an established foreign market, the sufficient condition is that the source-country firm not be at a substantial profitability disadvantage. One reason the foreign bank will be at a profitability disadvantage is the costs of economic distance; a second is the difficulty in achieving scale economies comparable to those of host-country banks, and especially in marketing of deposits. Foreign banks can enter a national market through a take-over of established banks or through establishment of new offices; where the national market is characterized by a small number of firms, take-overs are unlikely. The establishment of new offices encounters the handicap difficulty of achieving scale economies comparable to those realized by the established banks. The result is that entry of foreign banks is much more likely in those countries characterized either by several regional markets, or a large number of domestic banks, or both. Hence the structure of the industry *might* reflect economic factors rather than regulation - or likely both economic factors and regulation.

6. Conclusion

The thrust of this paper is to examine whether the structure of the international banking industry has been significantly affected by protection. The activities of banks can be segmented into the production and sale of deposits, and the purchase of loans and investments. International banking traditionally has been primarily concerned with the purchase of loans and investments. One characteristic of the sale of deposits is that individuals prefer to deal with a banking office in their neighborhood; the costs of dealing with banking offices at some distance are too high. Banks find it expedient to site offices near clusters of people - and most of these banking offices are operated by domestic firms. Foreign-owned firms account rarely for more than 20 percent of the offices, or 20 percent of deposits. Indeed in most countries, foreign-owned firms account for less than 5 percent of the banking offices and of total deposits.

Hence, the key question is whether the near-monopoly of domestically owned firms in producing bank deposits reflects one or several economic factors, or whether instead the small share of foreign-owned banks in the production of deposits in most countries reflects protection. The economic factors that might dissuade foreign banks from entry include that anticipated profitability is low, perhaps because foreign-owned banks would find it difficult to achieve scale economies, and also because the cost of capital of the host country is low.

The key presumption of this paper is that banks will expand their foreign offices and their retail activities in the production of deposits when they have a cost-of-capital advantage relative to their host-country competitors. Whether banks actually expand depends on whether they can obtain scale economies in the host country comparable to those of the domestic banks.

Bibliography

ALIBER, Robert Z., "International Banking: A Survey". Journal of Money, Credit, and Banking, Vol. 16, 1984, pp. 661-678.

DALE, Richard, The Regulation of International Banking. Cambridge 1984.

ECONOMIC COUNCIL OF CANADA, Efficiency and Regulation: A Study of Deposit Institutions. Ottawa 1975.

THE ECONOMIST, London, various issues.

FIELEKE, Norman S., "The Growth of U.S. Banking Abroad: An Analytical Survey". In: FEDERAL RESERVE BANK OF BOSTON, Key Issues in International Banking. October 1977.

MORGAN STANLEY CAPITAL INTERNATIONAL, Capital International Perspective. Geneva, various issues.

OFFICE OF TECHNOLOGY ASSESSMENT, CONGRESS OF THE UNITED STATES, International Competition in Services, esp. chapter 3, "International Competition in Banking and Financial Services", U.S. Government Printing Office, July 1987.

PECCHIOLO, R.M., The Internationalization of Banking: The Policy Issues. Organization for Economic Cooperation and Development, Paris 1983.

TERRELL, Henry S., Sydney J. KEY, "The Growth of Foreign Banking in the United States". In: FEDERAL RESERVE BANK OF BOSTON, Key Issues in International Banking. October 1977.

TSCHOEGL, Adrian E., "Foreign Banks in Japan". Bank of Japan, Monetary and Economic Studies, Vol. 6, No. 1, May 1988, pp. 93-118.

WALTER, Ingo, Barriers to Trade in Banking and Financial Services. Trade Policy Research Centre, London 1985.

Comment on Robert Z. Aliber, "Protection and the Structure of the Banking Industry in an International Context"

Norbert Walter   219-21

Aliber's paper is a very helpful contribution towards gaining an understanding of the behaviour of the banking industry, especially with respect to penetrating foreign markets. His hypothesis will be put to the test, for example, when the hitherto segregated EC market is unified after 1992. Then it will become obvious whether protectionism has been the villain of the piece in the modest internationalization of banking business or whether economic factors "naturally" protect home banks.

Aliber's eight stylized facts are very helpful towards an understanding of the unique structure of the banking industry. His first observation that concentration in the banking industry widely varies is very true. The impression that the US is unique with its large number of banks - mainly a result of regulation - is somewhat exaggerated. Germany with its numerous savings and co-operative banks might serve as another counter-example that big banks dominate the market: the three big commercial banks account for only some 10 per cent of the market.

It is certainly crucial in understanding banking structure and behaviour, to approve Aliber's second feature, that regulation of the banking industry is more extensive than that in the rest of business.

More surprising is his third stylized fact: that returns are not inconsistent with the competitive model. He points to the commodity-character of bank products as the probable explanation for this result.

The fourth feature seems to be at odds with this last observation. Image and brand names do play an important role in banking, the opposite of what you would expect in a commodity market.

The fifth factor adds to the paradox: relationships *between* banks are complex. They include competition for deposits and loans and co-operation for payments systems or syndicated loans.

The sixth stylized fact is almost trivial: retail banking is national, if not regional. Here, technological changes are possibly reasons for change in the future.

The seventh observation is that wholesale banking is much more international than retail business.

The eighth fact, that the larger the share of foreign banks, the smaller the concentration in a certain national market, is questionable. While it might be correct as a general observation, other factors, such as the regulatory framework for doing international business, do play a prominent role as well. London may be a particularly outstanding example with a high concentration of banking and a large market share of foreign banks. An opposite example is Germany with a relatively low concentration of banks, but nonetheless a small market share of foreign banks.

Aliber's argument that banking (especially retail banking) necessitates proximity has certainly lost validity over time. The domestic currency is obviously losing importance as a "natural" protection against foreign competition. Depositing no longer necessitates going to the branch. In Germany, the postal bank with its comfortable zero-cost mailing of all banking-related activities only foreshadows what will be possible if POS payments and other technologies are introduced.

One issue that Aliber did not address is the form of banking that is considered optimal: the Anglo-Saxon system of separating banking functions, or the continental universal bank. The crucial question is: are there synergies and is there cross-fertilization, or do universal banks suffer from unclear decision processes and from overdoses of bureaucracy?

In Section 2, Aliber describes the "Structure of Banking". This section is very traditional, it hardly exhibits surprises. He points out that economies of scale are very limited for banking products. This would leave one with the expectation of low barriers to entry and many banks as a result. Evidence shows that, in most cases, this is not so. Hints that there can be more prominent economies in marketing, in research, in education and training are not a convincing argument for the existence of so many oligopolistic structures in banking since these "functions" can be out-sourced. Other factors, however, namely the cost of creating a brand name, and the factual importance of "confidence" and "credibility" in this market might be better explanatory variables.

Section 3 develops the "Theory of International Banking". Aliber's first argument for a bank to go abroad is to accompany its customers who, themselves, are going international. This approach has a long historical tradition, especially if complemented by the thesis that business follows the flag. The move of US banks abroad in the 1960s can certainly be viewed as proof, as can the initial moves of Japanese banks recently. Home banks do have an information advantage about their clients over foreign banks.

A second factor explaining the international move is the cost of capital, since the disadvantage of the costs of economic distance have to be compensated for. Due to the large leverage in banking, this factor is limited to cases when equity capital is massively cheaper. Thus, it is of relevance today only to Japanese banks which have capital costs that are only one quarter of those in continental Europe. While the "follow the flag-business" strategy explains two-way internationalization of banking, the cost-of-capital argument leaves one to expect a one-way direction of foreign investment of banks.

In his final chapter, Aliber analyses whether economic factors or barriers to entry prohibit foreign banks entering national markets. The basic thrust is that, in many cases in retail banking, economic factors are the main obstacle to foreign penetration of national markets. This is, however, not true for wholesale and investment banking. Here, crude as well as subtle forms of protectionism do play a certain role.

This thesis can be tested in Europe when the unification of the European market is complete, since regulations will be harmonized, and entry - at least for EC banks including those third-country banks which are represented in the EC with a subsidiary - will be open. It looks as though a number of avenues to penetrate foreign markets will be tried: joint ventures, take-overs and the establishment of branches. Which strategy will be most successful will depend on a number of factors, among them the supply of management skill, financial resources and, in general, the time available to penetrate the foreign market.

4220. 6350

Brian Hindley

Integrated World Markets in Services: Problems and Prospects

222 — 44

1. Introduction

Everyone agrees that goods and services are different, though the on-going debate about the proper definition of services suggests that the boundary line is hard to draw. What seems to be less widely appreciated is the impact of the differences between goods and services on concepts such as that of an integrated world market, and on the problems to be anticipated and overcome in attempts to create one.

In this paper, I shall first discuss the nature of a service, and then explore the implications for the notion of an integrated world market in services. Finally, I shall discuss the prospects of achieving such a world market within the foreseeable future, and, in particular, the impact on such prospects of the Uruguay Round discussions on bringing services into the GATT.

2. Market Services

From the standpoint of international transactions, there are two important differences between goods and services. The first is that goods are tangible, so that, with more or less trouble or cost, they can be shifted from place to place. Hence, goods have simple and relatively homogeneous delivery systems. Services, on the other hand - being, as Hill [1977] remarks, a *change* in the condition of a good or a person - cannot themselves be shifted from place to place. The outcome of a service can be shifted from place to place, and so can the means of producing a service and the signifiers of property rights generated by a service - for example, an insurance policy. This is not possible, however, for the service itself.

Services therefore employ a much broader range of delivery modes than goods, and one result is that it is difficult to arrive at propositions that are both useful for policy purposes and that can be generalized to all services. This is a major factor leading to the idea that services are heterogeneous as compared to goods, though as noted elsewhere [Hindley, Smith, 1984], a bouquet of flowers and a ton of coal and a jet airliner are all goods but are also very different from one another.

The second major difference is that services are typically customised to a much greater extent than goods. A lawyer or a doctor advises you on one problem and one set of circumstances, and me on another. Hence, regulation of the *output* of service industries is difficult. It is less costly for governments to regulate the quality of *inputs* into the provision of services. Regulation of this kind, however, can readily be translated into controls on the entry of competitors. [1]

The activities that are generally referred to as services can be divided into three types, based upon the end-use of the service: locational services, intermediation services and knowledge or skill-based services. I am not certain that these three types exhaust the category "services", but they capture a very high fraction of it. More importantly, the members of the different categories raise different policy issues.

a. *Locational Services*

The essence of services in this category is the conveyance of something from one geographical location to another. Examples are the transport of persons or goods by air, land or water; posts and telecommunications; TV and radio; and the supply of water, gas and electricity...

Technical progress in the provision of locational services has been, and continues to be, extremely rapid. From the standpoint of public policy, however, their primary characteristic is that they are prone to

---

[1] Of course, direct regulation of inputs also occurs in goods trade. This is the case when a government, on health grounds, insists that it must inspect a food-processing or pharmaceuticals plant before the output of that plant can be sold in its territory. Restrictions of this type are almost certainly more prevalent in service industries than in goods industries, however. Moreover, such restrictions in goods industries provide classic examples of high protection, amounting to bans on importation. An example is British behaviour towards UHT milk imports: inspection of the milk was required by local authorities but no funds were available for the inspectors to travel abroad.

problems of natural monopoly. The provision of a locational service tends to require specialised routes (roads, rails, cables, pipes, satellites...) and/or specialised apparatus for transmitting and receiving (telephone exchanges, railway stations, airports, ports and harbours...).

There might, in principle, be an approximation of perfect competition between *users* of these facilities, for example between the owners of taxi cabs, ships, or aircraft. It appears to be typical of locational services, however, that somewhere in the complex of factors required for their provision, there is a large lump which cannot even in principle be reduced to perfect competition.

There is a variety of regulatory responses to this problem. Public ownership probably is the most common. Roads, ports and harbours, and airports, for example, are very often owned and operated by one or another level of government. Locational services themselves are frequently supplied by governments or their agencies (PTTs, electricity and gas supply, rail and air transport), or are directly regulated by them.

b. Intermediation Services

Banking, wholesale and retail trades, book-making, stock, commodity and real estate broking and employment agencies are all intermediation services. These activities provide a means of contact between pairs or groups of persons with off-setting excess demands.

A different group of intermediation services provides a means of organisation for persons who can gain by sharing. Insurance - the sharing of risks - is one example. Others are provided by sharing in the use of capital assets, as in the cases of auto and property rental, or key-cutting services and libraries.

In a world of zero search and transaction costs, intermediation services presumably would not exist, or would exist in a different form and with different primary functions. House-sellers and house-buyers, for example, would not need to pay an agent to find one another. Groups of persons could club together to buy books for their joint use or to make commitments to those of their number who suffered specified misfortunes, they would not need to use libraries or insurance companies for these purposes.

It follows that changes in search and transaction costs (as brought about by technical change in locational services) will affect the nature of these activities. A current manifestation is the internationalisation of many of the activities in this category. Suppliers of services within this group, in particular banking and insurance, have provided much of the pressure for the introduction of services into the GATT.

Natural monopoly is not typically a major issue in intermediation services. They are, however, often subject to regulation for fiduciary reasons.

c. Knowledge or Skill-Based Services

Lawyers, doctors, architects, hairdressers, sportsmen and other entertainers, TV repairers and electricians are examples of providers of knowledge or skill-based services. Many of the activities in this category require, or traditionally have required, geographical proximity of the provider of the service and the person or good that is the subject of the activity.

The extent to which this is true, however, depends upon the development of locational services. A person in London can now use a lawyer based in New York or San Francisco much more easily than would have been the case 100 years ago; and whereas 100 years ago a person in San Francisco could not have watched or heard an opera or play performed, or a game played, in London, he now can, and through a variety of means.

Haircuts and surgery still require physical proximity. There is, however, no obvious reason to suppose that that is a permanent state of affairs.

Natural monopoly is not a problem in this category. As with intermediary services, however, services based upon skills or knowledge are very often regulated. Typically, regulation takes the form of certification of the competence of suppliers by governments of by agencies appointed by governments. Such certification is often a necessary legal condition of practice.

Although natural monopoly is not an issue in the provision of skill-based services, they are often subject to elements of imperfect competition. Certificating authorities, for example, can, through their control of entry, create monopoly rents for members of the relevant profession or craft. A similar rent-creating potential derives from regulation in the other two categories, even though regulation has a different rationale there. A powerful theory of regulation holds that regulatory powers are "captured" by the suppliers putatively subject to them, and used by them to suppress competition.[1]

There are obvious overlaps and combinations between these three types of service activity. The provision of most services calls for specific knowledge or skills. Running an airline, for example, calls for the possession of specialised human capital - but the object of demand of the purchaser of airline tickets is transportation, not, except as a derived demand, the skill or knowledge of the manager of the airline. That manager might supply his skill directly to another airline as a consultant, however. In terms of the classification above, he then would be supplying a skill-based service.

On the other hand, some service industries offer a bundle of different types of services, in which skill-based services may play a prominent role as an object of demand. Banks, for example, typically offer both intermediation services and services based upon specialised skills or knowledge. Stock, real estate and commodity brokers make similar claims.

When the provision of intermediary or locational services depends upon a skill-based service as an input, or when they are offered in combination with skill-based services, they are likely to take on the characteristics of a skill-based service, that is, to require proximity of the service provider and the service user. From the standpoint of integrated world markets, this is a major difference between goods and services.

3. Integrated World Markets in Goods and in Services

For a good, the concept of an integrated world market is reasonably clear. It implies that the price of the good is equalized across national

---

[1] The classic sources on the capture theory of regulation are Stigler [1971] and Peltzman [1976]. Rottenburg [1980] provides a useful survey of relevant theory and evidence.

markets, taking account of the costs of transportation and of differences in national taxes. Tariffs may be compatible with a weakly integrated world market, insofar as an unchanging tariff permits the impact of events in the world at large - a reduction in the costs of production, for example - to affect the domestic market. Quotas insulate domestic producers from events in the outside world and are not in any sense compatible with an integrated world market.

The quota elements of the multi-fibre arrangement ensure that the world market for textiles and garments is not integrated. It is easy to conceive what an integrated world market in textiles and clothing implies, however, and it is also easy to specify the changes of policy that would be needed to create such an integrated world market.

The idea of an integrated world market for a service is less easy to come to grips with. Part of the problem is that in goods markets we expect some process of arbitrage to equalize prices in different national markets. If the price of a good is higher in one market than in another, shipments of the good will be diverted from the low-price market to the high-price market. Hence, the policies required to produce an integrated world market in a good entail the removal of obstacles to flows of the good.

In most services, such arbitrage cannot occur, at least not directly. Arbitrage in goods occurs without any change in the location of producers of the goods. For services, this typically is not possible. To some extent, the provider of the service has to be located in the market of the user of the service. If a service in a particular national market is over-priced relative to the rest of the world, the problem cannot be met by a diversion of trade flows. It requires a factor flow.

If the profits on the route from A to B are higher than those on the route from C to D, it is necessary to move ships or aircraft or trucks from the AB to the CD route. If the earnings of lawyers or doctors in country A are higher than those in country B, equalization of earnings by an arbitrage-like process will require the movement of lawyers and doctors from B to A. An integrated market for a service, therefore, requires something much more akin to the process by which we imagine that profits are equalized between different industries, or wages between different occupations, than to that by which we imagine that the prices of goods are equalized between different national markets.

Will this process produce similar prices in different national markets? One problem is that the local production of a service will almost inevitably involve local factors of production as well as imported ones. Hence, there is no evident reason to suppose that the price-quality combinations that A service suppliers can produce in A will be exactly reproducible by them in B. [1]

Possibly more important, establishment in B is likely to require conformity with the B regulatory system. A regulatory system will affect the costs of producers subject to it. Hence, there is no reason to suppose that the same supplier will be able to produce the same price-quality combinations when he is subject to the A regulatory system as when he is subject to B regulations.

In discussion of the concept of an integrated world market, moreover, the term "regulatory system" must be interpreted broadly. It obviously includes those matters taken into account by the usual meaning assigned to a regulatory system. It includes, for example, requirements for minimum levels of reserves or for minimum numbers of years of training at approved institutions. And the regulatory systems for international transportation include the bilateral agreements which currently form the basis of organisation for much civil air transport, and the market-sharing system of the UNCTAD liner code. But, since factor flows are entailed by the idea of an integrated market for a service, it must also include immigration rules and conditions imposed on employment generally, such as minimum wages and contributions to social security.

A Korean company, using Korean labour paid on Korean terms, may be able to construct a highway or a factory of a given quality in Germany more cheaply than could a European Community company using European Community labour. But a Korean company will have great legal difficulty in getting its Korean labour force into Germany. Even if it

---

[1] Of course, this is also true of goods at the retail level. The equality of price to be expected in an integrated world market for a good is the price at the dock, before any local services have been applied to it. The essential difference is that, for many services, there is no point short of delivery to the user of the service - such as the dockside - at which it would make any sense to talk about the price of a service.

could do so, it might not be able to produce more cheaply were that labour, once in Germany, subject to German employment laws.

I suggested above that tariffs might be consistent with an integrated world market for a good, but that quotas could not be. If that proposition is accepted, it raises the question of whether a particular restriction on service transactions is tariff-like or quota-like, or whether its direct effect is on the cost of providing the service or on the quantity of it that can be supplied.

There are numerous quota-like restrictions on the provision of services. The most evident is a ban or restriction on the establishment of foreign providers of a service. This is also probably one of the most frequent actions affecting service sectors, whether it is imposed de jure or de facto, and whether the prohibition primarily affects capital or labour.

4. Problems of Creating an Integrated World Market for a Service

The problems of creating an integrated world market in a service should be clear from this account of what an integrated world market implies. The difficulties occur primarily at two levels. These are (a) the requirement of freedom of location for factors of production; and (b) national regulation of the provision of services or of conditions relevant to their supply.

a. Freedom of Location

The difficulties raised by issues of factor location are political rather than economic. Before discussing political issues, however, it is useful to enquire whether it is always true that the integration of any national market for a service into the world market for that service requires freedom of service suppliers to locate in the national market.

One exception is the class of "tradeable services", services that can be provided by a supplier in country A to a user in country B without relocating either of them. Such services (long-distance services in the terminology of Bhagwati [1984]) do exist. If I can conduct business with my bank by computer terminal, so can a person in another country. Any service transaction that takes place within a country entirely by mail, fax, or phone, without direct personal contact, can also, in principle, be traded internationally. This does not currently appear to be a very large class in relation to the service sector as a whole. It is obviously growing, however, and might be expected to grow even faster in the future.

The scope of tradeable services can be extended somewhat by adding to the category services whose provision requires only brief periods of relocation, rather than permanent or semi-permanent residence. An architect or consulting engineer, for example, may be able to function effectively with a few brief visits to the site of a project. A bank, on the other hand, is likely to need a permanent presence in a country if it is to provide a full range of banking services successfully.

A second possible exception occurs when potential users of the service can move to the location of foreign suppliers of the service (or if both are able to meet in some third location). Even if there is no freedom of service suppliers to locate in the national market, temporary relocation of users of a service might produce many of the consequences of a national market that is integrated with the world market. Evidently, this is more likely to be true the lower the cost of transportation services; and this suggests that it is more likely to apply to Luxembourg than to New Zealand.

A third exception might occur when arbitrage is possible between a free market and a restricted one. Cabotage laws may prevent foreign vessels or aircraft from competing on the internal routes of a country, for example; but if that country's vessels or aircraft compete successfully in the international market, and have entered, or could enter, the cabotage routes, then those routes may be supplied at a reasonable approximation of the prices that would prevail were they open to international competition.

Similarly, when a service uses a primary input that is supplied under conditions of international competition, a closed market in the service itself may be consistent with an approximation of the outcome of an internationally-integrated market in the service itself. Reinsurance and direct insurance might be an example of this. Another might be ocean transportation, where a ship owned in one country may be flagged in another and therefore able to hire crews from yet other countries.

All such apparently evadable restrictions raise the question of why the restrictions exist in the first place. One possible answer is that they are largely irrelevant, and that their maintenance is a mistake or oversight by someone or other. Another answer is that the arbitrage process is incomplete, whether for economic or legal reasons, so that suppliers favoured by the restriction are still able to make super-normal profits.

In any event, these exceptions do not appear to make a major breach in the general rule that factor flows are required to produce an integrated world market in a service. The idea of permitting such flows, however, is not popular anywhere.

Why this should be so is an interesting question. Suppose that a Korean construction firm, allowed to locate temporarily Korean labour in Europe, can construct a road or an airport in Europe more cheaply than any European firm supplying a similar quality of output. Or, alternatively, that an airline headquartered in a developing country could fly the London-Paris route more cheaply than the incumbents on the route.

If the output were motor cars or television sets, produced in Korea and sent to Europe, many economists would jeer at the notion that the relative cheapness of Korean labour was a valid reason for resisting the import of those goods. An airport, of course, cannot be built in Korea and shipped to Europe - if it is built, it has to be built in Europe. But the logic of comparative cost that applies to cars and television sets seems to apply to airports, and that logic suggests that if the Koreans can build it at a lower cost, then they should be allowed to locate temporarily in Europe for that purpose. Nevertheless, the idea seems to many - including some who instinctively attack the pauper labour argument applied to trade - unthinkable. I do not mean that they regard it as politically infeasible, which is a very plausible judgement, I mean that they find it unthinkable.

And under present arrangements, of course, not even a German (or any other European Community) airline can offer a London-Paris service. That state of affairs is unlikely to change in the near future.

Developing countries, symmetrically, reject the notion that service suppliers from the rest of the world should be able to set up local establishments in order to provide their services - even though it is often conceded, implicitly of explicitly, that foreign suppliers are more efficient than local ones.

b. *National Regulation*

National regulation of service suppliers raises problems at two levels. It is important to separate them clearly.

There is first the issue raised by "grey-area" measures - non-tariff barriers (NTBs) to trade or investment which in services often derive from the regulatory process. Regulation of service industries, of course, is widely held to have strong social justification. Even accepting that, however, it also might be agreed that particular regulations, or particular actions of the regulatory authorities, are difficult to justify in terms of the standard rationale for regulation, which is protection of the interests of users of the service.

Such "grey-area" measures are a major problem in efforts to liberalise international service transactions. In the first place, they probably comprise the bulk of the measures by which local service industries are protected. In the second place, it is difficult to obtain a consensus on which measures fall on the wrong side of the line. This is especially true when, as in many developing countries (but not only in developing countries), infant-industry and balance-of-payments reasons are invoked as justifications for extending regulatory action beyond the need to protect the local users of the regulated service.

Although the NTB problem in services is serious, however, it is not substantively different from similar problems in goods trade. That is not to suggest, of course, that it is tractable: the GATT process has not been markedly successful in dealing with NTBs in goods trade, and there is no reason to suppose that it will be more successful where services are concerned. But the nature of the problem is clear, and no new conceptual issues appear to arise in consideration of "grey-area" barriers to service transactions. [1]

---

[1] The fact that services are protected almost entirely by such measures, and typically *cannot* be protected by border measures such as tariffs or quotas, does raise problems in the context of the GATT. It is unclear, for example, how a services equivalent to Article XIX - which

The second problem, however, arises from the mere fact of regulation. Regulation is likely to affect the costs of producers of the service. Hence, when producers subject to the regulations of country A are free to sell services in country B without being subject to the B regulatory system, there is not only competition between A and B producers - there is also competition between the national regulatory systems of A and B. Thus, suppliers subject to a system which requires larger reserves, more years of education, or higher minimum prices will claim that they are at a competitive disadvantage against suppliers who are subject to less stringent requirements.

The problem can appear either as a trade or as an establishment issue. It is likely to occur as a matter of establishment in skill-based services, where transactions demand proximity. If standards of certification for medical practice are higher in A than in B, for example, but certification in B implies a right of establishment in A, practitioners in A are likely to protest against the dilution of standards.

It occurs as a trade issue when producers established in B are free to sell services in A without being established in A or otherwise subject to the A regulatory system, and vice versa. Suppliers subject to the heaviest regulatory requirement are likely to claim that they are penalized in such competition.

In either case, the authority with the most stringent regulations is likely to come under pressure to relax them, and it will probably regard this as a threat to the integrity of the national regulatory structure. Whether regulatory powers have been used for purposes which are socially beneficial, in the view of the regulators, or for protecting local service suppliers, local suppliers and regulators are likely to unite in opposition to competition from suppliers not subject to those powers, whether the competition is by means of trade or establishment.

There is a political and an economic component to the problem thus raised. The political problem is simply that a coalition of both producers and regulators in an industry is capable of inflicting political costs on a government - thus casting doubt on that government's ability to enter an agreement that entails competition between regulatory structures. That

---

allows tariff or quota protection against a sudden surge of imports - could be formulated.

problem might be easier to avoid were the economics of the situation clearer. But while the economic case is less straightforward than those claiming necessary dilution of regulatory standards might wish to suggest, it is not clear cut.

The argument that standards will be diluted by competition between regulatory regimes assumes one of two things. Either it assumes that the more stringent requirements are not valuable to buyers of the service (or, more precisely, that buyers do not value them at a level commensurate with their cost), or that buyers are ignorant of the advantages that will accrue to them from dealing with suppliers subject to these more stringent requirements. If regulations are not valuable to buyers, however, there is no obvious reason why they should not be eliminated in competition.

The mainstay of the standard case for regulation, though, lies in the suggestion that buyers are ignorant. That contention raises much more difficult issues. Clearly, the contention raises a question of the cost of the policy alternative to regulation, which is to ensure that buyers are better informed. In the presence of ignorance, however, it is not clear that a looser regulatory regime is to be preferred to a more stringent one on economic grounds (Hindley [1987b] gives a fuller discussion of these issues).

The problem of competition between regulatory systems could be avoided by harmonizing the requirements of the A and B regulatory systems. Yet that suggestion inevitably raises the issue of the structure of an optimal regulatory system. Should A accept B's regulations or vice versa or what compromise should be struck? In the absence of a decisive economic answer, such a discussion will be dominated by political considerations, and may have no conclusion.

This outcome is particularly evident in the EEC. The Treaty of Rome is a much stronger instrument than it would be possible to negotiate in the world at large, and includes an independent Court of Justice to rule on its interpretation. Despite that, progress towards liberalisation of trade in services within the EEC has been stalled on exactly the issue of competition between regulatory systems. [1] It is difficult to ima-

---

[1] Hindley [1987b] gives a detailed discussion of the problems of the service sector in the EEC as they stood in mid-1986. The 1992

gine that a negotiated harmonization of regulations is feasible in the world at large in the foreseeable future.

Another solution to the problem raised by competition between regulatory systems is to combine a right of establishment with an agreement that the national regulations of the host country apply to establishments. That solution avoids, or begs the question of appropriate regulatory structure. Moreover, it runs into the difficulties with rights of establishment discussed in the first part of this section.

5. Prospects of Creating Integrated World Markets in Services

In discussing prospects for the creation of integrated world markets, it is useful to distinguish between transport and other services. In air and maritime transport, quota-like restrictions are the main barrier to integration. In each case, the restrictions have come about under the aegis of international organisations other than the GATT, and are therefore unlikely to be a subject of the GATT negotiation. It is quite possible that these services will be discussed in the GATT, but, if so, the discussion seems more likely to be about discriminatory practices (in particular discriminatory access to port and airport facilities) than about the fundamental organisation of the industries.

a. Air and Sea Transport

Maritime transport is one of the few services that has in the past exhibited many of the characteristics of an integrated world market. Now, at least so far as liner trade is concerned, it is subject to different conditions for trade between the developed countries and trade involving the developing countries - a characteristic of other services also, and it might be feared, one that will spread.

The UNCTAD Liner Code is not the only division in the industry: the United States and the Europeans (or, more correctly, the Consulta-

---

initiative contains proposals that will improve matters if they come into force. Nevertheless, the general comment stands.

tive Shipping Group (CSG), which also includes Japan) disagree over interpretation of, and appropriate action towards the Conference system; and, even within the EEC, cabotage is a source of dispute. Nevertheless, the Liner Code is the primary barrier to integration in the industry.

The Code is based upon an asserted right of a "cargo-generating country" to carry one half of the goods it sends into or receives from foreign trade. To make this right operational, the Code calls for the negotiation of a cargo-sharing formula between vessels of the countries engaged in trade. Under the Code, third-flag ships have no rights to carry cargo between the two countries engaged in trade. However, in the event that those two countries cannot agree on a formula, the Code suggests that cargo should be shared 40:40:20, i.e. 40 per cent to vessels of each of the trading partners and 20 per cent open to competition by vessels under third flags.

In fact the position is worse than this would suggest. The Code is supposed to apply only to Conference shipping, but in fact is often applied to all trade. Some developing countries have established freight bureaus through which all outgoing or inbound cargo must pass, thereby setting up machinery for an even more thorough discrimination between vessels of different flags.

A review conference on the Liner Code is due five years after the entry into force of the Code, which occurred in October 1983. It seems extremely unlikely, however, that members of the Group of 77 will be inclined to review their general policy. The interesting question is whether the CSG and the United States will be able to agree on some common position to resist the further spread of bilateralism in the industry (Böhme and Schrier [1989] discuss this issue in detail).

They have so far failed to arrive at such a common position. The CSG negotiating stance can possibly be summarised by reference to "the Brussels Package", which accepts the asserted right of a developing country to carry 40 per cent of its own trade, but insists that the 40 per cent allocated to the trading partner should be open to competition by ships of any flag. The United States, after accepting bilateral deals to cope with unilateral legislation by Brazil and Argentina in the early 1970s, now favours a more aggressive stance. It rejects the Brussels Package. Attempts by some countries to follow the example of

Brazil and Argentina have been met by American threats to close US ports to ships flying the flags of those countries. The Europeans would find this option more difficult to follow: the arguments deployed by the developing countries in liner shipping are essentially the same as those deployed by the Europeans in civil aviation.

The basic framework of civil aviation was established at the Conference on International Civil Aviation, held in Chicago in 1944, and at Bermuda in 1946, when the British and United States' governments negotiated bilateral agreements that became the model for most other bilaterals. At Chicago, one option tabled by the United States – the draft International Air Transport Agreement – would have created in civil aviation a system closely akin to the open maritime system strongly favoured by the British.

The British and the Europeans, however, suspected that the United States possessed a comparative advantage both in the provision of air transport services and in the production of large aircraft. Yet, both a capacity to construct large aircraft and the possession of nationally-owned air transport facilities had strategic significance, particularly for those countries still in possession of far-flung colonial empires. The Europeans were unwilling to take the chance that the United States would dominate a multilaterally-organised civil aviation industry. Hence, the bilateral system emerged – created for protectionist purposes.

Three points are of particular interest in the present context. The first is that the Europeans took their stand upon an undisputed national right: that of a government to prevent aircraft from picking up or discharging passengers in its territory. In maritime transport and civil aviation and many other services, it is not the rights of governments that are at issue but the good sense of exercising those rights in particular ways.

The second point is the simple one that the bilateral system permits groups of countries to liberalise as they see fit. This has been the basis for the recent history of liberalisation in international civil aviation, and liberalisation might be expected to continue in that way. A world-wide conversion to liberal aviation policies is not in prospect.

The third point, best illustrated by civil aviation, is the power of a protectionist structure to resist change, even when the rationale for its existence has wholly or largely disappeared. The European airlines,

238

charging prices that are multiples of those charged over similar distances in the United States [CAA, 1983] maintain that they could not fly their routes more cheaply. They may be right: some of them cannot make a profit even at those high fares! But in assessing their claim, a central issue is that of who has captured the rents created by the bilateral system. A good deal of evidence suggests that the staffs of airlines have done so [Pryke, 1987]. If that is the case, then liberalisation of air transport will eliminate the rents and produce lower costs of operation. Such an outcome appears to have been a primary result of deregulation in the United States.

An important general point follows from this. It is that, where industries have been subject to regulation, predictions of comparative advantage are likely to be subject to considerable error. Deregulation, or competition that is tantamount to deregulation, may itself have profound effects on the costs of providing a service.

b. Other Services

The modes of organisation of most other services are in principle possible subjects for discussion in GATT. What is likely to happen, however, is that a framework of principles will emerge, together with applications to a small number of service industries. Which industries will be selected for this purpose is not yet public information. There is in fact disagreement between the EEC and the US as to whether the general principles should be enunciated before the specific-industries have been discussed (the US position) or simultaneously with, or after, that discussion (the EEC position).

A variety of papers have been presented to the Group of Negotiations on Services, most notably by the EEC and the US. It would be foolish to try to infer too much from the early submissions to a negotiation of any kind. It is notable, however, that the US, which before the start of the negotiation firmly maintained that the negotiation would be about trade in services, now expressly refers to rights of establishment: "The framework should apply to cross-border movement of services as well as to the establishment of foreign branches and subsidiaries for the

purposes of producing and delivering the service within the host country" [US Submission, 1987, p. 3].

The EEC paper is primarily concerned with the problems raised by
regulation. It suggests two forms of notification to the GATT. Firstly,
governments might notify the GATT of those of their regulations that
they perceive as appropriate. Secondly, governments whose service providers feel impeded by the regulations imposed by another government
could notify the GATT of the fact. Clearly, the lists of regulations emerging from these two processes are likely to be different. The actual
appropriateness of regulations would be subject to review by a standing
regulations committee. The EEC paper notes that the agreement is to be
about "trade in services" (quotation marks in original). It continues with
the comment that: "... since it is now generally accepted that trade in
services usually has characteristics which distinguish it from trade in
goods, an agreed concept of 'trade in services' will be a central element
of the agreement and will to a large extent determine its sectoral coverage" [EC Submission, 1987, p. 2].

A central issue in the GATT negotiation is the country coverage of
any agreement. In the developed world, there is already a good deal of
integration, especially in the establishment sense. If developed countries
were negotiating among themselves in the GATT, it is possible and even
likely that this state of affairs could be formalised and codified, and the
remaining protectionist practices diluted, to a degree that would produce
some approximation of integration. However, the GATT negotiation is not
merely between developed countries. It is the presence of the developing
countries at the negotiating table that creates the primary difficulty in
reaching a substantial agreement.

Some developing countries have always been hostile to the idea of
including services in the GATT [Bhagwati, 1987b]. There is a major
irony in this since it is probable that the most restrictive regimes for
services are to be found in developing countries (especially in those
most hostile to the negotiation) and it is accordingly they who have the
most to gain - in terms of economic welfare - from liberalisation
[Hindley, 1988]. However, there is a very substantial probability that
the negotiation will fail to convert them. In that event, the developed
countries may face a choice between a vacuous agreement - so vacuous
that unenthusiastic or even moderately hostile countries can adhere to it

- with a large number of signatories or a strong agreement with a much smaller membership.

In a legal sense, it appears that the developed countries can conclude an agreement on services in the GATT without the adherence of any developing country. Moreover, the obligations of signatories of an agreement on services apparently do not have to be extended to non-signatories, as would be the case with an agreement elaborating some existing part of the GATT. Hence, the position of the developed countries is strong, at least formally. It is clear, however, that they would prefer a services agreement which obtains the assent of at least some developing countries. The question, therefore, is what they will be willing to give up in order to achieve that assent.

The developed countries could follow two routes. One is to make genuine and economically meaningful concessions. The other is to make a phoney concession. The Punta del Este Declaration calls for the negotiation "to establish a multilateral framework of principles and rules for trade in services ... as a means of promoting economic growth of all trading partners and the development of the developing countries" [GATT, 1986, p. 11]. Some developing countries apparently are pressing for a development clause to be included in a services agreement which would have effects equivalent to those of Part IV of the GATT, that is, to permit developing countries to share in the benefits negotiated between developed countries, but to remove from developing countries any obligation to "make concessions" in return. The problem is that, however *politically* painful "concessions" may be, it is exactly in the giving of them that the primary *economic* benefits of GATT membership arise.

The case for a development clause in a services agreement is weak - weaker, even, than that for the similar clauses already in the GATT (Hindley [1987c] gives an analysis of these). The argument for such a clause has two principle components: infant industries and the balance of payments. [1]

---

[1] There are also genuine issues of sovereignty and national security in particular services (the United States, for example, places nationality restrictions on the ownership of airlines and television stations). Currently, the loudest allusions to these issues come from among the developing countries: nevertheless, the issues have nothing to do with development and concern all countries.

Though the infant industry argument for protection is hallowed in GATT terms by its inclusion in Article XVIII, its intellectual rationale has shrunk as a result of recent economic analysis [Johnson, 1961]. It requires (as a necessary but not sufficient condition) some form of first-mover disbenefit. It is more difficult to see what this might be in the case of service industries than in that of industries producing goods. Hindley [1982] discusses the application of the argument to the insurance industry.

Trade restrictions by developing countries for balance-of-payments reasons are also included in Article XVIII. Again, however, recent economic analysis has largely removed the rationale for such responses to balance-of-payments difficulties [Johnson, 1961; McKinnon, 1981]. To expect that conclusion to be carried into a revision of existing GATT articles may be unduly demanding. To expect it to be reflected in new additions to the GATT seems very much less demanding.

Nevertheless, there is a distinct possibility that the developed countries will decide to follow the phoney concession, development clause, route. In the first place, it is not obvious what real concessions they might make that are politically feasible. Within the service sector itself, the developed countries appear currently to have a comparative advantage in most of the services that can be traded across borders or that require merely a local "presence". The problem, therefore, in GATT terms, is that, so long as discussion is limited to such services, the developing countries have nothing to gain from adherence to a multilateral services agreement. They will almost certainly experience economic gains as a result of liberalising their service sectors. Those gains, however, they can obtain by unilateral action: the developing countries do not need to engage in a multilateral trade negotiation (MTN) to get them. To rationalise any "concessions" they make in the MTN, the governments of the developing countries need to be able to point to gains that they could obtain only by participation in the MTN.

In principle, the obvious exchange to be made between developed and developing countries is of rights of establishment for rights of temporary abode for labour engaged in the provision of services [Bhagwati, 1987a]. The question, evidently, is whether that exchange is politically feasible [Hindley, 1987a].

In the second place, the developed countries have followed the route of enticing the developing countries into GATT agreements before - indeed, into the GATT itself - by promises that membership would carry no obligations [Hudec, 1987]. They may now regret the consequences. Nevertheless, in the final stages of the negotiation, current expediency might outweigh anticipated regret.

Measured against the notion of an integrated world market for services, it would be foolish to expect too much from the GATT. That is not a criticism of the GATT or of the GATT process. The GATT is the type of institution in which progress is more appropriately measured in decades than in years or months.

What *is* to be expected of the GATT, however, is that the outcome of one negotiating round will not foreclose sensible outcomes in future rounds. In this case, that implies that nothing done in the Uruguay Round should close routes to integrated world markets - that nothing is done that will make it more difficult in future negotiations to move towards solutions of the regulatory problem and meaningful rights of establishment for all factors engaged in the provision of services.

Bibliography

BHAGWATI, Jagdish, "Splintering and Disembodiment of Services and Developing Countries". The World Economy, Vol. 7, 1984, pp. 133-143.

-- [1987a], "International Trade in Services and Its Relevance for Economic Development". In: Orio GIARINI (Ed.), The Emerging Service Economy, Services World Economy Series 1. New York 1987, pp. 3-34.

-- [1987b], "Trade in Services and the Multilateral Trade Negotiations". World Bank Economic Review, Vol. 1, 1987, pp. 549-569.

BÖHME, Hans, Elliot SCHRIER, A Perspective on European and American Shipping Policies. Trade Policy Research Centre, London 1989, forthcoming.

CIVIL AVIATION AUTHORITY (CAA), A Comparison between European and United States Fares. CAA Papers, 83006, London 1983.

EC SUBMISSION TO THE GROUP OF NEGOTIATIONS ON SERVICES, A Possible Conceptual Structure for a Services Agreement, MTN.GNS/W/29. 10 December 1987.

GENERAL AGREEMENT ON TARIFFS AND TRADE (GATT), Ministerial Declaration on the Uruguay Round, GATT/1396. 25 September 1986.

HILL, T. P., "On Goods and Services". The Review of Income and Wealth, Vol. 23, 1977, pp. 315-338.

HINDLEY, Brian, Economic Analysis and Insurance Policy in the Third World. Trade Policy Research Centre, Thames Essays, 32, London 1982.

-- [1987a], "A Comment on Jagdish Bhagwati's Geneva Association Lecture". In: Orio GIARINI (Ed.), The Emerging Service Economy, Services World Economy Series 1. New York 1987, pp. 35-39.

-- [1987b], "Trade in Services within the European Community". In: Herbert GIERSCH (Ed.), Free Trade in the World Economy: Towards an Opening of Markets. Symposium 1986. Tübingen 1987, pp. 468-486.

-- [1987c], "Differential and More Favorable Treatment of Developing Countries - and Graduation". In: J. Michael FINGER, Andrzej OLECHOWSKI (Eds.), The Uruguay Round - A Handbook on the Multilateral Trade Negotiations. Washington 1987, pp. 67-74.

--, "Service Sector Protection: Considerations for Developing Countries". World Bank Economic Review, Vol. 2, 1988, pp. 205-224.

--, Alasdair SMITH, "Comparative Advantage and Services". The World Economy, Vol. 7, 1984, pp. 369-390.

HUDEC, Robert, The Participation of Developing Countries in the GATT Legal System. Trade Policy Research Centre, Thames Essays, 50, London 1987.

JOHNSON, Harry G., "Towards a General Theory of the Balance of Payments". In: Harry G. JOHNSON (Ed.), International Trade and Economic Growth. Cambridge, Mass., 1961, pp. 153-168.

--, "Optimal Trade Intervention in the Case of Domestic Distortions". In: Robert E. BALDWIN et al. (Eds.), Trade, Growth and the Balance of Payments. Chicago 1965, pp. 3-34.

McKINNON, Ronald I., "The Exchange Rate and Macroeconomic Policy: Changing Postwar Perceptions". The Journal of Economic Literature, Vol. 19, 1981, pp. 531-557.

PELTZMAN, Sam, "Towards a More General Theory of Regulation". The Journal of Law and Economics, Vol. XIX, 1976, pp. 211-240.

PRYKE, Richard, Competition Among International Airlines. Trade Policy Research Centre, Thames Essays, 46, London 1987.

244

ROTTENBURG, Simon (Ed.), Occupational Licensure and Regulation. American Enterprise Institute for Public Policy Research, Washington 1980.

SAMSON, Gary P., Richard H. SNAPE, "Identifying the Issues in Trade in Services". The World Economy, Vol. 8, 1985, pp. 171-181.

STIGLER, George J., "The Theory of Economic Regulation". The Bell Journal of Economics, Vol. 2, 1971, pp. 3-21.

US SUBMISSION TO THE GROUP OF NEGOTIATIONS ON SERVICES, Concepts for a Framework Agreement on Services, MTN. GNS/W/24. 27 October 1987.

245-47

Comment on Brian Hindley, "Integrated World Markets in Services: Problems and Prospects"

Jürgen Müller

Hindley has provided us with an interesting framework in which to study the current negotiations of the GATT and the role of the different national players.

The major policy issue in on-going service liberalisation is the policy of "excessive" regulation, which may curtail the production of services, the right to establish, and trade in services. As an economist, Hindley finds that many of the reasons for government intervention and regulation are not linked to market failure (such as natural monopoly and externality arguments), but rather to equity and distributional considerations. These pertain to the case of infant industries, structural adjustment of disadvantaged factors as a consequence of trade, and the possible elimination of rents connected to regulation etc. As a consequence, the political economy arguments for why such regulatory barriers are introduced in the first place become much more important in understanding the current scope for trade liberalisation in services.

Government regulation has an impact on the location of services, since it affects the movement and costs of inputs (and therefore acts in a quota-like fashion) or it affects the cost of producing such services and therefore acts as a tariff restriction. After having shown the analogy to the goods trade (and the effects of trade restrictions there), the lessons learnt from the literature of trade liberalisation in general ought to apply here as well.

However, as Hindley points out, there are limits to the world-wide integration of services. This is due to the peculiarity of services themselves, (i.e., requiring continuous, or occasional, proximity of inputs), since there are very few services which are truly independent of distance. Rather, service-providers need to be at least partly near a user or to rely on partial mobility of inputs.

For those services for which trade is currently impossible, government regulation or "apparent market failure reasons" act as major barriers to trade. To the extent that regulation is only related to different standards of quality (either for output or input), extended trade in services would eventually result in competition between different regulatory systems. Countries with higher regulatory standards for inputs and outputs would then be at a disadvantage. Taken to its ultimate extreme the competition of such systems should result in a lifting, or at least a lessening, of regulations in order to maintain a country's comparative advantage in service provision (unless it is ready to forego certain income streams as a consequence of higher regulatory demands). To some extent, these tendencies can be seen in the case of ocean shipping, and perhaps in insurance regulation.

Hindley examines a number of such tradeable services in detail, but then concentrates more on the effects of multilateral trade agreements, such as the UNCTAD liner code and the Conference on International Civil Aviation. In these and other agreements, the potential for fully liberalised service markets is greatly reduced to protect a country's own service markets. Naturally, those negatively affected by service liberalisation protest strongly and to some extent successfully. In other words, the limits to trade liberalisation can clearly be seen as a result of established interest groups using the regulatory framework to maintain the status quo and to use regulation as a rent-seeking device in the international trading arrangement.

It is at this point that a marriage between the political economy approach, which Hindley hints at, and the case studies, which he uses to exemplify his ideas, could have benefited from amore in-depth analysis: Which sectors and political groups benefit from the current arrangements and which are most seriously threatened by further liberalisations? What are the potential gains from further trade liberalisation in services and how will the gains be distributed in different sectors? Will locational services be affected differently from intermediation services or knowledge and skill-based services?

Once the quantitative dimensions of these questions are more clearly seen, it will be easier to understand the current impasse in the trade of services negotiations and to show perhaps some way forward in which both parties, in other words the developed countries (DCs) and the less-developed countries (LCDs), could gain. At the moment, it seems that the benefits of trade might largely be precipitated or squandered in the process. Hindley believes that the LDCs cannot really see that they would gain from increased liberalisation of the services trade with the DCs, given their established lobbying mechanisms in protecting their industries. This makes bilateral agreements between countries or between trade blocs (such as DCs, OECD or CSG countries on the one hand and LDCs on the other) quite likely. In bilateral agreements, the gains from trade liberalisation may be smaller, but they can be more easily identified and redistributed. The free-rider problem is reduced and the cost of ignoring uncontrolled side effects reduced.

This hypothesis needs to be tested further, however, by analysing specific bilateral agreements and looking at the sectorial implications. It is not clear if Hindley's assertion that the LDCs can gain little is really true. What happens if one links the negotiation in the liberalisation of services with the liberalisation in commodities (as for example in agriculture), where the LDCs could gain?

I would also like to see Hindley's proposal that the outcome of current negotiations do not foreclose sensible outcomes of future negotiations tested in more detail on the available case studies. What economic dimensions are we considering? If we are merely thinking of trade in services, such as insurance, tourism, air and maritime transport, banking and telecommunications, I believe that the major volume would be covered by the trade between the OECD countries. By coming quickly to more sensible policy proposals in this group of countries, valuable gains from trade could probably be realised earlier. Less-developed countries might then move in parallel by having their own service liberalisation.

This allows one to move more quickly on the time trajectory than in a fully multinational negotiation. At the same time it would allow the LDCs to free ride on some of the benefits that accrue from service liberalisation in the DCs. One could then negotiate in a step-wise fashion those policies of service liberalisation where the major structural adjustment of the LDCs is feared, and some of the gains of liberalisation could be distributed in a more incentive-compatible way.

Such an exercise would allow one to draw stronger policy conclusions on the basis of Hindley's current theoretical framework as well as to point out the future research steps which would have to be undertaken in order to make such work flow more fruitfully into the negotiation process he discusses.

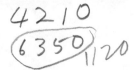

248-71

IV. SERVICES AND INTERNATIONAL DIVISION OF LABOUR

Rolf J. Langhammer

North-South Trade in Services: Some Empirical Evidence

1. Introduction

During the last two decades the rapid progress of many developing countries to restructure their export supply from primary commodities towards manufactures and to gain sizeable shares in growing world markets has been widely documented and explained. As a contrast, however, very little information exists on global North-South trade in services because of considerable barriers to both concept and documentation. [1]

On the other hand, scattered facts on specific service industries, for instance transport and travel, suggest that services contain an important element of continued structural change in developing countries' export supply. For instance, shipping lines and airlines operating in

---

[1] To mention only two of various relevant barriers, a clear-cut definition of what would be subsumed under "services" is still lacking. Controversies mainly exist with respect to foreign direct investment (FDI) and its income. Income derived from FDI can be interpreted as a remuneration for firm-specific skill advantages crossing the border [Rugman, 1987, p. 662] but it is usually not subsumed under internationally-traded services taken out of consideration [Lee, Naya, 1988; Grubel, 1987; Sapir, 1982; 1985; Gray, 1983; Arndt, 1987, p. 713]. Thus, it is mostly trade in service industries rather than trade in services which is dealt with. Yet, even in more narrowly defined service industries, there is no unanimity whether in addition to "visible" services (travel, transport) so-called "non-visible" services (fees and royalties and "other services") should also be included. Next to conceptual problems, data problems are the second large barrier. Only very few national balance of-payments statistics are regionally disaggregated, because in many countries detailed data on transactions with non-residents are not collected through the banking system. Furthermore, unlike in merchandise trade, services are often registered not on the basis of transactions crossing borders but on that of financial flows between residents and non-residents. Overlaps between both concepts of documentation seem to be large in "visible" services but they decrease rapidly along with a growing importance of "non-visible" services.

developing countries have succeeded in capturing rising parts of the World's merchandise and passenger transport [Böhme, 1986; Sichelschmidt, 1986]. Furthermore, evidence on international design contracts confirms that sizeable shares of contracts have been awarded to firms in Brazil, India, Korea, and Taiwan [Sapir, 1986, Table 3]. With respect to imports, it was mainly the rapidly growing demand of countries in the Gulf region and other OPEC member states for construction services and related activities which opened up new markets for both Northern and Southern suppliers.

This paper will try to summarize information on trade in services with developing countries of four OECD countries, that is, the United States, Japan, France, and West Germany. These four countries publish regionalized balance-of-payments statistics on goods and services so that the development of trade in services can be viewed against the performance in merchandise trade.

In Section 2, major trends and patterns of the four OECD countries' trade in services with developing countries are exposed. In Section 3, some hypotheses concerning the regional and sectoral pattern are introduced. Section 4 presents some in-depth analysis on the link between West German trade in manufactures and in services with developing countries. Section 5 summarizes the results.

2. Trends and Patterns in US, Japanese, French, and West German Trade in Services with Developing Countries

In this paper, services are defined as private services only. Thus, government services and income from foreign direct investment (FDI) are excluded for both conceptual and practical reasons. Government services comprise non-market transactions and do not signal competitiveness in international trade. With respect to income from FDI, most developing countries are net importers of private risk capital and do not yet figure as recipients of investment income. "Non-visible" services (fees, royalties), as far as they are recorded in the national balance-of-payments statistics, are taken into consideration.

a. US Trade in Services

Table 1 records US merchandise and service trade with developing countries in total, two sub-regions (Latin America, Africa and Asia) and for two periods, 1974/75 and 1985/86. Several findings are worth special notice.

Firstly, US service exports to developing countries grew faster than US merchandise exports, and developing countries account for roughly the same share in US exports of services as in goods, that is, about one third.

Secondly, while Latin American countries still absorbed one half of US exports of services to developing countries in 1985/86, Asian and African countries have proven to be the most rapidly growing export market for US services. Very probably, this record has to be booked on the account of Asian countries only. So-called "disembodied" services[1] - in the terminology introduced by Bhagwati [1984] - such as management fees, insurance, communications, summarized under "other private services", form the export stronghold of the US in terms of growth rates.

Thirdly, services still play a minor role in total US exports of goods and services to developing countries (about 17 per cent in 1985/86), but this is not a peculiarity of North-South exports. It holds true for US world exports of services as well.[2]

Fourthly, important US export markets for merchandise and services are not identical. Asian (and African) developing countries were by far the major LDC export markets for US goods in the mid-1970s and mid-1980s, whereas they were at the same level as Latin America as regard to services. One may suggest that the activities of US commercial banks

---

[1] Bhagwati has coined the term "embodiment" for traditional person-to-person related services (transport, travel) and "disembodiment" for services which are characterized by the availability of modern information and communication techniques. As such techniques are mainly available in industrialized countries, the hypothesis that these countries are internationally competitive in disembodied services, seems plausible. Furthermore, "disembodied" services enjoy decreasing transaction costs because of the advance of modern technology and thus may rapidly expand in future.

[2] As will be shown below, this percentage is in the range of shares in other OECD countries, too.

Table 1 - US Trade in Goods and Services with Developing Countries, 1974/75 and 1985/86 (a) (mill. US $)

	World			Latin America(b)			LDCs in Asia and Africa			Total LDCs			Share of LDCs in US world trade	
	1974/75	1985/86	Growth rate	1974/75	1985/86	Growth rate	1974/75	1985/86	Growth rate	1974/75	1985/86	Growth rate	1974/75	1985/86
US exports														
Merchandise(c)	106110	227287	7.2	16565	31239	5.9	20437	46468	7.8	37002	77707	7.0	34.9	34.2
Services (credits)	17723	46228	9.1	3634	7859	7.3	2237	7655	11.8	5871	15514	9.2	33.1	33.6
travel	4454	12296	9.7	1797	3650	6.7	173	962	16.9	1970	4612	8.0	44.2	37.5
passenger fares	1084	3185	10.3	175	525	10.5	143	343	8.3	318	868	9.6	29.3	27.3
other transportation	5707	14340	8.7	716	1804	8.8	1041	3701	12.2	1757	5505	10.9	30.8	38.4
fees, royalties(d)	4045	6318	4.1	427	242	-5.0	347	367	0.5	774	609	-2.2	19.1	9.6
other private services(e)	2433	10090	13.8	520	1639	11.0	534	2284	14.1	1054	3923	12.7	43.3	38.9
Total exports of goods and services	123833	273515	7.5	20199	39097	6.2	22674	54123	8.2	42873	93220	7.3	34.6	34.1
US imports														
Merchandise(c)	105764	366111	12.0	17646	44154	8.7	25139	77132	10.7	42785	121286	9.9	40.5	33.1
Services (debits)	15486	44575	10.1	3626	10551	10.2	1320	5653	14.1	4946	16203	11.4	31.9	36.3
travel	6195	17146	9.7	2518	6117	8.4	455	1435	11.0	2973	7552	8.8	48.0	44.0
passenger fares	2196	7078	11.2	188	667	12.2	129	523	13.6	317	1190	12.8	14.4	16.8
other transportation	5451	16221	10.4	514	1757	11.8	655	3740	17.2	1168	5497	15.1	21.4	33.9
fees, royalties(d)	416	968	8.0	12	32	9.3	5	-3(f)	-	17	29	5.0	4.1	3.0
other private services(e)	1228	3163	9.0	395	1978	15.8	77	-43(f)	-	471	1935	13.7	38.4	61.2
Total imports of goods and services	121249	410686	11.7	21272	54705	9.0	26459	82785	10.9	47731	137490	10.1	39.4	33.5

(a) Two-year average. - (b) Including Central America and the Caribbean. - (c) Including military sales and purchases. - (d) Receipts and payments for the use or sale of intangible property rights, including patents, industrial processes, trade-marks, copyrights, franchises, designs, know-how, formulas, techniques and manufacturing rights. - (e) Includes non-merchandise insurance, communications, processing and repairs, advertising, brokerage, leasing, fees for management, professional and technical services. - (f) Credits.

Source: US Department of Commerce [September 1975; September 1976; March 1987]; own calculations.

in Caribbean banking centres, the debt issue and the concomitant drain on US services needed for debt management have contributed to this result.

Fifthly, the US turned from a surplus country in trade in services with developing countries to a deficit country during the decade under observation. As a matter of fact, US service imports from developing countries grew much faster. Asia, as a supplier of services, clearly out-stripped Latin America in terms of growth rates. Nevertheless, Latin America has still remained the major source of services supplied by de-veloping countries. While travel and transportation are the backbones of services exported to the US from both regions, a growing number of transactions under "other private services" have been credited to Latin American residents. Given the heterogeneity of this segment of services and the large element of "disembodiment", this figure is not easy to in-terpret.

To summarize, in terms of growth rates US exports and imports of services have risen faster than trade flows in goods. It is basically in "embodied" services such as passenger and other transportation where developing countries have demonstrated their competitiveness, whereas on the US export side other private services seem to have gained mo-mentum compared with the traditional "smokestack" service industries.

It is not surprizing that in a comparative setting Asian exporters have performed better than Latin American ones. As transportation ser-vices are to a large extent by-products of merchandise trade, fast rising US merchandise imports from Asia stimulate imports of related services. In addition, a rapidly expanding infrastructure for tourism in Asia and very competitive Asian airlines seem to have challenged the locational ad-vantages of Caribbean and South American tourist sites.

"Disembodied" other private services which in a two-way trade are expanding with Latin America may have their roots in a strong involve-ment of US commercial banks in Latin American borrowing. Yet, the stat-istical basis does not allow for any verification of this assumption.

b. *Japanese Trade in Services*

Japan's regionalized balance-of-payments statistics allow for but a cursory view on trade in services with developing countries. [1] Available data for two periods in the 1980s, however, suggest that an even larger share of exports and imports of services than in the US case is directed towards or originate from developing countries (Table 2). In 1985/86 about 38 per cent of Japanese world imports of services (and 35 per cent of its exports) stemmed from developing countries (and were absorbed by developing countries). Services supplied by developing countries accounted for one fifth of total Japanese imports (including merchandise) from this group of countries, whereas only 11 per cent of Japanese total exports can be attributed to services. As a result, Japan has been a clear net importer of services in its bilateral trade with developing countries, and this is probably due to the shipment of primary commodities mostly under "flags of convenience" to Japan. In 1985/86, more than 50 per cent of total Japanese imports of services in transportation industries were credited to the accounts of residents in developing countries. Japanese tourism in neighbouring Asian developing countries and a relatively large amount of payments of fees, royalties and non-merchandise insurance premia to developing countries have also contributed to the Japanese trade deficit in services. Whether the latter source of this deficit is related to large Japanese FDI and trading activities in Asian developing countries and to payments received by firms in which Japanese parent companies hold minority equity shares, cannot be verified here but could provide scope for further research.

---

[1] Developing countries do not appear as explicit entities in the Japanese regionalized balance-of-payments statistics. They are labelled "other countries" besides OECD countries, Communist bloc countries and international institutions. There is no regional disaggregation within developing countries, and the sectoral composition of services is much broader than in the US case, comprising only three groups of services.

Table 2 - Japan's Trade in Goods and Services with Developing Countries, 1982-1986 (mill. US $)

	World		LDCs		Share of LDCs in Japan's world trade	
	1982/83(a)	1985/86(a)	1982/83(a)	1985/86(a)	1982/83	1985/86
			Japanese exports			
Merchandise	141565	189803	62491	59715	44.1	31.5
Services	20081	21173	8113	7488	40.4	35.4
transportation(b)	12764	11880	5414	4424	42.4	37.2
travel	790	1300	313	452	39.6	34.8
other private services(c)	6527	7993	2386	2838	36.6	35.5
Total exports of goods and services	161646	210976	70604	67203	43.7	31.9
			Japanese imports			
Merchandise	116799	115396	67940	58831	58.2	51.0
Services	33941	35791	13899	13505	41.0	37.7
transportation(b)	16114	14473	7949	7396	49.3	51.0
travel	4272	6021	1424	1822	33.3	30.3
other private services(c)	13555	16297	4526	4286	33.4	26.3
Total imports of goods and services	150740	152188	81839	72336	54.3	47.5

(a) Two-years average. - (b) Freight, insurance on international shipments, port disbursements, passenger fares, time charters, ocean vessels, aircraft. - (c) Management fees, patents, royalties, fees, agent's fees, advertising, film rentals, non-merchandise insurance.

Source: The Bank of Japan [current April issues]; own calculations.

c. French Trade in Services

The decomposition of French trade in services by regions faces a number of problems of compatibility due to two different concepts of measurement applied.[1] Hence, the regional breakdown of trade flows presented in Tables 3 and A1 should be evaluated with caution.

As far as two sub-regions of developing countries, OPEC countries and Latin America, are concerned, the OPEC region proved to be an important importer of French construction services. After the end of the oil price boom, this importance slowed down. Yet, in 1985/86, still more than 26 per cent of total French exports of construction services were directed to OPEC countries. It is due to this flourishing demand that OPEC countries accounted for a larger share in French world service exports than in French world merchandise exports. On the other hand, the Latin American market has proven just as sluggish for French exports of services as for goods.

On the import side, the relatively large share of construction services "imported" from OPEC countries (about 13 per cent of French world imports in this service industry in 1985/86) deserves attention. One may assume that this "import" either reflects the participation of foreign firms registered in OPEC countries in large turn-key infrastructure projects, as a "local content" substitute, or payments of subscription fees to OPEC residents.

More important partner regions of France for trade in services than Latin America are the three Maghreb states Algeria, Tunisia, and Morocco, and especially the francophone African member states of the

---

[1] Whereas the global balance-of-payments statistics record "transactions", bilateral balance-of-payments statistics (with regions of individual countries) are compiled on the basis of "règlements bilatéraux" between residents of the partner country (credits and debits). Differences between real flows of goods and services and financial flows may basically arise if trade is financed by credits. Furthermore, bilaterally, there is no record on trade between France and "developing countries". This group can only be formed as a residual from the global balance of payments (based on transactions) minus two bilateral balance of payments with the OECD countries and Socialist countries (both in terms of "règlements"). For subgroups of developing countries, bilateral balance of payments, again in terms of "règlements" with OPEC countries, Latin America, Maghreb states and member countries of the Franc Zone (basically francophone Sub-Saharan African countries) are published.

Table 3 - Share of OPEC, Latin American Countries and Franc Zone
Countries in French World Exports and Imports of Goods and
Services, 1979/80 and 1985/86 (a)

	OPEC		Latin American countries		Franc Zone countries		Share of all LDCc in French world trade(b)	
	1980	1985/1986	1979/1980	1985/1986	1979/1980	1985/1986	1979/1980	1985/1986
	French exports							
Merchandise	10.6	7.7	3.5	2.3	3.9	3.6	16.5	15.6
Total services	10.6	8.4	1.8	1.8	10.2	6.8	36.1	31.3
freight	6.6	11.4	0.8	3.4	12.6	5.3	74.3	27.0
transport	6.3	5.3	1.7	1.1	9.7	5.4	25.8	42.9
insurance	3.1	3.7	3.3	1.5	6.8	4.0	18.3	20.3
travel	4.9	4.1	0.7	0.6	9.4	7.1	13.6	11.3
construction	31.8	26.3	4.0	4.8	10.9	10.8	65.3	62.3
patents, licences	0.5	2.2	1.1	0.7	2.9	2.6	8.8	7.3
other services	5.8	4.7	1.3	1.7	11.2	6.7	27.7	24.1
Total exports of goods and services	10.6	7.9	3.1	2.2	5.1	4.3	20.2	18.8
	French imports							
Merchandise	22.4	9.6	1.9	2,4	3.9	4,0	26,4	18,0
Total services	3.2	3.9	1.9	1.6	4.9	3.7	25.6	25.6
freight	2.2	7.8	2.0	2.1	0.5	1.7	52.8	20.2
transport	3.1	4.5	3.4	2.4	6.0	4.3	20.4	43.3
insurance	1.8	1.0	1.9	1.0	1.3	1.8	8.1	15.1
travel	0.7	0.8	0.6	0.4	2.8	5.3	15.8	17.7
construction	12.1	12.9	2.9	3.1	11.0	6.0	38.8	37.0
patents, licences	0.1	0.1	0.2	0.1	0.2	0.2	0.5	0.7
other services	4.9	2.3	1.4	1.3	10.7	2.6	21.4	12.0
Total imports of goods and services	19.5	8.6	1.9	2.3	4.0	3.9	26.3	19.3

(a) Two-year average. - (b) Estimated as a residual of total French
external transactions minus "règlements" (financial flows) with OECD
countries and socialist countries.

Source: Ministère de l'Economie [1979; 1980; 1985; 1986]; own calculations.

Franc Zone.[1] This mirrors the relatively strong links in merchandise trade and monetary relations between the francophone countries and the former Metropolitan country.

As far as French exports in services to all developing countries are concerned, a similar figure as in the US case emerges. That means that about one third of total services sold abroad was directed to developing countries.

In general, developing countries accounted for higher shares in both French exports and imports of services than in merchandise trade. There are strong parallels between growth rates of trade in goods and services with specific developing regions. As an example, after the end of the two oil-price hikes service exports to the OPEC countries slowed down considerably compared to other developing regions and so did merchandise exports.

With respect to imports, France seems to have been more absorptive to services originating from developing countries than to goods. Between 1979/80 and 1985/86, merchandise imports from developing countries rose by 4 per cent annually whereas imports in services (mainly transport and travel) grew by almost 13 per cent annually. There is much evidence from the French trade pattern that developing countries captured rising shares in the international transport market at a time when excess capacities were high and freight rate competition was very aggressive. In 1979/80 as well as 1985/86, about 25 per cent of total French imports in services stemmed from developing countries but an overproportionate share of more than 40 per cent was gained in maritime and air transport (Table 3).

d. *West German Trade in Services*

Figures presented on West German trade in services with developing countries are the most detailed ones among the four OECD countries. In addition to published data on trade with the developing countries in total, unpublished data for 16 major developing countries have been made

---

[1] In 1985/86, about 7 per cent of French service exports and 4 per cent of imports were with Franc Zone countries.

258

Table 4 - West German Trade in Goods and Services with Developing Countries (per cent)

	Average annual growth rate				Share of all developing countries in West German world trade			
	World	Four Asian NICs(a)	Latin American Six(a)	All developing countries				
	1971/86	1971/86	1971/86	1971/86	1971	1975	1980	1986
West German exports								
Merchandise	8.6	13.8	4.8	8.1	11.7	16.7	15.2	11.0
Services	9.2	16.5	6.3	11.6	12.4	17.6	21.8	17.1
travel	6.5	24.9	6.6	16.8	1.7	5.9	7.1	6.7
total transport	6.6	13.7	6.0	7.2	16.7	20.7	19.0	18.2
freight	5.0	11.1	7.2	4.3	19.4	24.7	20.1	17.6
passenger fares	8.0	16.4	5.5	10.8	16.1	20.5	24.2	23.6
port services	8.8	23.9	4.1	12.0	9.3	10.5	13.0	14.2
repairs	9.6	4.7	-1.9	n.a.	17.4	14.2	n.a.	n.a.
other transport	3.7	n.a.	n.a.	11.2	0.0	1.1	11.9	18.0
insurance	14.0	12.9	7.2	8.1	12.7	14.0	10.8	5.7
other private services	13.4	21.6	6.5	15.9	16.7	21.8	33.5	23.0
Total exports of goods and services	8.6	14.1	5.0	8.6	11.8	18.5	16.2	11.7
West German imports								
Merchandise	7.8	16.2	8.2	11.8	7.4	18.9	20.5	12.7
Services	7.9	16.5	6.1	9.3	10.7	11.7	13.7	12.9
travel	8.1	20.1	10.9	17.1	2.3	3.2	5.8	7.6
total transport	4.8	14.5	7.3	4.9	17.0	15.0	17.0	17.2
freight	3.2	11.4	7.2	4.4	14.7	16.5	16.0	17.5
passengers fares	8.6	28.0	11.1	16.9	5.0	8.5	14.7	15.2
port services	6.5	12.2	4.0	6.7	15.4	15.1	16.7	15.8
repairs	6.0	n.a.	n.a.	n.a.	1.8	11.1	n.a.	n.a.
other transport	-0.7	24.3	10.5	-3.5	60.1	21.7	32.8	33.6
insurance	12.9	12.9	2.1	13.2	9.7	9.9	13.3	10.0
other private services	9.5	17.6	4.4	10.6	13.8	18.7	21.5	16.2
Total imports of goods and services	7.9	16.2	7.8	11.2	8.1	17.1	19.1	12.8

(a) Four Asian NICs: Hong Kong, Singapore, South Korea, Taiwan. Latin American Six: Argentina, Brazil, Chile, Colombia, Mexico, Venezuela.

Source: Deutsche Bundesbank [No. 7, July 1973; No. 7, July 1978; No. 7, July 1983; No. 6, June 1988]; Deutsche Bundesbank (Unpublished data); own calculations.

available. Tables 4 and A2 provide a breakdown of West German merchandise and service trade with the world, developing countries and two
important subgroups, the four Asian NICs (Hong Kong, Singapore,
South Korea, and Taiwan) and the six largest Latin American countries
(Argentina, Brazil, Chile, Colombia, Mexico, and Venezuela). It emerges
that:

- West Germany has been a net importer of services from developing
  countries during the 1970s and 1980s whereas it used to be a net exporter of goods except for 1980 when the second oil-price hike had its
  impact on imports (in value terms);

- developing countries turned out to be more important export markets
  for West German services than suppliers of services (in 1986 about
  17 per cent of West German service exports were directed to developing countries whereas about 13 per cent of West German imports orig-
  inated from developing countries; cf. Table 4);

- services rather than goods make up a more dynamic segment of total
  West German exports to developing countries;

- on the import side, services supplied by developing countries kept
  growing after the end of the oil-price boom in the 1980s whereas
  merchandise imports in value terms declined as commodity prices decreased;

- there is no clear evidence of inter-industry specialization except for
  travel, fares, advertising, and fees where West Germany appears to be
  a clear net importer and for construction where it is a net exporter.
  In transportation services, West German exports and imports have by
  and large been balanced;

- in regional terms, the four Asian NICs outstripped the other major
  LDC group, the six large Latin American countries. Whereas in 1971,
  the latter group comprised about 22 per cent of West German imports
  in services from developing countries compared to only 6 per cent for
  the Asian NICs, the relation drastically turned by 1986 to 14 and 15
  per cent respectively. Strongholds of the NICs which started their
  catch-up process in the late 1970s and early 1980s were not only the
  traditional services such as travel and transport, but also management
  activities and construction services summarized under "other services"
  (Table 5).

Table 5 - Composition of West German Exports and Imports in Services with Selected Developing Countries, 1971-1986 (per cent) (a)

Trading partners		Travel				Transport				Insurance				Other services			
		1971	1975	1980	1986	1971	1975	1980	1986	1971	1975	1980	1986	1971	1975	1980	1986
Singapore	exports	7.7	4.0	3.3	12.1	76.9	74.0	68.9	32.3	7.7	4.0	3.3	1.7	7.7	18.0	24.6	53.9
	imports	13.5	7.7	14.7	13.7	43.2	47.9	5.0	37.2	2.7	2.1	1.6	1.6	40.5	42.3	26.7	47.5
ASEAN	exports	7.3	2.1	3.8	7.3	66.9	38.5	57.0	37.2	5.6	3.3	4.4	2.7	20.2	56.1	34.9	52.7
	imports	8.9	12.9	18.1	18.2	45.7	32.1	43.9	38.0	1.3	1.6	2.5	1.7	44.0	53.3	35.5	42.1
Hong Kong	exports	5.9	2.4	5.5	18.3	86.3	78.4	66.0	61.3	3.9	4.0	2.0	1.5	3.9	15.2	26.5	18.8
	imports	10.3	8.4	19.5	21.8	43.1	18.5	30.3	26.1	6.0	4.2	6.2	3.0	40.5	70.9	44.1	49.1
South Korea	exports	0.0	0.0	2.6	1.2	37.0	78.9	64.5	49.6	3.7	7.9	3.9	2.3	59.3	28.9	28.9	46.9
	imports	3.0	3.8	3.1	3.9	15.2	55.1	40.4	27.5	3.0	5.1	9.9	3.9	78.8	35.9	46.6	64.8
Taiwan	exports	0.0	1.4	0.9	0.5	81.5	81.9	55.7	54.9	3.7	6.9	5.7	9.2	14.8	9.7	37.7	35.4
	imports	3.0	2.0	1.5	2.9	57.6	47.5	43.1	39.7	6.1	5.1	5.0	5.5	33.3	45.5	50.5	51.9
India	exports	2.4	3.5	2.8	2.3	71.4	65.9	55.4	53.7	6.0	5.9	2.3	3.8	20.2	27.4	39.5	40.3
	imports	13.7	15.3	38.9	37.5	42.5	55.0	28.2	17.7	8.2	3.6	6.3	3.1	35.6	26.1	26.6	41.7
Saudi Arabia	exports	0.6	2.2	0.3	2.8	6.1	12.5	6.0	11.1	0.6	1.3	0.5	1.6	92.7	84.0	93.1	84.4
	imports	8.0	10.3	2.9	9.8	17.5	26.3	11.6	8.4	0.7	1.7	1.1	1.2	73.7	61.6	84.5	80.6
Argentina	exports	14.3	13.9	9.4	11.0	42.9	62.0	40.9	26.7	1.7	1.9	0.6	1.3	41.2	22.2	49.1	61.0
	imports	4.0	3.9	3.6	5.0	28.0	25.5	20.7	54.1	2.0	1.3	1.2	1.8	66.0	69.3	74.6	39.2
Brazil	exports	9.9	8.1	9.4	10.8	41.8	57.9	48.8	50.1	1.4	1.9	1.2	1.6	46.8	32.2	40.6	37.6
	imports	4.8	7.6	8.6	12.8	49.1	44.5	50.4	60.0	3.3	1.6	1.7	2.2	42.7	46.3	39.3	24.9
Mexico	exports	11.5	3.0	8.4	10.8	46.0	36.6	46.6	46.2	16.1	6.9	6.0	12.8	26.4	53.4	39.0	30.3
	imports	16.2	15.8	25.7	16.2	12.1	13.8	15.4	9.7	8.1	6.6	10.3	26.2	63.6	63.8	48.6	47.9
Venezuela	exports	9.0	5.5	8.6	6.4	32.8	46.6	36.9	51.2	6.0	5.5	6.3	13.4	52.2	42.3	48.2	29.1
	imports	3.5	5.7	8.3	4.6	42.1	29.3	22.1	36.4	1.8	5.1	11.1	8.1	52.6	59.9	58.5	50.9
LDC Sample	exports	7.1	4.3	3.0	6.8	48.3	47.0	26.3	39.4	3.8	3.2	1.6	3.2	40.8	45.5	69.1	50.6
	imports	7.3	9.1	10.8	15.4	39.1	32.8	28.9	32.2	3.3	2.8	3.4	3.8	50.4	55.3	56.9	48.6

(a) Deviations from 100 are due to rounding.

Source: Deutsche Bundesbank (unpublished data); own calculations.

3. Hypotheses Derived from Main Empirical Observations

Given the extraordinary conceptual and statistical barriers, it comes as no surprize that empirically-tested hypotheses on determinants of North-South trade in services are very rare. Basically, the few studies available lend support to the use of the same set of analytical tools to explain trade in services as they are well-established in merchandise trade. [1] The empirical evidence presented here cannot add more to this literature as the factor content of services is disregarded in this paper. The following hypotheses derived from the four OECD countries' bilateral or regional balance of payments hence refer to the direction of trade in services rather than to its structure.

Firstly, developing countries have no reason to be concerned about their participation in world trade in services as they seem to suggest in the Uruguay Round of the GATT [Bhagwati, 1987]. Quite a number of them have proven to be very competitive and successful on OECD markets. On the other hand, they are important markets for OECD countries' exports. In some cases growth rates of trade in services have exceeded those in merchandise trade, and this is not always the result of a low initial level.

Secondly, as argued by Sapir and Lutz, Lall and others, inter-industry specialization seems to be more dominant in North-South trade in services than intra-industry specialization. Disaggregated data on US, French and especially West German trade in services lend support to the view that industries in which developing countries are clear net exporters can be separated from those in which they are net importers. "Embodied" services such as travel and maritime transport form the core of

---

[1] The pioneer study in this respect has been the study by Sapir and Lutz [1981] which takes a strong parallel to factor proportions theory as it has been applied for North-South trade in goods. Capital abundance and the availability of human capital are exposed to be the main determinants of comparative advantages for instance in freight and passenger services. This view is basically supported by Lall [1986] who argues that developing countries can be net exporters of relatively physical capital-intensive services, if this stock of physical capital has been built up in the course of developing a competitive manufacturing base. Simultaneously, developing countries can be net importers of those services being at the upper end of the human-capital intensity scale. Hence, inter-industry specialization is said to be dominant instead of intra-industry specialization.

the first group; management activities and construction industries belong to the latter one. Peculiarities such as the temporarily high OPEC demand for construction services and concomitant payments to non-residents in OPEC countries booked as "imports" do not change this general pattern. Yet, this hypothesis requires much more in-depth analysis in order to be consolidated.

Thirdly, in regional terms, there is much overlap between the groups of major exporters of manufactures and successful suppliers of services among the developing countries. This is probably the most important result and has to be specified further. Both the US and West German data suggest that South-East and East Asian NICs were able to surpass Latin American countries in terms of export growth rates both in goods and services. This supports Lall's view of a dynamic manufactured export base as an important determinant of a similar service infrastructure [Lall, 1986, p. 136].

The concrete relationships between LDC exports of goods and services can be hypothesized as follows:

(i)   Trade in services is not autonomous but is induced to some extent by merchandise trade. This mainly refers to transport and merchandise insurance. If factor availability allows for building up own transport facilities for own exports, government interventions such as adherence to strict cargo-sharing principles agreed upon in liner conferences between importing and exporting countries contribute to tighten this link (UNCTAD Shipping Code). Such government interventions in this industry may lead to a bias in bilateral trade relations towards intra-industry specialization.

(ii)   To be successful, relatively outward-oriented trade strategies in the goods sector require the permanent exploration of new foreign output markets and the knowledge of competitive input markets. Both foreign and local investors can offer such services if close connection to local producers and their needs is maintained. Successful production centres for merchandise are therefore also service centres on a national as well as international scale. Singapore which owes its existence to the role of a service centre is a case in point.

(iii)   It is empirically well-founded that trade relations between partners are relatively strong where flows of FDI are strong as well. For-

eign investors and their subsidiaries are per se excellent producers and transmitters of services, no matter whether investment is
in the service or manufacturing sector.

(iv) Business travel, conferences, fairs, and leisure tours are by-
products of intensive international exchange of goods. Successful
LDC suppliers of goods have hence invested extensively also in
travel and aviation services in order to offer both information on
new goods and facilities for recreational activities in their countries.

(v) Capital requirements for shipping and shipping-related services are
such that the minimum economic size is rather large. Only those
countries with a rapidly growing volume of trade can achieve such
minimum levels, and these are exporters of manufactures rather
than of commodities. An additional argument for regarding service
exports and imports of an individual country as a by-product of
its manufactured trade is that manufactures are mostly shipped by
direct liner services (including air cargo transport). Such services
are subject to bilateral bargaining between exporting and importing
countries and their agencies, i.e. pool services, so that bilateral
flows of goods are commensurate with bilateral flows of related
services. This overlap may be much smaller in trade with commodities where tramp services have a larger importance.

4. The Directionality of North-South Trade in Goods and Services: The Case of West Germany

Trade in manufactures between individual countries is expected to
create trade in related service activities between the same trading partners. This hypothesis assumes developing countries to be successful
suppliers of service activities if they are able to compete on world markets with manufactures. Such success, however, cannot only be the outcome of comparative advantages but may also be influenced by govern-
mental interventions into the distribution of related services between the
trading partners (i.e. cargo preferences).

To test the link between trade in manufactures and services, several cross-country regressions were run with changes in per capita income

Table 6 - West German Trade in Manufactures and Services with Developing Countries (Cross-Country Regression Results on Changes in Trade Shares)

Endogenous variable	Constant	Exogenous variable		$\bar{R}^2$	F
		change between 1971 and 1986			
Δx^s_i	-0.13 (-1.97)**	$0.0001\Delta y_i$ (4.59)*	$+0.41\Delta x^g_i$ (2.07)**	0.57	10.87*
		change between 1975 and 1986			
Δx^s_i	-0.10 (-1.42)	$0.00006\Delta y_i$ (1.91)**	$+0.7\Delta x^g_i$ (3.63)*	0.53	9.48*
		change between 1971 and 1986			
Δm^s_i	-0.08 (-1.10)	$0.00006\Delta y_i$ (3.28)*	$+0.20\Delta m^g_i$ (1.33)	0.40	6.01*
		change between 1971 and 1986			
$\Delta x^s_i + \Delta m^s_i$	-0.25 (-1.99)**	$0.00002\Delta y_i$ (4.44)*	$+0.42(\Delta x^g_i + \Delta m^g_i)$ (2.14)**	0.56	10.68*
		change between 1975 and 1986			
$\Delta x^s_i + \Delta m^s_i$	-0.15 (-1.39)	$0.00001\Delta y_i$ (2.00)**	$+0.91(\Delta x^g_i + \Delta m^g_i)$ (3.76)*	0.55	10.17*

Note: Δx^s_i = absolute change in the share of country i in West German exports of services between ...

Δx^g_i = absolute change in the share of country i in West German manufactured exports between ...

Δy_i = absolute change in the per capita income of country i (in US $) between ...

Δm^s_i = absolute change in the share of country i in West German imports of services between ...

Δm^g_i = absolute change in the share of country i in West German manufactured imports between ...

* Statistically significant at the 5 per cent level. - ** Statistically significant at the 10 per cent level. - t-statistics in brackets.

Source: As for Table 4; own calculations.

and country shares in West German manufactured exports and imports as independent variables, and changes in country shares in West German exports and imports of services as dependent variables. The sample covers 16 major developing countries.[1] Both regression coefficients are hypothesized to be positive. The change in per capita income is a catch-all proxy for various demand and supply factors, such as rising absorptive capacity, human and physical capital formation and development level, whereas the change as supplier and purchaser of manufactures reflects the changing openness of the economy, skill availability and the demand for trade-related services.

In general, the regression results confirm the hypothesis (Table 6). Yet, the catch-all variable of changes in per capita income has always a stronger impact on changes in shares of service trade than shares in manufactured trade and their changes. Furthermore, the relationships are more stable on the export side than on the import side. Finally, it is mainly the period of the mid-1970s to mid-1980, where links between trade shares in services and manufactures can be measured, not the earlier period of 1971-1975. Hence, this link is a recent phenomenon directly related to the process of rising income levels and the concomitant capital formation. The intensity of trade relations in general (including trade in commodities) and not only of manufactured trade seems to influence trade in services positively. This is supported by the observation that West German residents credited relatively large amounts under service accounts to resource-rich developing countries such as Saudi Arabia and Venezuela, both of them did not export manufactures worth mentioning during the reference period.

5. Final Remarks

North-South trade in services is neither quantitatively negligible nor exclusively a "transport and travel" topic. Exports of developing countries still have their strongholds in these two service industries

---

[1] In addition to the four Asian NICs and the six largest Latin American countries listed in Table A2, the four ASEAN member states Indonesia, Malaysia, Philippines, and Thailand as well as India and Saudi Arabia have been included.

which are strongly related to merchandise trade. Yet, other private services have become more relevant too. Unfortunately, very little is known about their underlying determinants and the concrete nature of the transactions. In addition, given their high degree of "disembodiment" it is debatable whether one can force them into bilateral matrices of partner and reporting countries as in merchandise trade.

Regional balance-of-payments statistics presented in this paper are at best useful for finding very broad relationships between merchandise trade balances and those in services. Though the analyses of at least three OECD countries' data suggest more inter-industry specialization in services than intra-industry specialization, the results are not fully conclusive. Parallels to merchandise trade appear strong with respect to regional shifts in trade. Asian developing countries, including the four NICs Hong Kong, South Korea, Singapore, and Taiwan, proceeded more rapidly in exports of services than Latin American countries, and this has also been a key element of recent developments in merchandise trade.

Wide differences emerge between the four OECD countries as far as the importance of developing countries in total and certain subregions for their service exports is concerned. Countries like the US and Japan which have strong merchandise export bases in neighbouring developing countries and operate in these countries with a large number of FDI subsidiaries, also direct a sizeable share of their total exports in services to developing countries. France sells a large share of its services to francophone Mediterranean and Sub-Saharan African countries where it still keeps a dominant trading position as a former Metropolitan country. West Germany seems to have profited especially from high import demand for services in OPEC countries which in 1986 accounted for more than 40 per cent of its total service exports to developing countries.

In general, such surveys are no substitute for industry studies because sectoral aggregation is very high in the balance-of-payments statistics and because serious accounting problems emerge especially in modern "disembodied" services. Only detailed studies on international activities of service industries can provide the basis for analyzing to what extent flows of services between developing and developed countries are determined by the relative factor endowment and which part is generated by policy interventions.

Appendix Tables

Table A1 – French Trade in Goods and Services with Developing Countries, 1979/80 and 1985/86 (mill. Francs) (a)

	OPEC		Latin American countries		Franc Zone countries(b)		All developing countries(c)	
	1980	1985/86	1979/80	1985/86	1979/80	1985/86	1979/80	1985/86
	French exports							
Merchandise	58212	74595	17764	22165	19845	35234	84422	150990
Total services	13879	20547	2116	4370	12228	16563	43273	76305
freight	1113	1335	115	400	1924	617	11372	3152
transport	1798	3495	457	709	2546	3551	6742	28063
insurance	164	634	164	256	340	691	921	3469
travel	1688	2836	210	435	3005	4914	4352	7862
construction	8103	10477	939	1925	2552	4289	15270	24831
patents, licences	10	104	22	33	56	119	172	342
other services	1003	1668	211	613	1805	2382	4447	8537
Total exports of goods and services	72091	95142	19880	26535	32073	51797	127695	227295
	French imports							
Merchandise	134740	95631	10155	24277	20927	39616	142537	179309
Total services	3412	7921	1893	3201	4774	7434	25158	51401
freight	458	1613	364	430	93	344	9702	4208
transport	835	2772	834	1462	1445	2620	4955	26629
insurance	101	168	98	162	65	285	412	2448
travel	174	352	143	177	671	2278	3752	7620
construction	1032	2225	235	537	883	1024	3100	6394
patents, licences	3	11	9	9	6	21	19	60
other services	809	782	212	426	1611	862	3220	4043
Total imports of goods and services	138152	103552	12047	27478	25701	47050	167695	230709

(a) Two-year average. - (b) Benin, Cameroon, Comoros, Ivory Coast, Gabon, Equatorial Guinea, Upper Volta, Mali, Niger, Central African Republic, Senegal, Chad, Togo. - (c) Estimated as a residual of total French external transactions minus "règlements" (financial flows) with OECD countries and socialist countries.

Source: Ministère de l'Economie [1979; 1980; 1985; 1986]; own calculations.

Table A2 - West German Trade in Goods and Services with Developing Countries, 1971, 1975, 1980, and 1986 (mill. DM)

	World				Four Asian NICs			
	1971	1975	1980	1986	1971	1975	1980	1986
West German exports								
Merchandise	145054	214794	335232	497246	1230	2197	4348	8584
Services	19456	32782	53806	73103	131	285	504	1291
travel	5340	7014	11539	13685	5	6	18	140
total transport(c)	8526	12329	18122	22146	96	224	224	663
freight	5067	7346	9770	10554	69	176	195	334
passenger fares	1606	2187	3493	5091	18	33	68	175
port services	1491	2275	4061	5308	6	12	53	150
repairs	253	344	537	1003	2	4	5	4
other transport	109	177	261	189	n.a.	n.a.	n.a.	n.a.
insurance	843	1501	2723	6033	6	13	17	37
other private services(c)	4747	11938	21422	31239	24	42	145	451
fees, advertising, fairs	529	841	1743	3237	0	5	16	50
licences, patents	545	796	1101	1981	1	2	20	26
wages and salaries received								
from non-residents	1569	2447	4209	6145	2	2	12	40
construction, assembly	1219	3057	7056	7536	12	17	47	122
overhead costs (receipts)(d)	301	829	1015	1253	0	0	12	47
receipts of repayments, discounts, liability, payments	318	413	649	893	4	4	3	11
miscellaneous(e)	266	3555	5649	10193	3	10	31	156
Total	164510	247576	389038	570349	1361	2482	4852	9875
West German imports								
Merchandise	122395	174528	320578	380130	1254	3754	8319	11893
Services	35521	56208	88855	111314	219	724	1163	2175
travel	12292	20940	36609	39384	19	50	143	297
total transport(c)	11223	13126	18929	22738	90	233	509	690
freight	6353	6485	8711	10224	54	101	194	273
passenger fares	1703	2337	3860	5903	5	16	43	204
port services	2196	3422	5154	5658	28	81	119	158
repairs	56	45	79	134	n.a.	n.a.	4	4
other transport	914	837	1124	818	2	34	49	52
insurance	1129	2424	3747	6990	11	21	56	68
other private services(c)	10877	19718	29570	42202	99	420	455	1120
fees, advertising, fairs	3164	5122	7297	10224	58	107	199	501
licences, patents	1483	2052	2624	4159	1	0	1	1
wages and salaries paid								
to non-residents(f)	2767	3877	6774	8557	10	14	33	90
construction, assembly	1694	3058	4823	4764	3	211	37	102
overhead costs (payments)(g)	370	1389	2237	1955	4	13	28	84
repayments, discounts, liability payments	970	1786	2261	3937	19	14	32	71
miscellaneous	429	2435	3555	8607	4	62	126	273
Total	157916	230736	409433	491444	1473	4478	9482	14068

(a) Four Asian NICs: Hong Kong, Singapore, South Korea, Taiwan. - (b) Latin American Six: Argentina, Brazil, Chile, Colombia, Mexico, Venezuela. - (c) Deviations from the sum of sub-items are due to rounding and to missing information on sub-items - (d) Payments of foreign subsidiaries to parent companies for participation in overhead costs. - (e) Mainly wages received in outward processing and services of the West German postal service. - (f) Excluding payments to guestworkers which are defined as residents. - (g) Grants of parent companies to foreign subsidiaries. - n.a.: Not available.

Table A2 (continued)

	Latin American Six				Developing countries			
	1971	1975	1980	1986	1971	1975	1980	1986
West German exports								
Merchandise	4164	6508	9429	8435	16977	35953	51121	54478
Services	680	1118	1690	1704	2411	5776	11729	12495
travel	72	76	142	189	89	414	821	920
total transport(c)	325	621	807	780	1423	2550	3435	4031
freight	166	347	429	468	982	1815	1968	1858
passenger fares	94	139	222	210	258	448	845	1204
port services	49	117	133	90	138	238	527	754
repairs	16	18	24	12	44	49	n.a.	n.a.
other transport	n.a.	n.a.	n.a.	n.a.	0	2	95	215
insurance	28	40	47	80	107	210	294	344
other private services(c)	255	381	694	655	792	2602	7179	7200
fees, advertising, fairs	16	18	80	79	49	74	227	409
licences, patents	94	98	39	70	115	154	129	180
wages and salaries received from non-residents	11	30	116	67	36	178	554	858
construction, assembly	103	172	290	284	531	2031	5725	4633
overhead costs (receipts)(d)	3	7	14	14	16	32	91	179
receipts of repayments, discounts, liability payments	8	11	15	17	30	26	67	70
miscellaneous(e)	10	42	138	125	16	106	384	871
Total	4844	7626	11119	10139	19388	45729	62850	66973
West German imports								
Merchandise	3351	4813	7817	10899	9038	32931	65814	48459
Services	816	1158	1665	1982	3795	6573	12205	14414
travel	46	100	161	216	280	675	2124	2980
total transport(c)	327	396	581	937	1906	1967	3212	3901
freight	217	237	257	616	932	1068	1390	1789
passenger fares	29	64	86	140	86	198	568	900
port services	79	92	136	143	338	516	860	892
repairs	n.a.	n.a.	n.a.	n.a.	1	5	n.a.	n.a.
other transport	2	3	2	9	549	182	394	320
insurance	30	37	78	41	109	240	500	698
other private services(c)	413	625	845	88	1500	3691	6369	6835
fees, advertising, fairs	245	391	511	456	740	1601	2259	2639
licences, patents	1	0	2	2	5	5	13	8
wages and salaries paid to non-residents(f)	36	41	79	89	122	146	499	544
construction, assembly	76	85	84	60	407	1138	2295	2023
overhead costs (payments)(g)	13	17	89	44	56	447	656	265
repayments, discounts, liability payments	39	58	51	88	150	234	353	485
miscellaneous	1	30	31	51	20	118	293	869
Total	4167	5971	9482	12881	12833	39504	78019	62873

(a) Four Asian NICs: Hong Kong, Singapore, South Korea, Taiwan. - (b) Latin American Six: Argentina, Brazil, Chile, Colombia, Mexico, Venezuela. - (c) Deviations from the sum of sub-items are due to rounding and to missing information on sub-items. - (d) Payments of foreign subsidiaries to parent companies for participation in overhead costs. - (e) Mainly wages received in outward processing and services of the West German postal service. - (f) Excluding payments to guestworkers which are defined as residents. - (g) Grants of parent companies to foreign subsidiaries. - n.a.: Not available.

Source: Deutsche Bundesbank [No. 7, July 1973; No. 7, July 1978; No. 7, July 1983; No. 6, June 1988]; Deutsche Bundesbank (unpublished data); own calculations.

Bibliography

ARNDT, Heinz W., "GATT and the Developing Countries: Agenda for a New Trade Round". Weltwirtschaftliches Archiv, Vol. 123, 1987, pp. 705-718.

THE BANK OF JAPAN, Balance of Payments. Tokyo, various issues.

BHAGWATI, Jagdish, "Splintering and Disembodiment of Services and Developing Nations". The World Economy, Vol. 7, 1984, pp. 133-143.

--, "Trade in Services and the Multilateral Trade Negotiations". The World Bank Economic Review, Vol. 1, 1987, pp. 549-569.

BÖHME, Hans, "Weltseeverkehr: Kein Ende der Krise?" Die Weltwirtschaft, 1986, H. 2, pp. 144-167.

DEUTSCHE BUNDESBANK, Reihe 3: Zahlungsbilanzstatistik. Supplement to Monatsberichte der Deutschen Bundesbank. Frankfurt/M, various issues.

GRAY, H. Peter, "A Negotiating Strategy for Trade in Services". Journal of World Trade Law, Vol. 17, 1983, pp. 377-388.

GRUBEL, Herbert G., "All Traded Services are Embodied in Materials or People". The World Economy, Vol. 10, 1987, pp. 319-330.

LALL, Sanjaya, "The Third World and Comparative Advantages in Trade Services". In: Sanjaya LALL, Frances STEWART (Eds.), Theory and Reality in Development. London 1986, pp. 122-138.

LEE, Chung H., Seiji NAYA, "U.S.-ASEAN Trade and Investment in Services: The American Viewpoint". In: Loong-Hoe TAN, Narongchai AKRASANEE (Eds.), ASEAN-U.S. Economic Relations: Changes in the Economic Environment and Opportunities. Institute of Southeast Asian Studies, Singapore 1988, pp. 146-173.

MINISTERE DE L'ECONOMIE, DES FINANCES ET DE LA PRIVATISATION, La Balance des Paiements de la France. Paris, various issues.

RUGMAN, Alan M., "Multinationals and Trade in Services: A Transaction Cost Approach". Weltwirtschaftliches Archiv, Vol. 123, 1987, pp. 651-667.

SAPIR, André, "North-South Issues in Trade in Services". The World Economy, Vol. 8, 1985, pp. 27-42.

--, "Trade in Services: Policy Issues for the Eighties". The Columbia Journal of World Business, Vol. 17, 1982, pp. 77-85.

--, "Trade in Investment-Related Technological Services". World Development, Vol. 14, 1986, pp. 605-622.

SAPIR, André, Ernst LUTZ, Trade in Services: Economic Determinants and Development Related Issues. World Bank Staff Working Papers, 480, Washington 1981.

SICHELSCHMIDT, Henning, "Weltluftverkehr: Verlangsamte Zunahme des Personenverkehrs". Die Weltwirtschaft, 1986, H. 2, pp. 168-178.

US DEPARTMENT OF COMMERCE, Survey of Current Business. Washington, various issues.

Comment on Rolf J. Langhammer, "North-South Trade in Services: Some Empirical Evidence"

J. Michael Finger

No topic at the Uruguay Round of multilateral trade negotiations has been more controversial than the establishment of multilateral rules for the treatment of international trade in services. There remains a significant split between developed and developing countries as to the appropriateness of the GATT approach to services. This split reflects perhaps a shared perspective of the underlying economics - that services is an area of trade in which developed countries have the advantage over developing countries. The mercantilist instinct of the developed countries is to want services in the GATT system while the same instinct propels developing countries' efforts to keep it out.

Perhaps the most important finding Langhammer's work provides is that this presumption - that the developing countries deal less in world trade in services than in merchandise - is not true.

The evidence Langhammer provides on this point is summarized in Table 1. For each of the four developed countries included in his study, at least as large a fraction of services exports as of merchandise exports goes to developing countries. And for three of the four developed countries, at least as large a share of services imports as of merchandise imports originate in developing countries. Japan is the only exception - 38 percent of Japanese services imports as compared with 51 percent of merchandise imports come from developing countries.

"Services" are not a homogeneous collection of activities. As is generally accepted in the case for merchandise, different service activities may have entirely different bases of comparative advantage. Services trade between developed and developing countries, as Langhammer's results show us, displays much the same pattern as merchandise trade. As with merchandise trade, some types of services tend to flow South-North, others North-South. Also in parallel with a merchandise trade, North-North flows of services are in significant part *intra*-industry flows, while North-South trade in services, as in merchandise, tends to be predominantly *inter*-industry trade.

Table 1 – Developing Countries' Share of Selected Developed Countries' Trade in Merchandise and Services, 1985 and 1986 (a) (percent)

Developed country	Developing countries' share			
	exports		imports	
	services	merchandise	services	merchandise
United States	34	34	36	33
Japan	35	32	38	51
France	31	16	26	18
West Germany(b)	17	11	13	13
(a) Ratios based on total trade for 2 years. – (b) 1986 trade only.				

Source: Langhammer, "North-South Trade in Services: Some Empirical Evidence". In this volume, p. 248-271.

In conclusion, Langhammer's work shows that the sources and the location of comparative advantage in various services activities are as disparate as the sources and location of comparative advantage in different sorts of merchandise. The issue of market access for internationally-traded services is not one on which a sorting of countries by developing versus developed provides a particularly robust distinction between countries with relatively restrictive versus relatively open policy regimes. To insist that the services issue be addressed at the Uruguay Round as a North versus South issue is to insist that it not be addressed in a constructive way.

List of Contributors

Prof. Robert Z. Aliber, Ph.D.	University of Chicago
Prof. Richard Blackhurst	General Agreement on Tariffs and Trade, Geneva
Axel Busch, Dipl.-Volksw.	Institut für Weltwirtschaft, Kiel
Prof. John H. Dunning, Ph.D.	University of Reading, UK; The State University of New Jersey, USA
Prof. Gerald R. Faulhaber, Ph.D.	University of Pennsylvania
J. Michael Finger, Ph.D.	The World Bank, Washington
Prof. Dr. Drs.h.c. Herbert Giersch	Institut für Weltwirtschaft, Kiel
Prof. H. Peter Gray, Ph.D.	Rensselaer Polytechnic Institute, Troy
Prof. Herbert G. Grubel, Ph.D.	Simon Fraser University, British Columbia
Brian Hindley, Ph.D.	Trade Policy Research Centre, London; London School of Economics
Prof. Seev Hirsch, Ph.D.	Tel Aviv University
Dr. Henning Klodt	Institut für Weltwirtschaft, Kiel
Prof. Dr. Günter Knieps	Rijksuniversiteit, Groningen
Dr. Rolf J. Langhammer	Institut für Weltwirtschaft, Kiel
Dr. Jürgen Müller	Deutsches Institut für Wirtschaftsforschung, Berlin; INSEAD, Fontainebleau
Dr.h.c. Tyll Necker	Bundesverband der Deutschen Industrie; Hako-Werke GmbH & Co., Bad Oldesloe
Prof. Domenico Siniscalco	University of Turin
Dr. Herbert Ungerer	EC Commission, Luxembourg
Prof.a.D. Dr. Norbert Walter	Deutsche Bank, Frankfurt/M.

Michael A. Walker, Ph. D.	The Fraser Institute, British Columbia
Dr. Frank D. Weiss	Institut für Weltwirtschaft, Kiel
Prof. Pan A. Yotopoulos, Ph. D.	Stanford University, USA; Kyoto University, Japan